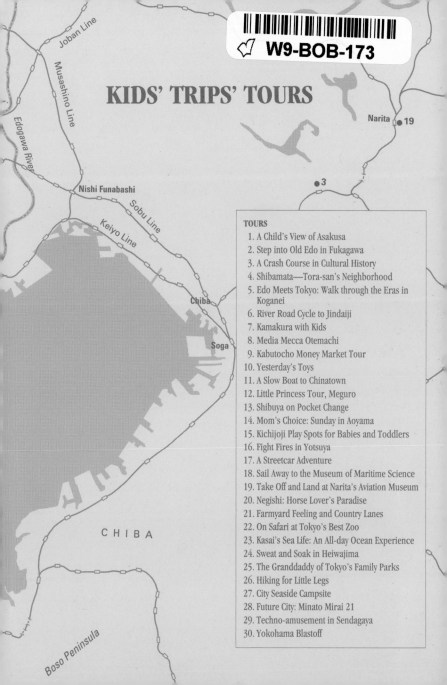

KIDS' TRIPS' TOURS

Joban Line

Musashino Line

Edogawa River

Nishi Funabashi

Sobu Line

Keiyo Line

Narita ● 19

● 3

Chiba

Soga

CHIBA

Boso Peninsula

W9-BOB-173

KIDS'
TRIPS
in Tokyo

KIDS' TRIPS

TRIPS

in Tokyo

Ivy Maeda

Kitty Kobe

Cynthia Ozeki

Lyn Sato

A Family Guide to One-Day Outings

KODANSHA INTERNATIONAL

Tokyo • New York • London

Maps by Tadamitsu Omori

Published by Kodansha International Ltd., 17-14 Otowa 1-chome, Bunkyo-ku, Tokyo 112-8652, and Kodansha America, Inc.

Distributed in the United States by Kodansha America, Inc., 575 Lexington Avenue, New York, New York 10022, and in the United Kingdom and continental Europe by Kodansha Europe Ltd., 95 Aldwych, London WC2B 4JF.

2 3 4 5 6 7 8 9   05 04 03 02 01

ISBN 4-7700-2040-6

CONTENTS

● S E C T I O N T W O ●
A DAY WITH A THEME

● S E C T I O N T H R E E ●
UPTOWN TOURS

• SECTION FOUR •
THINGS THAT GO!

• SECTION FIVE •
FINS, FUR, AND THINGS WITH WINGS

• SECTION SIX •
NATURE IN THE CITY

INTRODUCTION

Despite all of the concrete and crowds, Tokyo is a great place for children, with scores of imaginative play spots at surprisingly inexpensive prices. As Western wives of Japanese, we missed outdoor play space, and wanted to teach our children about the world around them. So we started looking for places where we could have some quality family time. We read Japanese guidebooks for families, scanned local papers, and tuned into Japanese TV shows highlighting leisure spots, and soon we were putting together outings that would fill our photo albums with fun.

From these good times sprang the idea to put what we were learning into a guidebook for all non-Japanese parents, a resource for making happy memories rather than frustration. So we've put together a collection of excursions, each with enough attractions to fill a whole day for even the most active families. You won't find Disneyland or Tokyo Tower in this book, but you don't need us to tell you about the obvious. We purposely selected many spots not found in other guidebooks, as well as things to do near places all foreign parents have to visit, like the immigration office and the airport. There is plenty for everyone in this guidebook—we've included places that will appeal to toddlers, teens, and especially moms and dads.

This is a selective collection of places to go, not an exhaustive one. We picked the very best the city has to offer, searching for value in terms of learning opportunities, sheer entertainment, and cost. There we have a pleasant surprise: the entrance fees for many of our outings total less than ¥1,000 per person. We tried to select places that have enough English to help answer children's questions and get you through the day with a minimum of language problems. To this end, we have a number of tours in Yokohama, where museums and other public facilities have, on average, far more in the way of English explanations than you find in Tokyo.

We wanted the book to be as reliable and informative as possible, so every tour has been parent-and-child tested, most by two or more families. For parents of infants and toddlers we give complete information on feeding and diaper-changing facilities.

Maps and the "Where & When" section in each chapter give detailed instructions on how to get to the fun.

It has taken over two years to piece together this book, to narrow the offerings down to thirty tours that will provide something for every family. Along the way we've also shared many happy memories with our families, and we hope you will with yours.

About This Book

Each of our tours describes a full day of places for your family to visit, and many list other things to do in the area or similar places to visit another time. Quite a few tours have more spots than you could possibly see in one day, so we've provided information to help you cut and shape them to fit your family. This also lessens the boredom when a child falls in love with a particular place and begs to go there often—you can combine it with something different every time you go.

We tried to describe each spot so that you will have a good idea of what you can find there, and we've provided background information to make things easier in places where you'll find lots of fun but little English. Special sections on the last few pages of each tour assist you with the mechanics—as well as the pleasures—of the day.

The "Eating Options" section lets you know where you can find restaurants or places to eat food from home. One word of caution here: aside from a few noteworthy exceptions, we made no effort to critique restaurants. The fare available at most museums, amusement parks, etc., is more or less the same across the board, with few places aimed at pleasing sophisticated palates. "For Infants and Toddlers" lets you know about nursing or diapering facilities (see Appendices for information on department stores) and whether your stroller will be more of an asset than a liability, as well as offering other information useful to parents of very young children. The "Where & When" section lists addresses, phone numbers, prices, directions, station exits, and parking facilities. Note that even when a site has no parking of its own, you may be able to find a place nearby—we put as many lots as possible on our maps to help. We tried to give not only directions from one spot on the tour to the next, but also general directions to each place to help parents who might want to skip earlier stops. At the end of each "Where & When" entry, we comment on how much English you'll find, whether there is a spot for nursing, and if you need reservations. We also give you an idea of the target age group for most places, although of course this is just a general guide; after reading the descriptions you'll have a fairly good idea of what will appeal to your own children.

TIPS FOR TAKING TOURS

Phone First

We've been careful to select only spots we think will be around for years, but places are constantly closing temporarily to add new attractions or tear down old ones, changing holidays and hours, raising prices, and sometimes disappearing altogether. Based on our own experience, we recommend you pick up the phone and make sure any spots you really want to visit are open before you set out. See our "Some Useful Phrases in Japanese" section at the back of the book for the expressions you'll need.

Bring the Essentials

If you are traveling by public transportation, put your gear in backpacks and waist pouches to keep your hands free and to balance your load if you have to carry a sleeping child.

Large supermarkets and department stores sell sturdy, lightweight, waterproof picnic sheets. These are much easier to carry than a heavy blanket, can be used as either a picnic tablecloth or a ground cover, and wash up easily with a wet sponge.

If your children are small, a lightweight stroller is essential. Some of the

> Japanese children learn early never to leave the house without tissues and a handkerchief. Public toilets often have no hand towels and sometimes no toilet paper, so these are essential. You might also want to pack *oshibori* (damp hand towels) to take care of sticky fingers and faces. Sanrio gift and stationery shops in department stores and neighborhood shopping areas sell cute little *oshibori* as well as plastic cases, both of which can be used over and over again.

Japanese models can be folded and opened with one hand, but the handles may be too low for tall non-Japanese parents. Check out the local infant carriers, too; several styles double as a small bag for snacks, wipes, and other items. If you're using mass transit, you'll also want a good English map of the rail system, available at English bookstores, and a copy of the Toei bus map, which you can get from the Tourist Information Center in Yurakucho—☎ (03) 3502–1461. If you are taking a small child on a cycling tour, bring your own child seat—they are generally not available from bike rental shops.

Winter in the Tokyo area is mild, but cold enough to warrant putting on a few layers. Dress warmer if you are going to Sakura City or Narita, where the days get a little cooler. Summer, on the other hand, is very hot (a bit cooler in Kamakura and Yokohama). It's best to put hats on small children to keep them safe from the tropical sun, and give them plenty to drink. During the rainy season from mid-June to mid-July you'll probably want to carry a folding umbrella in your backpack—Japan has a wide selection of ultralight models. Bring insect repellent if you are going to a park or wooded area in the summer. Pack light if you're taking the train and don't worry about forgetting something. Japan has twenty-four-hour convenience stores nearly everywhere, selling everything from hot lunches to batteries.

Getting Around

All destinations in the book can be reached by public transportation, and many have parking attached or in their vicinity. Reading the "Where & When" section will help you decide how you want to go. There are stairs at nearly all stations, something to remember when your kids are in strollers. Train, subway, and bus lines all have the same systems for child and adult fares. Two children under the age of six per adult can ride free on buses, subways, and trains. If you bring three or more children under the age of six, the extra children pay the child fare, which is half of the adult fare. Infants under age one ride free. Children six to twelve pay the child fare; children twelve and older pay the adult fare. Most stations on our tours have English signs to guide you to the platform you want, but some don't have fare maps posted in Roman letters. If this is the case, you can always buy the cheapest ticket and pay a fare adjustment at your destination without penalty.

If you want to bring a bicycle on a train or bus you must carry it in a bag; you can pick up one made for this purpose at a local bike or sporting goods store. You must take the front wheel off the bike to fit it in the bike bag.

Discount Fares

Trains, subways, and buses have several types of discount tickets, most of which you can buy at the automatic ticket-dispensing machines. Multiple-trip tickets (*kaisu ken*) offer eleven tickets for the price of ten. Japan Rail (JR) sells Orange Cards, prepaid fare cards that you can use to purchase tickets at the ticket vending machines. Larger denominations of the card have discounts. JR also sells an IO card to use for adult fares only. There are no discounts with this card, but there is definitely a timesaving advantage: no figuring out what fare to pay and no lining up to buy tickets. You simply insert the card in the electronic ticket wicket as you enter and when you leave. Your fare is automatically calculated and deducted from the card. Note the IO card does not work for child fares, so there is little advantage in buying them if you have children between the ages of six and twelve. You can also use the IO cards to purchase tickets at the automatic vending machines.

Tokyo subway stations sell T cards, which operate the same as JR's IO cards and can be used for both subway systems in Tokyo: Toei and Eidan. The Toei subway system has a one-day pass that can be used for the Arakawa line Toden Streetcar, Toei buses, and Toei subways. The pass, called *Ichinichi Josha Ken*, costs ¥700 for adults and ¥350 for children.

There are two types of buses: those that charge a flat fee and those with fares based on the distance you travel. On a flat-fare bus you enter near the front of the bus, pay the fare, and go as far as you want. On a bus where fares are based on distance, you enter at the middle of the bus and take a slip of paper with a number on it. The number corresponds to a fare displayed on a board at the front of the bus. Pay the fare at the box near the driver as you get off. Most buses have automated change makers that can accept ¥1,000 bills as well as coins. Buses also have a prepaid card that offers discounts for larger denominations. The card, Bus Kyotsu Card, can be used in Tokyo's twenty-three wards, Musashino, Mitaka, Komae, and Chofu cities of the Districts of Tokyo, Yokohama, and Kawasaki.

Rush hour on any type of mass transit will be dangerous for small children, especially in the morning. Train and subway cars get so packed that even adults can be crushed. Rush hours vary from line to line, but as a rule stay off the trains and subways from 7:30 to 9 A.M. The evening rush hour starts slowly from about 4 and continues through 6:30. Adjust these times if you are farther out in the suburbs; trains leaving Yokohama, for example, are packed from 7 A.M. with workers who must travel all the way to Tokyo to get to the office by 8.

Trains, subways, and buses all have "silver seats," reserved for the elderly and handicapped. The general pattern of etiquette here—though often ignored—is for teenagers and young adults (usually young women) to give up seats for the elderly. You'll often

Taxis

Taxis here have a hefty initial meter charge, but the fare increases more slowly as you go along than in many other major cities. The left taxi door opens and closes automatically. You cannot enter or exit a taxi from the right. You'll find taxi stands near train stations, department stores, and hotels, but you can also hail one from the street. Bring a map and have a general idea of where you are going—you may have to direct the driver.

find a kind soul, usually a woman with kids of her own, willing to relinquish a seat for a parent carrying a sleeping toddler. And, though not a local custom, often Japanese men will give up a seat to a foreign woman. Japanese don't eat on the street or local trains but this rule is relaxed for small children. It's okay to give them some crackers and juice to tide them over till the next meal. It's also okay for kids to climb all over the seats as long as they remove their shoes.

Lost and Found

As careful as you may be, with kids, it seems something always gets left behind. Taxis have a central lost and found used by all companies. If you lost the item on a train or subway, inquire at the last station on the line. If you lost it on a bus, inquire at the bus office on the route. If you don't inquire about the lost article in a day or two it will be taken to a lost and found center. Here are some numbers for lost and found centers:

❏ JR	(03) 3231–1880
❏ Eidan subways	(03) 3834–5577
❏ Toei bus and subways	(03) 3431–1515
❏ Taxi	(03) 3648–0300

Something for Your Scrapbooks

Most museums, zoos, aquariums, amusement parks, and train stations have commemorative rubber stamps you can stamp into a scrapbook. Kids love these. Buy a special book to put them in and help your child fill it up with memories from enjoyable outings.

Map Symbols

P Parking
T Taxi
✟ Baby room

Old Japan for the Young

To really understand modern Japan, you need to examine its cultural and historical roots. This section is packed with places where history remains, or has been recreated in amazing detail. You can also experience lasting traditions like sipping ceremonial tea, watching craftsmen fashion Edo-period toys, or attending a temple festival.

Asakusa, the birthplace of Tokyo, is the city's most famous temple, and the area around it is crowded with traditional souvenir shops and fun family activities that don't appear in ordinary guidebooks. If you're in the mood for a quieter Japanese experience, stroll the friendly old-fashioned streets of **Shibamata**, lined with tiny sweet shops. On weekends you can rent bikes and cycle the Edogawa river levy to a park where you can wade and fish, then admire the water and greenery in the traditional garden of a wealthy merchant. Chances are there won't be another foreigner in sight. A pleasant riverside bicycle ride through a nature preserve and shops specializing in delicious fresh-made soba make a trip to woodsy **Jindaiji temple** a special outing. A nearby cycle rental shop has bikes available all week. For a dose of ancient Japan, visit the temples, shrines, gardens, and statues of historic **Kamakura**. We've weeded out the spots that won't appeal to kids and ordered your day so you can see as much as possible with a minimum of transportation hassles.

There's more to this section than shrines and temples, though. Wander through a life-size recreation of a working-class neighborhood in Edo-period Tokyo, fingering cooking utensils, sake bottles, and furnishings as you listen to the sounds of old **Fukagawa.** Just minutes away from the indoor museum you can follow steppingstones around a large traditional garden complete with a teahouse and ducks in a pond. The scale is much larger at **Koganei Park**'s open-air architectural museum, where you can walk into historical farmhouses, shops, and mansions that have been moved here from all over Tokyo. Because the buildings come from different eras, you can get a feeling for how the Musashino plain was developed over the years. If you're looking for a lot of easy-to-digest background on Japan, visit the **National Museum of Japanese History** in Sakura, where outstanding displays and detailed information in five languages bring history to life.

1

A Child's View of Asakusa

Karakuri Clock • Sensoji Temple and Nakamise • Hanayashiki Amusement Park • Drum Museum

Before undertaking a difficult role, Kabuki actors go to Asakusa's Sensoji temple to pray. Sumo wrestlers dressed in traditional attire visit the temple in preparation for tournaments. Kimono-clad Japanese dancers, intent on purchasing makeup, fans, and props, mingle with the thousands of tourists who come to Asakusa to admire the temple and buy gifts at the tiny traditional shops crowding the area.

Asakusa was once just a small farming village. But it became the heart of

Sensoji, said to be the birthplace of Tokyo, got its start back in 628, when two brothers found a small gold statue of Kannon, the goddess of mercy, while fishing. They gave it to their village headman, who kept it in his home until a temple was erected to house it. Asakusa Shrine, located east of the main temple building, is dedicated to these three men.

Japan's entertainment industry when the area, then called Edo, was made the capital of the country. Stalls selling toys, souvenirs, and sweets sprang up around Sensoji, competing with acrobats and street musicians for the attention of the crowds. Among the most popular wares were woodblock prints (*ukiyo-e*) of leading Kabuki actors; Asakusa was home to the country's leading Kabuki theaters from the 1840s until the mid-twentieth century, and the Asakusa Kokaido hall still features Kabuki plays for the entire month of January. The first movie theaters were built in this district, alongside watering holes ranging from cheap bars to expensive geisha establishments. Much of Asakusa was destroyed by the firebombings of World War II, but the area was quickly rebuilt. Although Ginza, Shibuya, Roppongi, and Shinjuku are better known for their nightlife today, Asakusa is still the best place to experience a traditional Japanese carnival atmosphere any day of the year.

A festive air overtakes you as soon as you exit the station. Try to time your arrival so you can be outside the nearby **Asakusa Culture and Tourism Center** on the hour. As Seiko's large *karakuri* **clock** above the entrance chimes the hours from 10 A.M. to 7 P.M., mechanical revelers hoist a portable gold *mikoshi* shrine and shout *"seya"* to the beat of a traditional Japanese melody, just as they do at real Asakusa festivals. Small costumed figures perform actual dances from the area's most important *matsuri*, or festival. The show lasts only 3 minutes, but superb craftsmanship and ¥100 million went into its production, and the results are impressive. Inside, the tourism center with its comfortable benches and clean bathrooms is a good place to regroup, meet friends, and gather English-language information on all of Japan. The English-speaking staff will provide free maps and answer questions.

Look across the big street and you'll quickly spot the famous red gate that leads to Asakusa's delights. Decorated by a huge paper lantern, the Kaminarimon, or Thunder God Gate, is one of the most famous symbols of Tokyo. As you pass through you can see impressive carvings of the god of thunder on your left and the god of wind on your right.

Tiny shops selling everything from Noh masks and good luck charms to paper umbrellas and kimono crowd the long *nakamise* shopping street that leads to Sensoji. This is a great spot to shop for Japanese-style gifts for friends and family back home. **Ichibanya**, halfway up on the right side, is the source of the delicious aroma you notice as you walk toward the temple. Pick up one of their freshly made *senbei* rice crackers and nibble as you browse. Ichibanya also has another large cracker store directly behind this one. Two stores closer to the Kaminarimon, Ichibanya's sister store, **Iidaya**, serves the Japanese dance community. This famous shop is a good place to look for fans, paper umbrellas, colored *tabi* socks, and other souvenirs. The shop has a small stage they rent out, and you can often catch a glimpse of women in beautiful dance kimono on their way to a performance.

Sukeroku, the tiny shop next to the end of the *nakamise*, sells traditional hand-crafted miniatures. The Kimura family, which has always owned this nationally famous one-of-a-kind shop, sold books here when Sukeroku opened in 1866. When they introduced a few miniatures, the immensely popular figurines soon took over the bookshelves. The current Mr. Kimura can help you select a collectible in English. His brother runs the last shop in the row, **Kimuraya Honten**, which sells one of the sweets Japanese visitors to Tokyo often buy as a souvenir for the folks back home: *ningyo yaki*.

The large and impressive Hozonmon gate at the end of the street marks the entrance to the **Sensoji temple** grounds. Notice the enormous straw sandals hanging behind the guardian gods on either side. They were a gift from a village famous for its weaving techniques, provided in case the gods felt like going for a stroll. On your left is a beautiful five-story pagoda, one of several buildings that share the grounds with Sensoji. To the east of the temple you'll find Asakusa Shrine, the traditional red building that gave the area its start. Before heading up the steps of the main temple, pause a mo-

A variety of Japan's ubiquitous sweet-bean-filled cakes called *ningyo yaki* are often shaped like religious figures; the ones in Asakusa are cooked in molds of the thunder god, pigeons, pagodas, and *akachochin*, the red lanterns hung outside drinking establishments. The area's most famous treat is *okoshi*, a sweet crunchy rice snack sold throughout the *naka-mise*. It is shaped into bars that resemble their American cousins, Rice Krispy Treats.

ment to join the people wafting incense smoke toward their faces; this is said to prevent bad luck. Sensoji is an impressive temple, and the area around the altar glitters with gold. The big golden lanterns in the main hall were donated by local geisha organizations, yet another sign of the strong ties the entertainment industry has to Sensoji.

It seems appropriate that Japan's very first amusement park is less than 50 meters away. The recently renovated **Hanayashiki Amusement Park** attracted huge crowds when it was built back in 1853. Today this small park has twenty rides that appeal mainly to preschoolers and elementary school children, including a small roller coaster and a merry-go-round. A Japanese haunted house maintains the flavor of old Asakusa. You can buy tickets for each attraction as you go or buy your kids a Flower Free Band all-day pass and let them ride as much as they want.

To fully appreciate the flavor of the neighborhood, stroll back down the *naka-mise* when you've finished looking around the temple and the amusement park. Exploring Sensoji and its environs could take anywhere from 45 minutes to 3 hours. Shoppers may want to save some time to look into two small shops that stand across from each other on one of the side streets that leads to the Drum Museum, the last stop on our tour. **Takahisa Dolls** sells dolls and *hagoita,* beautifully decorated racquets for the traditional badminton games played at New Year's. **Asakusa Edo-ya** sells Japanese figurines and paper goods.

The **Drum Museum** is about a 7-minute walk from the *nakamise*. Continue down Mise Dori until you reach Kokusai Dori. Turn left and walk to the first intersection, and you'll see it across the street. Spotting the museum is easy; it's located above the Miyamoto Japanese Percussion and Festival Store, a corner shop whose windows are decorated with masks, *happi* coats, drums, and *mikoshi*, or portable shrines. You can buy a ticket to the museum at the store's counter, along with everything you'd ever need for a traditional Japanese festival. The clerks will direct you to the elevator that takes you up to the fourth-floor museum.

Inside, bang away. If you've ever wanted to try your hand at playing a steel drum, a set of bongos, or a huge *taiko* drum, this is the place. Preschoolers and anyone with a sense of rhythm will spend a delightful half hour or more testing out the sounds of drums from all around the world. Only the delicate or rare specimens marked with red dots are off limits, but they do ask that you just tap lightly to sample the sound of drums marked with blue. The museum, which has over three hundred percussion instruments, offers classes on different instruments and various styles of music, often with instructors from the instruments' native countries.

Asakusa is a big place, packed with adventure, but inside the drum museum and some of the small shops you can experience the friendly intimacy this part of town is famous for. Hard-working shopkeepers call out *"irasshaimase"* (please come in) 365 days a year here, and festivals are frequent. Check the schedule at the end of the chapter. If you're lucky, you may run into a Kabuki actor, geisha, or sumo wrestler.

Other Things to Do in the Area

Add another element of fun to your day at Asakusa: arrive by boat. Chug up the Sumida river past the Hama Detached Palace Garden, round the bend at the towering, modern River City 21 complex, continue past the sumo stadium and under the twelve bridges that cross this legendary waterway. A recorded English narration gives background information on the sights you pass. The 40-minute **boat trip** from Hinode Pier near Hamamatsucho takes you to Asakusa Pier, just 5 minutes' walk from Kaminarimon. (See Tour 18 for map of water bus routes.)

To make souvenir shopping a more personal experience, visit the second floor of **Kaminari Goro Goro Jaya**, where you can watch artists at work on Edo-period crafts on the weekends. The shop has a wide range of products to appeal to all tastes and budgets. Choose from *ukiyo-e* prints, kites, leather crafts, straw *tawashi* brushes and handmade brooms, and ingeniously crafted wooden tops. If you understand Japanese, buy a ticket to the third-floor mixed-media gallery for an in-depth look at the rich history of the Asakusa area. The first floor combines a Japanese restaurant with a souvenir shop specializing in *okoshi,* candy-coated rice shaped into bars. Kaminari Goro Goro Jaya is on the street behind Gojunoto Dori, or, in English, Pagoda Street.

A few streets beyond Hanayashiki is the **Traditional Crafts Exhibition Hall**. Here, too, you can watch artisans at work on traditional crafts and purchase souvenirs. Though there is only one craftsperson each day, the level of skill is usually exceptional—many of those invited to display their work have been officially honored as Living National Treasures.

Kappabashi means kitchenware to Tokyoites. A 6-minute walk beyond the drum museum will bring you to this neighborhood where restaurateurs come to shop for inexpensive wholesale dishes and the plastic food displayed in front of their eating establishments to attract customers. Some of the stores also have whimsical gift ideas that incorporate imitations of sushi and other popular dishes. Keep in mind that most of the stores are closed on weekends and national holidays.

Festival Schedule

Asakusa has festivals and fairs almost every month of the year. Unfortunately, some of the major events attract crowds so enormous and so packed they are unpleasant for families with small children. Use this schedule either to avoid or to attend, depending on your family makeup. Dates to expect crowds are marked with an asterisk.

- *January 1
  The crowds visiting the shrine at New Year's include many in kimono.
- February 3
  Setsubun Bean Scattering Festival and Fukuju-no-Mai, a dance festival.
- February 8
  Hari Kuyo is a service of thanks for used sewing needles.
- *March 18 and October 18
  Kinyu-no-Mai or Dance of the Golden Dragon celebrates the legend of the fishermen who discovered the missing image of Kannon, the Goddess of Mercy, on March 18, 628. When the Kannon was found in the Sumida river, it is said the scales of the dragon in the temple sparkled. The dance is held again on October 18 when chrysanthemums are offered to the Kannon.
- Late April
  Crying Sumo Tournament
- May 5
  Takara-no-Mai, a dance festival
- *Third Saturday and Sunday in May
  One of Tokyo's three biggest festivals, Sanja Matsuri, takes place at Asakusa Shrine. About one hundred *mikoshi* are paraded through the area. Sure to be exceedingly crowded with onlookers.
- Late May
  Asakusa Azalea Festival

- *July 9 and 10
  Worshippers believe a visit to the Kannon at Sensoji on July 9 or 10 is the equivalent of praying every day for 46,000 days. On these two days Sensoji holds Hozuki Ichi, or the Lantern Plant Festival. Vendors sell lantern plants, which supposedly drive away the summer's heat.
- Saturday in late August
  Asakusa Samba Carnival, where dancers in skimpy feathered costumes move to Brazilian music.
- A Sunday in October
  Edo Portable Shrine Festival
- Mid-October to mid-November
  Asakusa Chrysanthemum Exhibition
- *November 3
  Sensoji has two festivals on this day. Shirasagi-no-Mai, the more famous of the two, features dancers dressed in white heron costumes. Tokyo Jidai Matsuri celebrates Tokyo's past and present.
- December 14–19
  Gasa End-of-Year Fair
- *December 17–19
  Hagoita Ichi is a good festival to visit with children. The crowds are manageable, especially if the festival falls during the week. *Hagoita* are wooden racquets used for a Japanese version of badminton traditionally played during the New Year season. Although you probably wouldn't want to actually use the beautifully decorated *hagoita* on sale in the local stalls, displays of racquets emblazoned with women in traditional costume or Kabuki actors make for a festival atmosphere.
- December 31
  New Year's Bell Ringing at midnight

EATING OPTIONS

Restaurants Asakusa has plenty of Japanese-style restaurants in every price range. The area around the temple is crowded with places selling *soba* noodles and sushi, *tonkatsu* (fried pork cutlets) and tempura. A Kentucky Fried Chicken and a McDonald's with highchairs cater to those starved for Western food.

Picnic Possibilities Unfortunately, there isn't really a family-oriented park we can recommend for eating outside in the area. Nearby Sumida Park is a haven for the homeless. Volunteers from the Franciscan Chapel Center and other churches distribute meals here on many Saturday evenings. Kids help too; call ☎ (03) 3401-2141 if your family wants to participate.

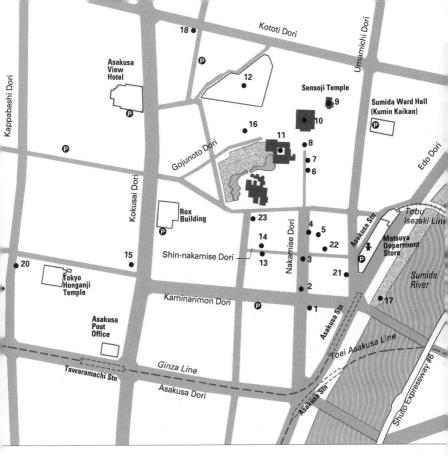

PLACES TO VISIT

1. Asakusa Culture and Tourism Center
   (*Karakuri* Clock)
2. Kaminarimon Gate
3. Sensoji Nakamise
4. Ichibanya Senbei
5. Iidaya Dance Accessories and Souveniers
6. Sukeroku (miniatures)
7. Kimuraya Honten Ningyo Yaki Shop
8. Hozomon Gate
9. Sensoji Temple
10. Asakusa Shrine
11. Pagoda
12. Hanayashiki Amusement Park
13. Takahisa Dolls & Hagoita
14. Asakusa Edo-ya Souvenirs
15. Drum Museum
16. Kaminari Goro Goro Jaya
17. Sumida River Boat Terminal
18. Traditional Crafts Exhibition Hall
19. Kappabashi Shopping Street
20. Plastic Food Shop
21. Kentucky Fried Chicken
22. McDonald's
23. Asakusa Kokaido

FOR INFANTS AND TODDLERS

Hanayashiki has diaper-changing areas near the restrooms. Ask a park attendant if you want to nurse; they will direct you to a second-floor office you can use. The Asakusa Culture and Tourism center has clean bathrooms, free English maps, comfortable benches, and English-speaking receptionists who are happy to answer questions. There are no diaper-changing facilities or nursing rooms, but it's a good place to get your bearings when you arrive or want to regroup later in the day. Asakusa is a big, exciting place with activities for all ages, but some infants and toddlers may find it overwhelming.

WHERE & WHEN

Asakusa Culture and Tourism Center
浅草文化観光センター (Asakusa Bunka Kanko Center)

2–18–9 Kaminarimon, Taito-ku, Tokyo 111–0034

☎ (03) 3842–5566

東京都台東区雷門2-18-9　〒111-0034

OPEN: daily 9:30 A.M. to 8 P.M.; *karakuri* clock chimes on the hour from 10 A.M. to 7 P.M.

DIRECTIONS: opposite Kaminarimon gate. See directions for Sensoji temple.

Sensoji Nakamise
浅草寺仲見世

• **Ichibanya Senbei**
一番屋煎餅

1–31–1 Asakusa, Taito-ku, Tokyo 111–0032

☎ (03) 3842–5001

東京都台東区浅草1-31-1　〒111-0032

OPEN: daily 7:30 A.M. to 7:30 P.M.

• **Iidaya Dance Accessories and Souvenirs**
民芸品の飯田屋 (Mingeihin Iidaya)

1–31–1 Asakusa, Taito-ku, Tokyo 111–0032

☎ (03) 3841–3644

東京都台東区浅草1-31-1　〒111-0032

OPEN: daily 10 A.M. to 7:30 P.M.

• **Sukeroku Miniatures**
助六ミニチュア玩具

2–3–1 Asakusa, Taito-ku, Tokyo 111–0032

☎ (03) 3844–0577

東京都台東区浅草2-3-1　〒111-0032

OPEN: daily 10 A.M. to 6 P.M.

• **Kimuraya Honten Ningyo Yaki Shop**
木村家人形焼本舗

2–3–1 Asakusa, Taito-ku, Tokyo

☎ (03) 3844–9754

東京都台東区浅草2-3-1

OPEN: 10 A.M. to 6 P.M.

CLOSED: Thurs

• **Takahisa Dolls & Hagoita**
高久人形 (Takahisa Ningyo)

1–21–7 Asakusa, Taito-ku, Tokyo 111–0032

☎ (03) 3844–1257

東京都台東区浅草1-21-7　〒111-0032

OPEN: daily 10 A.M. to 8 P.M.

• **Asakusa Edo-ya Souvenirs**
浅草江戸屋

1–29–4 Asakusa, Taito-ku, Tokyo 111–0032

☎ (03) 3844–3715

東京都台東区浅草1-29-4　〒111-0032

OPEN: daily 10 A.M. to 8 P.M.

Sensoji Temple and Asakusa Shrine
浅草寺と浅草神社

2–3–1 Asakusa, Taito-ku, Tokyo 111–0032

☎ (03) 3842–0181

東京都台東区浅草2-3-1　〒111-0032
OPEN: daily 6 A.M. to 5 P.M.

FEES: free, but most visitors make small donations when they pray at the altar

DIRECTIONS: a 3- to 5-minute walk from Asakusa station (Ginza line exit 1, Asakusa line exit A4) or Tobu Asakusa station. Walk toward the main street and look for the big red Kaminarimon gate. By car, you'll find Sensoji to the west of expressway #1 between Kototoi Dori and Kaminarimon Dori.

PARKING: none at the temple. Area lots are noted on the map, but parking is often difficult in this area.

COMMENTS: all ages, English pamphlets

Hanayashiki Amusement Park

浅草花屋敷 (Asakusa Hana-yashiki)

2–28–1 Asakusa, Taito-ku, Tokyo 111–0032

☎ (03) 3842–8780

東京都台東区浅草2-28-1　〒111-0032

OPEN: 10 A.M. to 6 P.M.

CLOSED: Tues, except during Japanese school hols

FEES: entrance for adults ¥800; children over 5, ¥400; attraction prices vary; all-day pass also available

DIRECTIONS: behind Sensoji temple

PARKING: none

COMMENTS: all ages, no English, nursing room

Drum Museum

太鼓館 (Taiko-kan)

Miyamoto Unosuke Shoten, 4F

2–1–1 Nishi-Asakusa, Taito-ku, Tokyo 111–0035

☎ (03) 3842–5622

東京都台東区西浅草2-1-1　宮本卯之助商店4階　〒111-0035

OPEN: 10 A.M. to 5 P.M.

CLOSED: Mon and Tues; Obon (mid-Aug) and New Year's hols (call for dates)

FEES: adults ¥300, children ¥150

DIRECTIONS: A 2-minute walk from Tawaramachi station (Ginza line) or a 6-minute

walk from Asakusa station (Ginza line exit 2 and Asakusa line exit A4). By car, you'll find it on Kokusai Dori at the T-crossing with Kaminarimon Dori.

PARKING: none

COMMENTS: all ages, English pamphlets

Kaminari Goro Goro Jaya

雷五六五六茶屋

2–7–3 Asakusa, Taito-ku, Tokyo 111–0032

☎ (03) 3844–5656

東京都台東区浅草2-7-3　〒111-0032

OPEN: 10 A.M. to 5 P.M. weekdays; until 6 on weekends

CLOSED: 2nd and 4th Tues

DIRECTIONS: on the street behind Gojunoto Dori, or Pagoda Street. Head west on the street behind the 5-story pagoda until you leave the temple grounds; it's the 1st shop on the right.

COMMENTS: all ages, no English

Traditional Crafts Exhibition Hall

江戸下町伝統工芸館 (Edo Shitamachi Dento Kogei-kan)

2–22–12 Asakusa, Taito-ku, Tokyo 111–0032

☎ (03) 3847–2587

東京都台東区浅草2-22-12　〒111-0032

OPEN: 10 A.M. to 5 P.M. weekdays; until 6 on weekends

CLOSED: Tues

FEES: none

DIRECTIONS: 6 minutes on foot from Tobu Asakusa station or a 10-minute walk from Asakusa station (Ginza line exit 2, Asakusa line exit A4). By car, near the intersection of Kototoi Dori and Hisago Dori.

PARKING: none

COMMENTS: all ages, no English

Sumida River Ferry Piers

隅田川観光汽船 (Sumidagawa Kankokisen)

☎ (03) 3457–7830 (Hinode Pier), (03) 3841–9178 (Asakusa Pier)

OPEN: Boats leave once or twice an hour every

day starting at 9:50 A.M., with the last boat leaving Asakusa at 7:35 P.M. (summer), 6:15 P.M. (winter).

FEES: adults ¥660 one way, children ages 6 to 11 ¥330

DIRECTIONS: see map for directions to Asakusa Pier. Hinode Pier is a 7-minute walk from Hamamatsucho station (Tokyo Monorail, JR Keihin Tohoku, and Yamanote lines). From the south exit take the covered overpass to exit S2 just after the river on left. Follow the tree-lined, winding road and take the 1st street on the left over the bridge. Cross Kaigan Dori and walk toward the red brick building. The pier is next to the building. It's also a 5-minute walk from Hinode station (Yurikamome line). By car, use expressway #1 or the Inner Circular line and exit at Hamazakibashi.

PARKING: there is no parking at the pier but you can use the lot at the World Trade Center near Hamamatsucho station where you pay by the hour.

COMMENTS: all ages

Step into Old Edo in Fukagawa

Fukagawa Edo Museum • Kiyosumi Garden • Nakamise Shopping Street • Fukagawa Fudoson Temple • Tomioka Hachiman Shrine

E vening falls in a working-class section of Edo: a fisherman's nets hang out to dry, while the poor-but-genteel widow next door softly strums her *shamisen*. Down by the riverfront, laughter drifts from the doorways of the local taverns.

Step into the past at the **Fukagawa Edo Museum** and experience Tokyo as it was a hundred and fifty years ago. Duck into the Masudaya Tavern, its low doorway built to suit the smaller stature of the people that populated this part of town when it was called Edo. The room is furnished exactly as it would have been back then, as are all ten or so of the buildings in this indoor museum's small but fascinating neighborhood. Slip off your shoes and explore the interiors; handle the craftsmen's tools and examine the sashes in the drawers of the waitress's wardrobe. Excellent sound and lighting effects take you through the day, from the cock's crow at dawn to the soft singing of the cicadas on a starry night.

Adults will want to buy the ¥600 English guide, a gossipy tour of the quarter and introduction to its inhabitants in the historical voice of Genzo-san, the local shopkeeper who manages the rice store. This well-written booklet brings the museum to life, giving detailed histories of the characters whose images greet you at the entrance to the museum. After you read it, listening to the sounds of these townspeople as they go about their daily business will make you feel surrounded by friendly ghosts. You are allowed to touch the houses and all their furnishings, although children should be carefully controlled to prevent them from breaking anything. An hour or two can easily slip by as you explore the truly outstanding displays.

Rocks, trees, water, carp, and ducks are the main attractions at the next stop, **Kiyosumi Garden**, about 6 minutes down the street from the museum. Originally the property of the wealthy merchant Bunzaimon Kinokuniya (no relation to the supermarket or bookstore), this peaceful garden also provides a glimpse of traditional Japan. Clever bridges, stepping-stones, artfully shaped trees, lanterns, and small islands vary the scene as you stroll the narrow gravel path around the pond. A graceful teahouse casts its reflection on the water. The traditional building, a reproduction of a lodge built to entertain British general H. H. Kitchener when he visited Japan in 1909, can be rented for special occasions. A quick trip around the garden takes about half an hour, longer if you stop to enjoy the animal life in the pond. Small children and out-of-town guests will be especially pleased with this beautifully landscaped garden.

The garden has only one gate; exit and walk along the outside of the wall, then follow Kiyosumi Dori south for about 15 minutes or take the bus to the **Monzen-Nakacho area**. This part of town retains the friendliness of Tokyo's old downtown district, especially on the fifteenth and twenty-eighth of each month when a temple fair is held. Stop to pick out a pair of traditional wooden *geta* (clogs), and the entire neighborhood will advise you on the best choice. The *geta* maker himself jokes and winks as he crafts each pair. Shops selling Japanese tea, rice crackers, and pickles line the narrow shopping street, or *nakamise*, that leads to the temple area, and on temple fair days vendors in booths sell *yakisoba* (fried noodles), *okonomiyaki* (a savory pancake), *takoyaki* (octopus fritters), and other Japanese treats. Japanese candies shaped like sushi, fruits, and vegetables, the specialty of a small shop called **Hana**, make fun gifts or entertaining snacks.

Fukagawa Fudoson, at the end of the street, is a living temple. On festival days it is festooned with brightly colored banners, and even on ordinary days many people come to pray and hold Buddhist ceremonies. In one corner you can see barrels of *sake* that have been donated to the temple; on New Year's Eve they are opened and used to make warm drinks for visitors. Across a narrow lane is **Tomioka Hachiman**, a spacious shrine whose grounds were the birthplace of the National Grand Sumo Tournament. Parents of boys come here to pray that their babies will grow up to be as strong as sumo wrestlers.

On display behind glass in the southern part of the grounds, the *mikoshi* is so heavy that even a huge group of people can support it for only a minute or two. Because it is impractical to shift bearers so often, the *mikoshi* remains in its display case for annual festivities and even during the big August festival the temple holds every three years. However, fifty or more smaller *mikoshi* are paraded through the streets.

The shrine also has one of the largest and most ornate *mikoshi* (portable shrines) in Japan.

Strolling the grounds of the temple and shrine and exploring the old-style shopping street should take about 45 minutes. When you're finished, the subway back to modern Tokyo is right across the street.

Other Things to Do in the Area

Active elementary schoolchildren will like the adventurous wooden climbing equipment in **Kiyosumi Park**, just next to Kiyosumi Garden. Plenty of open space and trees make this a nice spot to relax or eat lunch. Brightly colored slides, swings, and other equipment in the small playground located along the south wall of Kiyosumi Garden (walk around the outside of the garden) and at **Fukagawa Park** near Monzen-Nakacho station will delight children five and under.

Also off Kiyosumi Dori are Ryogoku Kokugikan, the **Sumo Stadium and Museum**, and the neighboring **Edo-Tokyo Museum**. Decorative sumo artifacts, woodblock prints of ancient wrestlers, and pictures of recent champions are the highlights of the small but worthwhile museum inside the stadium. The sumo matches themselves are a truly unique Japanese experience, although tickets can be hard to get. The futuristic Edo-Tokyo Museum's design was inspired by the traditional shape of a Japanese storage house. Inside, top-notch displays and models with moving figures teach about the lives of Edo-period peasants, merchants, warriors, and nobles, the move toward Westernization, and modern events like the Great Kanto Earthquake and postwar reconstruction. The museum offers pamphlets in English, Chinese, Korean, and French, and earphone sets with information in the first three languages are available near the ticket counter with a returnable ¥3,000 deposit. You'll also find a shop specializing in traditional handicrafts, and there's often a craftsman hard at work on the shop's second floor. The museum is a great way to give visiting friends and relatives a look at Tokyo's history, but on the whole it is more likely to be appreciated by adults than children. See Tour 5 for a description of the museum's open-air branch in Koganei Park, which is more likely to entertain the whole family.

The **Yasuda Garden** lies about 2 minutes on foot from the Edo-Tokyo Museum. A pond with carp and ducks, a traditional vermilion bridge, and pleasantly shaped pines and maples provide a restful view, especially in autumn when the maples turn red. Boat lovers can head to **Takabashi Pier** for a water bus ride (see map in Tour 18) to Yumenoshima (see Tour 27) or Tokyo Bay.

ONE

STEP INTO OLD EDO

Tour 2

EATING OPTIONS

Restaurants Across from the Fukagawa Edo Museum is Fukagawajuku, a small but famous restaurant specializing in an Edo-style simmered clam dish; there are few other restaurants in the neighborhood. You'll find more and better restaurant options in the Monzen-Nakacho area. The Edo-Tokyo Museum has a Japanese tea shop, a coffee shop, and two restaurants: one Western and one Japanese. There are also some fast-food restaurants near Monzen-Nakacho station.

Picnic Possibilities Bring food from home or stop and pick up something at Monzen-Nakacho's takeout restaurants; only ice cream, drinks, and snacks are sold in Kiyosumi Garden. The west corner of the garden has a grassy area with several picnic tables, but small groups will enjoy snacking on benches by the many scenic spots around the pond. Kiyosumi and Fukagawa parks are also nice spots for outdoor eating. You can eat your lunch outside on the Edo-Tokyo Plaza on the third floor of the Edo-Tokyo Museum; bring something from home or buy an *obento* boxed lunch from the stall near the main escalator on the same level. A bench near the pond in Old Yasuda Garden is another scenic lunch spot.

FOR INFANTS AND TODDLERS

While this tour is fun for small children, there aren't many facilities for them in the neighborhood. The toilets on the second floor of the Fukugawa Edo Museum are clean enough that you could spread a diaper-changing mat on the floor; hot water is available in the lounge near the entrance, where you can also get free tea for yourself. The Edo-Tokyo Museum has a diaper-changing table in the disabled toilet on the seventh floor.

Bringing a stroller is a good idea since there's a lot of walking involved in the main tour, but you'll want to leave it at the entrance to the Fukagawa Edo Museum and the gardens. In these places, stairs and rough ground will make it more of a hindrance than a help. The Edo-Tokyo Museum has strollers you can use for free at the sixth-floor entrance.

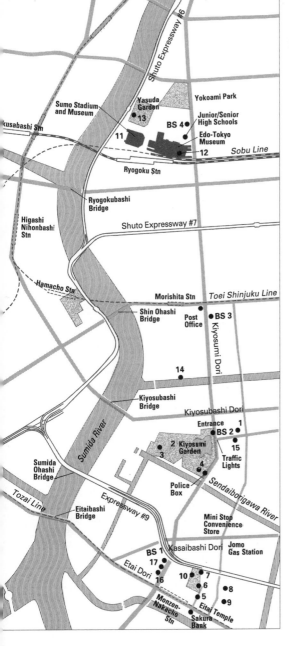

PLACES TO VISIT

1. Fukagawa Edo Museum
2. Kiyosumi Garden
3. Kiyosumi Park
4. Playground
5. Monzen-Nakacho Shopping Area
6. Hana (candy)
7. Fukagawa Fudoson Temple
8. Tomioka Hachiman Shrine
9. Mikoshi
10. Fukagawa Park
11. Sumo Stadium and Museum
12. Edo-Tokyo Museum
13. Yasuda Garden
14. Takabashi Pier
15. Fukagawajuku Restaurant
16. McDonald's
17. Kentucky Fried Chicken

BS 1. Bus Stop for Bus #33
BS 2. Kiyosumi Teien-mae Bus Stop
BS 3. Yokoami 1-chome Bus Stop
BS 4. Bus Stop for Bus #33

WHERE & WHEN

Fukagawa Edo Museum

深川江戸資料館 (Fukagawa Edo Shiryo-kan)

1–3–28 Shirakawa, Koto-ku, Tokyo 135– 0021

☎ (03) 3630–8625

東京都江東区白河1-3-28　〒135-0021

OPEN: 9:30 A.M. to 5 P.M.

CLOSED: 2nd and 4th Mon each month, late Dec and early Jan for New Year's hols; occasionally closed other days for administrative purposes

FEES: adults ¥300, elementary and junior high students ¥50

DIRECTIONS: a 20-minute walk or 7-minute ride on Toei bus #33 from exit 3, Monzen-Nakacho station (Tozai line); a 20-minute walk or 7-minute ride on Toei bus #33 from Kiyosumi Dori near Morishita station (Shinjuku line), get off at Kiyosumi Teienmae; a 20-minute walk or 5-minute taxi ride from Suitengu-mae station (Hanzomon line). By car, you'll find it just off Kiyosumi Dori between expressways #7 and #9.

PARKING: free parking for 6 cars is available in the garage below the museum

COMMENTS: school age and up, English pamphlet

Kiyosumi Garden

清澄庭園 (Kiyosumi Teien)

3–3–9 Kiyosumi, Koto-ku, Tokyo 135–0024

☎ (03) 3641–5892

東京都江東区清澄3-3-9　〒135-0024

OPEN: 9 A.M. to 4:30 P.M.

CLOSED: Dec 28 to Jan 3

FEES: adults ¥150, under 12 and over 65 (ID required) free

DIRECTIONS: see Fukagawa Edo Museum. The garden is half a block west of the museum.

COMMENTS: all ages, English photocopied handout

Hana (sweet shop)

華

1–14–8 Tomioka, Koto-ku, Tokyo 135–0047

☎ (03) 3643–7948

東京都江東区富岡1-14-8　〒135-0047

OPEN: daily 9 A.M. to 9 P.M., Sun and hols until 7 P.M.

DIRECTIONS: see Fukagawa Fudoson temple

Fukagawa Fudoson Temple

深川不動尊

1–17–13 Tomioka, Koto-ku, Tokyo 135–0047

☎ (03) 3641–8287

東京都江東区富岡1-17-13　〒135-0047

OPEN: daily; temple fairs on the 1st, 15th, and 28th of each month

CLOSED: late Dec and early Jan for New Year's hols; occasionally closed other days for administrative purposes

FEES: none

DIRECTIONS: a 3-minute walk from Monzen-Nakacho station (Tozai line), exit 1. By car, just off Eitai Dori between crossings with expressway #9 and Kiyosumi Dori.

PARKING: free parking for about 20 cars

COMMENTS: all ages, no English

Tomioka Hachiman Shrine

富岡八幡宮

1–20–3 Tomioka, Koto-ku, Tokyo 135–0047

☎ (03) 3642–1315

東京都江東区富岡1-20-3　〒135-0047

OPEN: grounds always open, *mikoshi* displayed 9 A.M. to 5 P.M. Annual festival on weekend closest to Aug 15; bigger celebration every 3rd year (1999, 2002, 2005, etc.)

FEES: none

DIRECTIONS: see Fukagawa Fudoson temple

PARKING: space for about 20 cars; parking free for visitors to the shrine; others pay an hourly rate

COMMENTS: all ages, no English

Sumo Stadium and Museum

両国国技館 (Ryogoku Kokugi-kan)

1–3–28 Yokoami, Sumida-ku, Tokyo 103–0015

☎ (03) 3623–5111

東京都墨田区横網1-3-28　〒103-0015

OPEN: call for sumo match dates and ticket prices; museum open 9 A.M. to 4:30 P.M.

CLOSED: weekends, Jan. 1–3, special hours/rules apply during major tournaments.

FEES: none

PARKING: none

DIRECTIONS: a 3 -minute walk from the west exit of Ryogoku station (JR Sobu line). From Monzen-Nakacho station (Tozai line) or the Kiyosumi Garden take Toei bus #33 to Yokoami 1-chome Edo-Tokyo Hakubutsu-kan bus stop and walk 3 minutes south to the museum. By car, on Kiyosumi Dori north of expressway #7.

COMMENTS: 8 and up, no English

Edo-Tokyo Museum

江戸東京博物館 (Edo-Tokyo Hakubutsu-kan)

1–4–1 Yokoami, Sumida-ku, Tokyo 130–0015

☎ (03) 3626–9974

東京都墨田区横網1-4-1　〒130-0015

OPEN: 10 A.M. to 6 P.M., until 8 P.M. Thurs and Fri

CLOSED: Mon (Tues if Mon is hol), Dec 28 to Jan 4

FEES: adults ¥600, students ¥300, under 6 and over 65 free (ID required)

DIRECTIONS: next door to Sumo Stadium

PARKING: no parking

COMMENTS: 8 and up, English pamphlets and earphones

Yasuda Garden

旧安田庭園 (Kyu Yasuda Teien)

1–12–1 Yokoami, Sumida-ku, Tokyo 135–0015

☎ (03) 5608–6291

東京都墨田区横網1-12-1　〒135-0015

OPEN: 9 A.M. to 4:30 P.M.

CLOSED: Dec 29 to Jan 1

FEES: none

DIRECTIONS: see Sumo Stadium. The garden is a 2-minute walk from the stadium.

PARKING: none

COMMENTS: all ages, English signboard

Koto Ward Water Bus

江東区水上バス

☎ (03) 3647–9111

OPEN: call for schedule

DIRECTIONS: a 7-minute walk from Morishita Station (Shinjuku subway line). By car, just west of Takabashi bridge on Kiyosumi Dori.

A Crash Course in
Cultural History

National Museum of Japanese History • Sakura Park • Sankeitei Teahouse

Japan's first human inhabitants appeared around 30,000 years ago; though they didn't learn to cultivate rice until around 200 B.C., the ancient Japanese had their own distinct culture as early as 7,500 B.C. Outstanding exhibits at the **National Museum of Japanese History** will help you trace the country's development from the rope-patterned pottery of the Jomon period to today's advanced technology.

The museum is a crash course on Japan. Developed as a resource for university-level research on Japanese culture and history, this top-notch facility is one of the best places to study the country—whether for a school report or personal satisfaction. It is on the way to Narita Airport and easy to reach by car. By public transportation it's about an hour and a half from Ueno. It is vast, modern, and equipped with multi-lingual earphones that guide you through the exhibits in English, French, Chinese, and Korean. Pick one up, free of charge, at the information desk. Wheelchairs and free brochures in English, German, and French are available in the same place. For ¥2,500 you can also buy a seventy-page guidebook that offers more detailed explanations.

The museum takes an objective look at Japan's past, including controversial issues like the Ainu, Japan's indigenous people, and the mistreatment of Koreans after the Great Kanto Earthquake in 1923. The focus is on general trends rather than individuals or political developments, so lists of names and dates won't bog down your understanding of the big picture. The exhibits incorporate lighting and display techniques that make the simplest items eye-catching.

Gallery 1 sheds light on the dawn of Japanese civilization with religious artifacts and everyday implements. Main topics in this section include Stone Age culture and pottery; the development of an agricultural society with rice-related rituals; fourth-century burial mounds; the advanced government of the seventh-to-ninth-century Ritsuryo State, based on the civil and penal codes of T'ang China; and splendid ceremonial offerings found in an island cave off Kyushu, thought to be associated with prayers for sea voyages to China and Korea.

In Gallery 2, *tatami* rooms are decorated with the traditional trappings of the court culture of the Nara and Heian periods. Wall exhibits show the development of *katakana* and *hiragana*—the Japanese phonetic syllabaries. While the elegance of Kyoto court life and developing commerce were central to life in western Japan, in the east events began to revolve around the military government in Kamakura. From the fourteenth to the sixteenth centuries, the power struggle extended to the lower levels of society, and displays illustrate how the manor system broke up in some areas, to be replaced by self-governing communities. In other regions, large landowners expanded their holdings to become powerful *daimyo* (feudal lords). The development of printing technology and the Tokugawa shogunate's policy of shutting out foreign influences are also discussed in this section.

In Gallery 3, maps and a detailed model of Edo, complete with boats in the water, help illustrate how towns and cities became more prosperous and important around 1600. Pilgrimages to distant shrines were popular; the displays show how people traveled along roads built by the military while goods were moved mainly by river and sea. The political intrigues of influential farmers and *daimyo*, and various forms of entertainment developed by commoners—highlights include puppets and a rather tame peep show from the late Edo period—round out the offerings in this gallery.

Gallery 4 contrasts lifestyles in different parts of Japan: urban areas, agricultural towns, mountain hamlets, fishing villages, and the southern islands. Japanese ideas of life after death are explored; one display shows small boats filled with dolls in kimono ready for travel to the other world, and a towering straw statue of a mountain folk god.

Books, colorful packaging, advertising posters, and the storefronts of a coffee shop and a beauty parlor recreate the atmosphere after the arrival of outside influences in Japan in Gallery 5. Everyday objects illustrate the dramatic changes that began with Commodore Perry's appearance in the famous black warships that forced open Japan's ports in 1853. The displays end with the period just before World War II.

Compare Western and Japanese culture by watching selections at the gallery's silent movie theater (the last show starts around 3:30 P.M., so check the schedule if you're interested). Younger children will probably enjoy the later galleries the most, so you may want to do the tour backward or go quickly through the first two or three sections. We suggest scheduling at least 3 hours for the museum, longer to enjoy the other attractions of the area.

The museum is constantly expanding; a botanical garden has recently opened on the grounds. Inside, plants are categorized by their use: mulberry and indigo for dyes, cotton and wisteria for weaving, plume grass and paulownia for tool-making, quince and plum for medicines, rape and *urushi* for lacquer, and soybeans and buckwheat for food. These and many other plants, landscaped to evoke the image of a samurai garden and surrounding fields, teach visitors about Japan's use of plants from ancient to modern times. In lush **Sakura Park**, which houses the museum, the moat that once surrounded Sakura castle still remains. On Sundays you can enjoy *matcha* (the strong tea used for Japanese tea ceremonies) and Japanese sweets at the park's **Sankeitei teahouse**. You can get an English map of the park at the information desk.

Other Things to Do in the Area

There is enough to do in Sakura to fill a day or even an overnight trip, but some things aren't easily accessible by public transportation and others have limited parking, so choose your activities based on your mode of transportation as well as your interests. If you are driving, the Kawamura Memorial Art Museum and Sakura Kusabue-no-Oka have ample parking. Choose one; you won't have time for both and the National Museum of History. If you come by train, the Bukeyashiki (Samurai Mansions) and the small Tsukamoto Sword Museum are within walking distance of the station and take little time to see.

Kids experience nature firsthand at **Sakura Kusabue-no-Oka** (Reed Hill), where you can plant or harvest peanuts and potatoes, pick fruit, and even camp out. Try your hand at pottery or ride the mini passenger train, then explore a two-hundred-year-old farmhouse, a mountain stream, two ponds, and the wildlife of Inaba Marsh. The pottery classes are held in Japanese on the second and fourth Saturdays of the month, Sundays, and national holidays from 1 to 3 P.M. About six weeks after the class, Kusabue-no-Oka will inform you that your piece has been fired in the kiln and is ready. You can pick it up in person or make arrangements during your class to have it shipped to you.

Rembrandts, Renoirs, Manets, Chagalls, Pollocks, Kandinskys, Picassos, Magrittes, and even a room full of Rothkos await you at the **Kawamura Memorial Museum of Art**. You may also want to visit the museum shop and restaurant inside. The museum sends a shuttle bus to Keisei Sakura station and JR Sakura station about once an hour. A schedule is posted at the bus stop.

The **Bukeyashiki** (Samurai Mansions) are the former homes of the Kawahara and Tajima samurai families. The Kawahara residence, built in the middle of the Edo period, has been restored to its original condition. You can only view the Kawahara residence from its entryway, but you can step into the Tajima home and have tea.

The **Tsukamoto Sword Museum**'s collection includes five hundred swords and two hundred and fifty sheaths, but the museum is very small so only a limited number of swords are displayed at one time. Items on exhibit are rotated every three months.

EATING OPTIONS

Restaurants The National Museum of Japanese History has a restaurant that offers a small selection of light, reasonably priced meals and a larger selection of overpriced beverages. There is also a tearoom that serves drinks and sweets. Outside the museum and surrounding park is a cheap noodle and sushi shop called Daikyo. It's a large, colorful place. Turn right out of the museum drive and you won't miss it.

Picnic Possibilities Sakura Park has lots of nice spots. You can buy cold drinks from the machines near the taxi stand in the parking lot closest to the museum entrance. You can also eat at the tables and chairs in the courtyard inside the museum or in the park. Keep your ticket stub if you want to reenter the museum. Kusabue-no-Oka also has many places to picnic. Call the park in Japanese if you'd like to barbecue there.

FOR INFANTS AND TODDLERS

There is nothing in the way of infant care facilities at the National Museum of Japanese History. At Kawamura Memorial Museum of Art, you'll find a diaper changing-table in the restroom for the handicapped, and you can borrow a stroller free of charge.

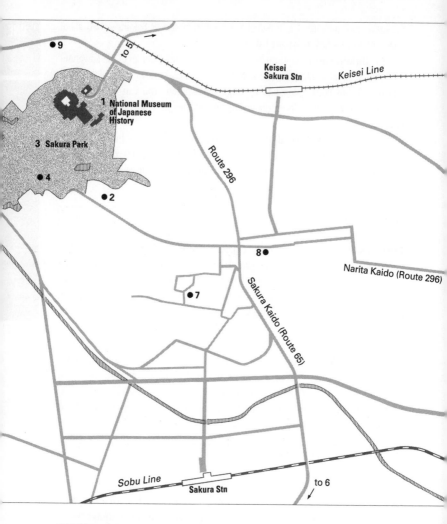

PLACES TO VISIT

1. National Museum of Japanese History
2. Botanical Garden
3. Sakura Park
4. Sankeitei Teahouse
5. Sakura Kusabue-no-Oka (Reed Hill)
6. Kawamura Memorial Museum of Art
7. Bukeyashiki (Samurai Mansions)
8. Tsukamoto Sword Museum
9. Daikyo Restaurant

National Museum of Japanese History
国立歴史民族博物館 (Kokuritsu Rekishi Minzoku Hakubutsu-kan)

117 Jonaicho, Sakura-shi, Chiba-ken 285–0017

☎ (043) 486–0123, ext. 229

千葉県佐倉市城内町117　〒285-0017

OPEN: 9:30 A.M. to 4:30 P.M. (admission until 4)

CLOSED: Mon (Tues when Sun or Mon is a hol), Dec 27 to Jan 4

FEES: adults ¥420, college/high school students ¥250, junior high/elementary school students ¥110

DIRECTIONS: a 15-minute taxi or bus ride from north exit of Sakura station (JR Sobu, Narita lines). Use bus at stop #1. A 15-minute walk or short bus ride from Keisei Sakura station (Keisei line). By car from the Tokyo area take the Shuto expressway to Keiyo Road and then the Higashi Kanto highway to the Sakura interchange. It takes about 70 minutes depending on traffic. From Narita Airport take the Higashi Kanto highway to the Sakura interchange. From there take Sakura Kaido (Route 65) north to Route 296 (west). It takes about 40 minutes depending on traffic.

PARKING: ample and free

COMMENTS: 8 and up, English pamphlets and earphones

Sakura Kusabue-no-Oka (Reed Hill)
佐倉草笛の丘

820 Iino, Sakura-shi, Chiba-ken 285–0003

☎ (043) 485–7821

千葉県佐倉市飯野820　〒285-0003

OPEN: 9 A.M. to 5 P.M. (admission until 4)

CLOSED: Mon (Tues if Mon is a hol), Dec 30 to Jan 4; no hols from July 21 to Aug 31

FEES: adults ¥310, junior/elementary school students ¥210, children 3–5 ¥100, children under 3 free; pottery classes ¥600

DIRECTIONS: there is no convenient way to get here by mass transportation. It is a 40-minute walk from both Keisei Sakura station and the National Museum of History. By car, turn left at the signal in front of the National Museum of Japanese History and drive about 2 km to a fork in the road. Take the left side of the fork and drive about 1 km till you come to the park.

PARKING: free, 70 spaces

COMMENTS: all ages, no English

Kawamura Memorial Museum of Art
川村記念美術館 (Kawamura Kinen Bijutsu-kan)

631 Sakado, Sakura-shi, Chiba-ken 285–0078

☎ (043) 498–2131

千葉県佐倉市坂戸631　〒285-0078

OPEN: 9:30 A.M. to 4:30 P.M. (admission until 4)

CLOSED: Mon and Tues except on national hols; Dec 24 to Jan 1

FEES: adults ¥800, college/high school students and seniors over 70 ¥600, junior high/elementary school students ¥400

DIRECTIONS: hourly museum shuttle bus leaves from south exits of JR Sakura station (Sobu line) and Keisei Sakura station (Keisei line) from 9 A.M. to 3 P.M. Taxis are also available. By car, take the Shuto expressway to Keiyo Road and then the Higashi Kanto highway to the Sakura interchange. From there, take Sakura Kaido (Route 65) to Route 51. Then take Yachimata Yokoshiba Dori to the museum.

PARKING: free, 250 spaces

COMMENTS: all ages, English pamphlets and picture titles

Bukeyashiki (Samurai Mansions)
武家屋敷

57–61 Miyakoji-machi, Sakura-shi, Chiba-ken 285–0016

☎ (043) 486–2947

千葉県佐倉市宮小路町57-61　〒285-0016

OPEN: 9 A.M. to 5 P.M. (admission until 4:30)

CLOSED: Mon (Tues if Mon is a hol), Dec 28 to Jan 4

FEES: adults ¥200, children ¥100

DIRECTIONS: a 10-minute walk from JR Sakura station or a 15-minute walk from Keisei Sakura station. By car, several blocks south of Route 296 and east of Sakura castle park.

PARKING: free but limited

COMMENTS: all ages, no English

Tsukamoto Sword Museum

塚本刀剣美術館 (Tsukamoto Token Bijutsu-kan)

1–4 Urashi-machi, Sakura-shi, Chiba-ken 285–0024

☎ (043) 486–7097

千葉県佐倉市裏新町1-4　〒285-0024

OPEN: 10 A.M. to 4 P.M.

CLOSED: Sun, Mon, and all but 3rd Sat of the month

FEES: none

DIRECTIONS: a 15-minute walk from either JR Sakura or Keisei Sakura stations. By car, just south of route 296 and east of Sakura Castle Park.

PARKING: free, only 2 or 3 spaces

COMMENTS: 5 and up, no English

4

Shibamata—Tora-san's Neighborhood

Shibamata Taishakuten Daikyo Temple and Nakamise • Yagiri-no-Watashi Ferry • Shibamata Park and Rent-a-Cycle Center • Mizumoto Park • Yamamoto Tei

Although relatively unknown to foreigners, Shibamata holds a warm spot in the hearts of the Japanese. Taishukuten Daikyo Temple became popular in the late eighteenth century after locals believed its deity was responsible for curing a famine and an epidemic. The fame of this quaint, old-fashioned neighborhood spread around the country when filmmakers selected it as the home of Tora-san, hero of the long-running *Otoko Wa Tsurai Yo!* movie series. Walking along the narrow street that leads to the temple, you'll be charmed by the confectioners who make Japanese sweets in the windows of their small, traditional shops. Two nearby attractions—an elegant Japanese-style home with an impressive garden, and an ancient ferry—help you feel that you have stepped out of modern Tokyo with its Western influences and bustle and into an unspoiled pocket of old-style Japanese working-class culture. Older kids will also enjoy cycling on the Edo River levy to Mizumoto Park.

The tiny shops lining the cobble-stone *nakamise* street to **Shibamata Taishakuten Daikyo Temple** tempt visitors with delicious surprises. Try fresh-made *taiyaki*, fish-shaped waffles filled with chocolate, cream, or sweet bean paste. With good timing, you may receive a piece of candy still soft and warm as

Tora-san, a good-natured but unrefined traveling salesman, falls in love at first sight in all of the forty-eight warm-hearted comedies he appears in, but he never manages to get the girl. Exactly which shop Tora-san lived in is something of a

43

a gift when you buy the traditional mild-flavored hard candies at **Matsuya-no-Ame**. But it is *kusa dango* (sweet "grass" green rice dumplings dyed with an herb called mugwort) that have made the temple shopping area famous. Tora-san's home base was above one of the *dango* shops.

Even if you aren't really interested in Tora-san, you'll enjoy the traditional, small-town atmosphere. The safe, quiet pedestrian street offers plenty of visual stimulation and the temple itself is lovely, similar in style to the buildings at Nikko, although unpainted. Founded in 1629, the temple is associated with the Nichiren school of Buddhism. As you enter the gate, look right: you'll see a small statue of the Jogyo Bosatsu. Worshippers believe this deity will cure whatever ails you if you wash the cor-

mystery. The proprietor of the **Tora-ya** claims that his shop was used as the site where the beloved salesman's relatives lived for the first four films. The folks at **Kame-ya**, which sells the best *dango* in the area, say their shop was used as the model for the studio setting where subsequent movies were shot. The movie company's PR department didn't know too much about earlier films, but told us that **Takagi-ya**, another *dango* and sweets shop on the street, was used for costume changes for the later movies when filming in Shibamata. Takagi-ya has two stores; the one on the right is where Tora-san buys gifts for his friends in the movies. The series, the world's longest ever, ended when Kiyoshi Atsumi, the actor who played Tora-san, died in 1996.

responding body part on the statue with one of the *tawashi* brushes available for the purpose. Don't miss the intricately carved wooden panels inside the Taishaku Hall. Each of the ten panels, commissioned from Tokyo's best woodcarvers in the 1920s, represents scenes from the most important of all Buddhist scriptures, the Lotus Sutra. The small fee also admits you to the temple's lovely garden. Toddlers will enjoy this experience as much as older people; the smooth, covered wooden walkway that takes you around the temple garden is a great place to practice walking, and there are plenty of things to look at. Depending on your child, however, you may want to steer clear of the gallery since the art is completely unprotected. Count on spending an hour exploring the sweet shops and the temple.

When you finish, go out the north gate of the temple, turn right, and walk down the street and over the levy. There you will find **Yagiri-no-Watashi**, one of fifteen ferry stations built in the Edo period, as well as a *sekisho,* an ID checkpoint that all travelers had to pass through when entering or leaving the city. Its name is regularly belted out in karaoke bars by amateurs singing one of the biggest *enka* hits of the early 1980s, a song called "Yagiri-no-Watashi" after the ferry. There is also a novel about this small ferry, built by the Edo *bafuku* government at the beginning of the seventeenth century to carry farmers to their fields across the Edo river. The sight that greets you at the riverbank—a crumbling ancient pier—is more impressive for historical than esthetic reasons, although kids always find it fun to try any kind of water transport. From December to March a long wooden boat is poled across the river; the motorboat used in the summer has considerably less ambiance.

Shibamata Park's perimeter starts south of the ferry pier and extends across the levy. Double back to get to the **Katsushika Tourist Center**, where you'll find a **Rent-a-Cycle Center** that lets bikes for the day on weekends and national holidays and, in the basement, the Tora-san Memorial Center. A few of the displays, like a model of the *nakamise* shops, appeal to children but unless you are a real Tora-san fan, it's not worth the entrance fee. Rent-a-Cycle has bikes for adults and children but no baby seats, training wheels or tricycles. To rent a bike, fill out a form and show some kind of ID. Bikes must be returned by 4:30 during summer hours (March to October) and 3:30 during winter hours (November to February). A cycling route runs atop the levy that separates Yagiri Ferry from the temple area. The bike path starts far up the Edogawa river in Saitama Prefecture and continues into Tokyo past Katsushika Ward and into Edogawa Ward. It follows the Old Edogawa river, takes a few turns through Kasai Seaside Park (see Tour 23), and then goes up the Arakawa river levy until it finally stops in Nishi Kasai, south of the Tozai line. For the most pleasant cycle from Shibamata, head north until you see the first golf hole on the west riverbank, exit the levy at the next ramp and cross the street to the cherry tree–lined road where the cycle path continues. Cycle a short distance to a five-way intersection; continue straight across two zebra crossings. Then turn left onto the bike path that borders **Mizumoto Park**, one of Tokyo's great parks.

You can cycle to the far end of the park to sprawl out on a wide lawn and go wading in a nearby water play area. Or, ride through the stands of poplar and sequoia trees to the bird sanctuary and peer at turtle doves, comorants, herons, egrets, coots, starlings, and finches. No matter what time of year you decide to see Shibamata, be sure to come back to Mizumoto Park for a whole day in late spring or summer. (In May, Katsushika Ward holds a children's festival in the park. Mid-June is also a good time because there is an exceptional iris festival.) Load the car up with fishing gear, beach sandals, extra clothes, towels, binoculars to watch birds, and magnifying glasses to inspect bugs. This is the only park in Tokyo with flowing and still water as well as marshy land, plus you can actually catch something. You'll see people here with respectable fishing gear stationed around the Obagawa river and the larger ponds and flowing streams catching blue gill and, crouching at the edge of the marshes, folks who have tied "bait" from their lunch box to a stick and are filling plastic bags with craw-fish. Young children net shrimp, sometimes scooping up a frog by mistake. You are supposed to throw the fish back in, but most people take their small hauls of shrimp and crawfish home. On the southeast side of the park, next to the parking lot, there is a little playground with simple obstacle course equipment and roller slides that the small ones like. Mizumoto Park is 62 hectares, but it's only about 4 kilometers from the center of the park back to the Rent-a-Cycle center where you return your bikes.

Before you go home, relax at **Yamamoto Tei** outside Shibamata Park just north of Katsushika Ward Tourist Center A Building. This Japanese-style home and its exquisite garden make a lovely Zen respite, a refreshing natural treat for eyes and ears. Pass through the gate and walk around to the back of the house to enter. Adults and children will love the garden with its waterfall and colorful carp. While you view the profusion of greenery and water from the elegant *tatami* rooms, you may want to treat yourself to some refreshments. Place an order at the reception desk, and you'll be served in any of the open rooms. Choose from *matcha,* the Japanese tea used in the tea ceremony, juice, or *ramune* soda. The beverages are accompanied by an appropriate sweet: candy for kids drinking juice or soda and an elegant Japanese confection with the *matcha*. You can also leave any excess baggage in coin lockers near the reception desk.

Built by a wealthy businessman in the early 1900s, Yamamoto Tei was donated to the government of Katsushika Ward, so entrance fees are very cheap. For a song you can rent out the teahouse on the grounds or one of the rooms in the main house for a morning, afternoon, or full day. To make reservations, call Technoplaza Katsushika at 3838–5555 in Japanese.

If you want to relax like Tora-san in a more working-class environment, amble back down the *nakamise* and sit in the little two-table dining room at the Takigi-ya shop on the south side of the street. It's the only *dango* place that stays open till 8 P.M. If you're not fond of sweet beans and sticky rice balls, try some of the other simple dishes on the menu written on the wall in Japanese. The other customers will most likely be avid Tora-san fans from other parts of Japan on a pilgrimage to pay homage to their fallen hero. Their conversations are often the same, "Seen 'em all... There's no other place like Shibamata... Did I tell you I've seen all forty-eight? Sure would have liked to have seen number forty-nine..."

Other Things to Do in the Area

Children ages two to seven who visit this area will definitely enjoy stopping at **Niijuku Transportation Park**—especially train-lovers. Child-size trains run in the mornings from 10 to 12 and in the afternoons from 1 to 4, except on Wednesdays and Thursdays. Bullet and diesel trains speed around the tracks on Fridays and Saturdays, while Sunday is the day to climb aboard a train powered by a steam locomotive. Kid-size go-carts, trains, bicycles, tricycles, overpasses, crosswalks, stations, stop signs, and traffic lights provide plenty of fun while teaching youngsters about safety, etiquette, and other rules of the road. There is even a small-scale city bus with a pint-size bus stop and a "shipwrecked" wooden boat that would-be mariners can climb on and pretend to sail across the sea. The different routes and vehicles will keep kids entertained for an hour or two. We like to come here in the morning and then spend the afternoon in Shibamata. Use the bus system with Kanamachi station as the transfer point to get from Niijuku to Shibamata.

Tsuri-no-Ie, a popular fishing hole, is just outside the main gate of Mizumoto Park. Bring your own gear; there are rental rowboats, but kids aren't allowed to use them, even with an adult. There are always lots of fully decked-out anglers here, but we've yet to see any of them reel one in.

EATING OPTIONS

Restaurants Small restaurants specializing in *unagi* (eel) and noodles line the street that leads to the temple in Shibamata. Prices can be surprisingly high, so be sure to look at the menus carefully. There is a Japanese noodle restaurant in the center of Mizumoto Park. A Denny's family restaurant near Niijuku Transportation Park is probably the best option in that area.

Picnic Possibilities Shibamata Park has many picnic spots, all with a pleasant view of the Edogawa river. Spread a cloth or grab a picnic table at Mizumoto Park or Niijuku Transportation Park.

FOR INFANTS AND TODDLERS

There is a shelf you can use to change diapers in the women's restroom just outside the temple gate. You'll find changing tables in the restroom reserved for the handicapped in Shibamata Park. Mizumoto Park has no designated facilities, but head for the wooded areas and you'll find lots of quiet spots. Request permission at the "station building" in Niijuku Transportation Park and you may be allowed to use the classroom on the second floor for nursing and diapering if it is unoccupied. If the wind picks up making the riverside uncomfortable for toddlers, take them to the little pocket part next to Shibamata Taishakuten Bus stop to work off their energy on swings and a sandbox.

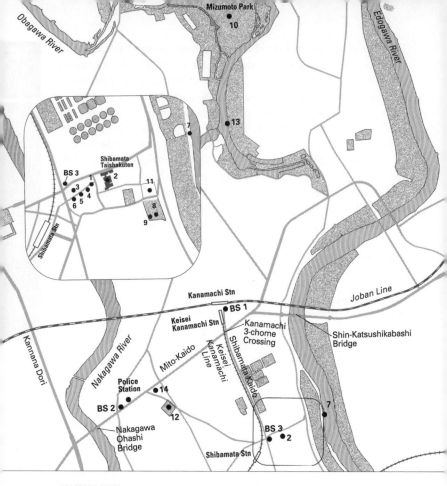

PLACES TO VISIT

1. Nakamise
2. Shibamata Taishakuten Daikyo Temple
3. Matsuya-no-Ame Candy
4. Tora-ya
5. Kame-ya
6. Takagi-ya
7. Yagiri-no-Watashi Ferry
8. Shibamata Park
9. Katsushika Tourist Center, Rent-a-Cycle, Tora-san Memorial Museum

10. Mizumoto Park
11. Yamamoto Tei
12. Niijuku Transportation Park
13. Tsuri-no-Ie (fishing)
14. Denny's Family Restaurant

BS 1. Bus Stop for Bus #3
BS 2. Kameari Keisatsucho Bus Stop
BS 3. Shibamata Taishakuten Bus Stop

Shibamata Nakamise Shops
柴又仲見世

See directions below for Shibamata Taisha-kuten Daikyo Temple. The *nakamise* shops line the street to the temple.

Matsuya-no-Ame Candy
松屋の飴総本店

7–6–17 Shibamata, Katsushika-ku, Tokyo 125–0052

☎ (03) 3657–1739

東京都葛飾区柴又7-6-17　〒125-0052

OPEN: 8:30 A.M. to 5:30 P.M.

CLOSED: usually on Mon

Kame-ya
亀屋本舗

7–7–9 Shibamata, Katsushika-ku, Tokyo 125–0052

☎ (03) 3657–6670

東京都葛飾区柴又7-7-9　〒125-0052

OPEN: 9 A.M. to 5:30 P.M.

CLOSED: Tues

Tora-ya (also known as Shibamata Dango)
とらや

7–7–5 Shibamata, Katsushika-ku, Tokyo 125–0052

☎ (03) 3659–8111

東京都葛飾区柴又7-7-5　〒125-0052

OPEN: 10 A.M. to 5 P.M.

CLOSED: usually for a few days before the New Year

Takagi-ya
高木屋本舗

7–7–4 Shibamata, Katsushika-ku, Tokyo 125–0052

☎ (03) 3657–3136

東京都葛飾区柴又7-7-4　〒125-0052

OPEN: daily 7 A.M. to 8 P.M.

Shibamata Taishakuten Daikyo Temple
柴又帝釈天題経寺

(Shibamata Taishakuten Daikyoji)

7–10–3 Shibamata, Katsushika-ku, Tokyo 125–0052

☎ (03) 3672–2661

東京都葛飾区柴又7-10-3　〒125-0052

OPEN: Outer grounds 9 A.M. to 7 P.M., inner garden and gallery 9 A.M. to 4 P.M.

DIRECTIONS: a 10-minute walk from Shibamata station on the Keisei Kanamachi line. Or take the Keisei bus bound for Koiwai station from bus stop #3 at the south exit of Kanamachi station on the JR Joban line. The easiest option is to jump in a taxi at Kanamachi station, and you'll get there before the meter starts clicking on extra yen. By car, exit Circular line expressway (Kanjosen) at Yotsugi interchange and take Mito Dori toward Matsudo City. Turn right on Shibamata Dori; the temple area will be on your left. Follow a good road map; it's about a 3-km drive from the Yotsugi interchange.

PARKING: space for 10 cars in the front of the temple and 60 cars in the rear, free except on Sun, when spaces are rented by the hour. Space goes fast.

COMMENTS: all ages, some English

Yagiri-no-Watashi Ferry
矢切の渡

7–17–13 Shibamata, Katsushika-ku, Tokyo 125–0052

東京都葛飾区柴又7-17-13　〒125-0052

OPEN: 9 A.M. to dusk; *closes when the weather is bad*

CLOSED: from Dec to late March the ferry is only open on weekends, special religious days at the temple, and throughout the New Year's hols from Jan 1 to 15

DIRECTIONS: see directions for Shibamata

Taishakuten Daikyo Temple. From the temple, turn right out of the north gate, then right again at the 1st street. The ferry pier is directly over the levy.

COMMENTS: all ages, no English

Katsushika-ku Tourist Center and Rent-A-Cycle

葛飾区観光文化センター (Katsushika-ku Kanko Bunka Center)

6–22–19 Shibamata, Katsushika-ku, Tokyo 125–0052

☎ (03) 3657–3455

東京都葛飾区柴又6-22-19　〒125-0052

OPEN: tourist center 9:30 A.M. to 4:30 P.M.; cycle center 9 A.M. to 5 P.M. (March–Oct), 9 A.M. to 4 P.M. (Nov–Feb) on Sat, Sun, and hols only

CLOSED: Mon, Dec 28 to 31

FEES: cycle rental ¥400 for adults and high school students, ¥200 for children. Tora-san Memorial Center ¥500 for adults and high school students, ¥400 for seniors over 65, ¥300 for children.

DIRECTIONS: by train, see directions for Yamamoto Tei. The center is in Shibamata Park next door. By car, take Mito Kaido to Shibamata Kaido and head south. Just before the Kanamachi Water Purification Plant turn east toward the riverbank. (You'll need to dogleg right on the way but generally stay straight.) Follow the road along the levy to the tourist center on your left.

PARKING: 190 spaces, daily rate

COMMENTS: no training wheels or tricyles

Mizumoto Park

水元公園 (Mizumoto Koen)

2–1 Mizumoto Koen, Katsushika-ku, Tokyo 125–0034

☎ (03) 3607–8321

東京都葛飾区水元公園2-1　〒125-0034

OPEN: 24 hours

DIRECTIONS: take Keisei bus #2 from Kana-machi station on the JR Joban line and get off at Mizumoto Koen-mae. By car, exit the Circular line expressway at Yotsugi interchange and take Mito Dori toward Matsudo City. Turn left at Kanamachi 1-chome crossing and you will find the park at the end of the street.

PARKING: 24 hours, 1200 spaces, hourly rate

COMMENTS: all ages, no English

Yamamoto Tei

山本亭

7–19–32 Shibamata, Katsushika-ku, Tokyo 125–0052

☎ inquire through Katsushika-ku Techno-plaza at (03) 3838–5555

東京都葛飾区柴又7-19-32　〒125-0052

OPEN: 9 A.M. to 5 P.M.

CLOSED: Mon (Tues when Mon is a hol), Dec 28 to Jan 3

FEES: ¥100 per person, children under middle-school age and adults over 65 free

DIRECTIONS: see directions for Shibamata Taishakuten Daikyo Temple. From the temple, turn left out of the south gate and take the next left. Follow the street to the end and you will come to Yamamoto Tei.

PARKING: none

COMMENTS: all ages, no English

Niijuku Transportation Park

新宿交通公園 (Niijuku Kotsu Koen)

3–23–19 Niijuku, Katsushika-ku, Tokyo 125–0051

☎ (03) 3608–2194

東京都葛飾区新宿3-23-19　〒125-0051

OPEN: 9 A.M. to 5 P.M.

CLOSED: Mon and Tues except for the 4th week of the month, when Sun and Mon are the scheduled hols. Closed Dec 27 to Jan 4 for the New Year.

FEES: free

DIRECTIONS: from Kanamachi station on either the JR Joban line (south exit) or the Keisei

Kanamachi line take Toei bus #39 bound for Asakusa Kotobuki-cho. Get off at Kameari Keisatsusho (Kameari Police Station). Walk back to the street just in front of Denny's Restaurant and across from the police station—you will see a sign pointing in the direction of the park. Turn right and walk along the street for about 5 minutes. The park is on the right side of the street. It's a very short bus ride so for a party with two adults taxi fare to the park won't be much more than bus fare. By car, exit the Circular line expressway at the Yotsugi interchange and take Mito Dori toward Matsudo City. Turn right after Nakagawa river when you see the police station on the left and Denny's on the right. If you are coming from the Shibamata Taishakuten area, walk down the *nakamise* to the 1st intersection, cross the street, and take a bus to Kanamachi station.

PARKING: a few spaces are available next to the park but only on weekends. You are requested to come by public transportation.

COMMENTS: toddlers to younger elementary school students, no English, nursing in classroom

Tsuri-no-Ie
釣の家
3–4 Mizumoto-koen, Katsushika-ku, Tokyo 125–0034
☎ (03) 3600–2757
東京都葛飾区水元3-4　〒125-0034
OPEN: 9 A.M. to 4 P.M. (winter), 8:30 A.M. to 4 P.M. (summer)
FEES: no entrance fee. Boat rental is ¥300. (Children cannot ride the boats.)
DIRECTIONS: see Mizumoto Park. Tsuri-no-Ie is next to the main entrance of the park.
PARKING: use the Mizumoto Park lot

5

Edo Meets Tokyo: Walk Through the Eras in Koganei

Edo-Tokyo Tatemono-en Open-Air Architectural Museum • Koganei Park

There is no water at the Kodakara-yu anymore, but looking at the deep tubs, the murals on the walls, and the gardens outside, you can imagine the voices of families from the past laughing as they scrub and splash in this former public bath. Antique cribs that held babies safe while their mothers soaked stand in a corner; the gods of good fortune guard the entrance. Built in 1929 in Adachi-ku, this *sento* is typical of the bathhouses that served as gathering places for every neighborhood in Tokyo before private baths became common. Down the street you can get a feel for an old-time shop at sixty-five-year-old Kodera, whose owner made and sold soy sauce—although *sake* was more popular with the customers. The ghostly officers of a late nineteenth-century police box, bedding neatly folded in a corner, watch over the homes and shops in the **Edo-Tokyo Tatemono-en**'s East Zone, which re-creates life in downtown Tokyo early in the twentieth century.

All of the buildings in this open-air architectural museum were selected because of historical or cultural significance. They were moved to this spot and restored instead of being torn down. Variety sets the museum apart from the many other collections of old buildings found throughout Japan. While temples, castles, and large government offices are built to symbolize an era and may remain in the same form for centuries, the designs of smaller buildings used by common folk are constantly changing, especially in Japan. The Edo-Tokyo Tatemono-en was built to showcase once-common mom-and-pop stores and traditional homes from the past so that people living in the Westernized Japan of the future will be able to get a glimpse of their cultural heritage.

The entrance to the museum is a ceremonial hall built in 1940 to commemorate the 2,600th anniversary of the mythical emperor Jimmu's succession. The Kokaden, as it is called, is an outstanding recreation of tenth-century palace architecture. Doubling as the visitor's center, the hall contains a museum shop, an audiovisual center, and displays that illustrate how Tokyo has changed over the years. All these are open to the public without charge, but you must purchase a ticket to explore the buildings that lie beyond. Stop to ask for one of the excellent brochures available in English, French, Korean, or Chinese. Attendants in each building can answer questions, and several of them speak a little English. If you understand Japanese, you can also watch videotaped interviews with the oldest living member of the families who once owned certain buildings.

Ancient history is the first stop on the tour; an exhibition room built onto the back of the hall houses archeological exhibits of the surrounding Musashino area from the Jomon period to modern times. Though the digs are historically important, don't linger too long over the pottery shards because there is a lot of territory to cover. To continue chronologically, head for the West Zone, walking behind the cannon just to the left of the door.

Slip out of your shoes and examine the contents of a nearby late-Edo-period farmhouse kitchen, including farm implements. The old wooden sink, open fire, and dirt floor are in stark contrast to the convenience of modern kitchens. Elsewhere in the house you can look over the tools and products of a craftsman skilled in weaving straw. The West Zone also has traditional granaries and the thatched home of an officer in the Hachioji Guards, the samurai warriors who led a police force in Hachioji during the Edo period (1603– 1867). Their small forces were unique, made up of farmers instead of career foot soldiers. Be sure to check out the old-style toilets in the corner of the house before heading off through the lush woods, which recreate the atmosphere of the Japanese countryside.

The houses of the wealthy are grouped together in the Central Zone. Here you can admire the charming Ogawa home, a Western-style mansion built in the 1920s in Den'enchofu, a real estate development project begun one month after the Great Kanto Earthquake of 1923 that quickly became one of the wealthiest and most famous neighborhoods in Tokyo. Down the street stands the house of Korekiyo Takahashi, interesting for both its architecture and its bloody past.

Despite its history, the house, with wide windows overlooking a Japanese-style garden, is a good place to relax. Tea, Japanese snacks, and light meals are served in a large *tatami* room in the back. The building is actually connected to the country home of a leading silk merchant. Izaemon Nishikawa selected only the best, most expensive materials—cedar, paulownia wood, and *hinoki* cypress—for the elegant Japanese-style guest house he had built in Akishima-shi in 1918. Step out into the garden and follow the pathway through thick green woods to a tiny spring, chosen to replicate Musashino Hake Spring and its environs. Here you can smell, touch, and feast your eyes on the native trees and flowering grasses of the area, which have fallen under the scythe of development on the Musashino plains, now northwest Tokyo.

Takahashi, a powerful cabinet minister, was shot in his second-floor study on February 26, 1936, as part of a famous coup attempt by a group of young army officers. Takahashi died, but the prime minister and the government survived. Several of Takahashi's possessions are on display in a glass case along with photos of the man himself. Among them is an English newspaper, marked with the fateful date; Takahashi learned to read English as a young man, and this paper was the last he ever read.

In the East Zone, a number of small businesses contribute to the illusion of a bustling shopping street in Tokyo's old downtown *shitamachi* district. The flower shop offers a tempting display of color; next door, brushes and paints for Japanese calligraphy line the shelves and fill huge walls of drawers at Takei Sanshodo, a stationery shop built around 1930. The wooden stools and *sake* bottles of Kagiya, a small neighborhood bar, look like a strong temptation for customers emerging from the bathhouse next door. On the other side of the bath is a kimono shop, complete with dressmakers' tools from the Taisho era.

In all, eighteen buildings have found a new home at the museum, which hopes to expand its collection to thirty-five by the year 2000. Even now, there's plenty of impressive detail to keep you occupied. Because of the museum's size, you should plan on spending at least 2 hours here before heading to **Koganei Park**.

Young or young at heart, you'll enjoy an afternoon in the grassy fields of this spacious park. Joggers and walkers can follow wandering paths and explore the park's many shady nooks. February and March, when pink, yellow, and cream blossoms decorate the large plum grove, are particularly good months for a picnic here. The park is also famous for its cherry blossoms, their beauty enhanced by the contrast with the park's many dark green pines—the area was picked for the open-air museum because it is beautiful all year round.

Children will be attracted to the east side of Koganei Park, where they can take turns circling a small cycling course on junior-size bicycles with training wheels. They can also zoom down a sledding hill covered with artificial turf. Beginning skateboarders, in-line skaters, and unicycle enthusiasts may want to bring their own equipment and practice on the small designated courses at the bottom of the hill. Nearby is Wanpaku Yama, a collection of slides, rope ladders, stairs, and sand that will delight elementary schoolchildren. Smaller kids will have more fun at the two playgrounds especially for them, one near the cycling course and another with a retired locomotive on the west side of the park.

The amount of time you want to spend will depend upon how fond you are of eating ice cream, soaking up sunshine, and relaxing in a natural world far removed from the bustle of the city—but the park closes at nightfall.

Other Things to Do in the Area

A large planetarium, a moonwalk simulator, and robots are the highlights of **Tama Rokuto Science Museum**, quite close to Koganei Park but unfortunately extremely inconvenient to reach by public transportation. This is a great place to come when poor weather spoils the regular tour, so if possible we recommend driving your own car on this outing. Located near the crossing of Koganei Kaido and Ome Kaido, the museum features excellent hands-on activities. An English handout explaining some of the exhibits is available at the entrance; explanations on the displays are in Japanese only, as is the narration at the star show. If you have basic Japanese language skills, you will enjoy the space shuttle simulator, a game that tests your hand-eye coordination, or the sound booth that lets you actually see the sound waves of different noises and your own voice. A taxi from one of the nearby stations is probably the best way to get there if you don't drive yourself, but you may have a hard time catching another cab for the return trip.

EATING OPTIONS

Restaurants A small restaurant in the Korekiyo Takahashi residence in the Edo-Tokyo Tatemono-en offers light Japanese meals and snacks in a *tatami* room overlooking the garden. Other restaurant options in the Koganei Park area are extremely limited. The Tama Rokuto Science Museum has a reasonably priced restaurant serving sandwiches and drinks on the first floor.

Picnic Possibilities Promising picnic spots abound in Koganei Park and the open-air museum. Bring a lunch and sprawl out in a grassy field or eat in more civilized fashion on one of the many picnic tables. Kiosks on the west and east sides of the park sell drinks, ice cream, and candy. At Tama Rokuto Science Museum you can eat on the benches near the second-floor library.

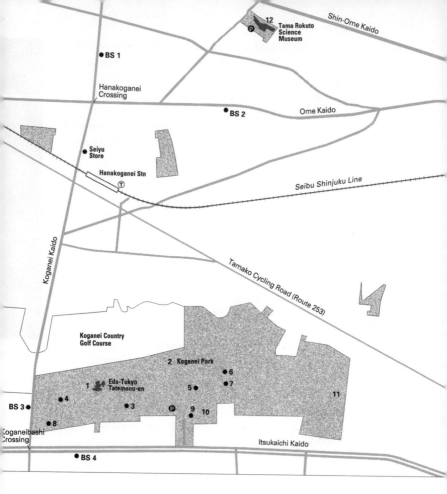

PLACES TO VISIT

1. Edo-Tokyo Tatemono-en, Open-Air Architectural Museum
2. Koganei Park
3. Plum Grove
4. Cherry Grove
5. Cycling Cener
6. Sledding Hill, Skateboarding, Unicycle Course
7. Wanpaku Yama
8. Steam Locomotive
9. Park Office
10. Koganei Gym
11. Sports Center
12. Tama Rokuto Science Museum

BS 1. Hanakoganei 5-chome Bus Stop
BS 2. Shibakubo Bus Stop
BS 3. Koganei Koen Nishi-guchi Bus Stop
BS 4. Edo-Tokyo Tatemono-en Bus Stop

FOR INFANTS AND TODDLERS

Diaper-changing facilities are located in the two outside toilet blocks at the architectural museum; there are none in the park. Strollers come in handy, but you can't take them inside the different buildings. Bring a baby carrier or be prepared for a lot of lifting. Also, make sure your child has easy-to-put-on shoes. You'll probably want anti-slip socks for toddlers, which you can find at any department store. The science museum has a crib between the two restrooms behind the red "Space Gym" stairwell on floor B1.

WHERE & WHEN

Edo-Tokyo Tatemono-en, Open-Air Architectural Museum
江戸東京建物園

3–7–1 Sakura-cho, Koganei-shi, Tokyo 184–0005

☎ (0423) 88–3311

東京都小金井市桜町3-7-1　〒184-0005

OPEN: April–Sept 9:30 A.M. to 5:30 P.M. (admission until 5), Oct–March 9:30 A.M. to 4:30 P.M. (admission until 4)

CLOSED: Mon (Tues if Mon is a hol), Dec 28 to Jan 4

FEES: adults ¥300, children 6–18 ¥150, seniors 65 and over free

DIRECTIONS: 5 minutes via any bus from the Seiyu Store near Hanakoganei station (Seibu Shinjuku line); get off at Koganei Koen Nishiguchi and walk through the park. 7 minutes by buses leaving from bus stops 1, 2, and 3 near the north exit of Musashi Koganei station (JR Chuo line); get off at Edo-Tokyo Tatemono-en or Koganei Koen Nishiguchi. By car, the park is south of Ome Kaido, accessible by Itsukaichi Kaido or Koganei Kaido.

PARKING: see Koganei Park

COMMENTS: 5 and up, English pamphlet

Koganei Park
小金井公園 (Koganei Koen)

1–13–1 Sekino-cho, Koganei-shi, Tokyo 184–0001

☎ (0423) 85–5611

東京都小金井市関野町1-13-1　〒184-0001

OPEN: daylight hours

DIRECTION: see Edo-Tokyo Tatemono-en

FEES: none

PARKING: available south of the park at an hourly rate, but both lots are generally full on weekends and hols

COMMENTS: all ages, no English

Tama Rokuto Science Museum
多摩六都科学館

(Tama Rukuto Kagaku-kan)

5–10–64 Shibakubo-cho, Tanashi-shi, Tokyo 188–0014

☎ (0424) 69–6100

東京都田無市芝久保町5-10-64　〒188-0014

OPEN: 9:30 A.M. to 5 P.M. (admission until 4)

CLOSED: Mon (Tues if Mon is a hol), Dec 28 to Jan 4

FEES: entrance for adults ¥500, children 4–18 ¥200; planetarium and plano-hemispheric projection shows adults ¥500, children ¥200

DIRECTIONS: a 20-minute walk from Hana-koganei Go-chome bus stop, a 20-minute ride on bus #2 from Musashi Koganei station (JR Chuo line). A 10-minute walk from Shibakubo bus stop, a 25-minute ride from Kichijoji station (JR Chuo, JR Sobu, Eidan Tozai, and Inokashira lines). Board bus #64 bound for Hashiba at bus stop #8. By car, the museum is located on the south side of Shin Ome Kaido next to the West Tokyo Sky Tower. If you are driving from Koganei Park, take Koganei Kaido to Shin Ome Kaido, turn right, and you will soon see the West Tokyo Sky Tower.

PARKING: 160 spaces, daily rate
COMMENTS: 5 and up, no English

River Road Cycle to Jindaiji

Nogawa River Bike Path and Park • Jindaiji Temple • Nakamise and Soba Shops

*S*oba noodles need lots of water. Water to raise the buckwheat, water to power the mills to grind it, water to knead it into the flour to make the noodles, and water for the final cooking. The Nogawa river brings this essential ingredient to Jindaiji temple and the traditional *soba* shops that surround it. Served hot or cold, plain or with traditional dishes like tempura, well-made *soba* can be a delicious treat, especially in this charming old-fashioned neighborhood. Spend an afternoon sampling *soba* dishes at local restaurants, strolling through the temple grounds, and examining the wares in the traditional *nakamise* shopping street. If your family is up for fresh air and exercise, you may want to make this a special day by including a long, leisurely cycle along the river's banks. The bike path cuts through scenic parks and quiet residential streets before bringing you close to the temple gates. For a slower-paced outing, go straight to the temple area, where you will still find enough to fill a day.

If you'd like to rent bikes in the area, call the day before to make reservations at Cycle Inn Matsushima, a National bike shop located near the south exit of Musashi Koganei station. The shop rents bikes for adults and school-age kids, and baby seats are available. It's also possible, of course, to bring your own bike by car or train (see the introduction for the rules on bringing bicycles on the train).

The **Nogawa River Bike Path** starts about a 10-minute ride from the station. Follow the map through the shopping district to the river. The first short section of the cycle route takes you past a quiet residential area, and the scenery gets greener and more wooded as you ride along. Elegant wading birds pick their way gracefully upstream, and you can catch an occasional glimpse of fish. The trees and greenery of small but beautiful **Musashino Park** line the path on one side. Beyond this park is a railroad, and just beyond that is **Nogawa Park**, which lines both banks of the river. The north bank, a fenced bird sanctuary and nature preserve, makes a great place for a cycle break. Stay on your bike until you see the Nature Center on the south bank; the gate that lets you into the nature preserve is on the north bank directly across from the Nature Center.

Inside the preserve, park rules ask you to stay on the wooded walkway and be careful not to disturb the ecosystem. Pick no wild grasses, net not a single bug. Water from the highlands owned by International Christian University (ICU) trickles down to the preserve's shallow water table where insects, mosses, and other plants thrive, inviting herons, woodpeckers, buntings, Japanese white-eyes, green finches, and others to set up homes here. Fireflies put on a spectacular light show in June. Remember to bring a magnifying glass for inspecting bugs, and your binoculars; there is even a little bird-watching blind on the outer west perimeter of the sanctuary. Japanese readers will also want to visit the Nature Center to see displays on the flora and fauna of the preserve and listen to taped bird calls.

If you are making good time and have plenty of daylight ahead, venture into the extensive park. Follow the path on the south bank beyond the Nature Center and across the bridge to Wanpaku Hiroba, a play space, and spend some energy on the child-sized obstacle course equipment, all made of natural materials. Several small groves of cherry trees make the park especially pleasant in April. In the summer, go further along the north bank and splash about in the water play area. But be sure to watch the time so you can make it to Jindaiji, another 3 kilometers along the riverside bike path, then a short jog up a residential road.

When you arrive in the temple area, park your bike and try your hand at painting pottery. **Rakuyaki**, a little wooden store across from the temple and flanked on both sides by shops selling sweets and *soba*, sells unpainted pottery, supplies the glazes, and fires your piece in about 20 minutes. You can choose from animal figurines, dishes, and other curios starting as low as ¥100. The highest-priced items cost around ¥2,500 and the firing is free. Once your work is ready for the kiln, explore the temple grounds and browse through the **nakamise**. You can come back for your masterpiece later.

Dating back to 733, **Jindaiji**, Tokyo's second-oldest temple, was built in honor of the water god Jinja Daio. The bronze Buddha inside the main building dates from the Nara period and is designated as an Important Cultural Property. The temple holds a *Daruma Ichi* festival on March 3 and 4, when papier mâché *daruma* dolls are sold in the stalls on the temple grounds. *Daruma* dolls have blank eyes; you make a wish to achieve a goal and color one eye black, then color in the other eye when it comes true.

You will need only a few minutes to see the temple and its wooded grounds. Then, explore the narrow wooden storefronts of the shopping street for a quick trip back in time. Pick up some *soba* noodles to cook at home or buy *soba manju* (buns filled with sweet bean paste) as a souvenir.

The trip back to the bike shop will take slightly less time because you will know the route and make fewer stops. If you want a shorter cycle course, bring your own bikes to Nogawa Park and start from there. For a longer ride, choose a stopping place further downstream.

According to legend, a young man from a poor family and the daughter of a rich family fell in love. To break up the couple, the parents of the young woman sent her off to a distant island. The young man prayed to Jinja Daio, who answered his prayers by sending a giant turtle to carry the man to his beloved. The couple married, lived happy lives, and bore a son who built the temple in honor of the water god.

The bike route continues for about 15 kilometers and goes all the way to Setagaya Ward, where the Nogawa river connects with the Tamagawa river near Futago bridge close to Futago-tamagawa-en station on the Tokyu Oimachi and Shintamagawa lines. From there, a cycle route along the Tamagawa continues as far as the area around Kawasaki station.

Other Things to Do in the Area

Dogwoods. Azaleas. Groves of plums, peaches, cherry trees, and magnolias. Beds of roses, peonies, and soft downy grasses—these are just some of the lush and fragrant plants that welcome you at **Jindai Botanical Garden**. The garden's style is European, but a thick stand of bamboo and several Asian fruit trees add local flavor. Tropical and subtropical plants grow in a big greenhouse overlooking large, European-style beds surrounding a monument to flowers where children wait for the hourly chime. Green-thumbed visitors may want to shop the nursery or inquire in Japanese about their plant problems at the Consulting Services Office. Throughout the year, the garden holds special botanical exhibitions like their famous mid-November Chrysanthemum Show. The small **Hydrophyte Garden** makes for a pleasant stroll in June when the irises are in bloom. The beds are planted so that there are blossoms in the park all year round.

The main garden has an entrance just behind Jindaiji temple. Its hydrophyte section is on the opposite side of the temple and, like the Consulting Services Office,

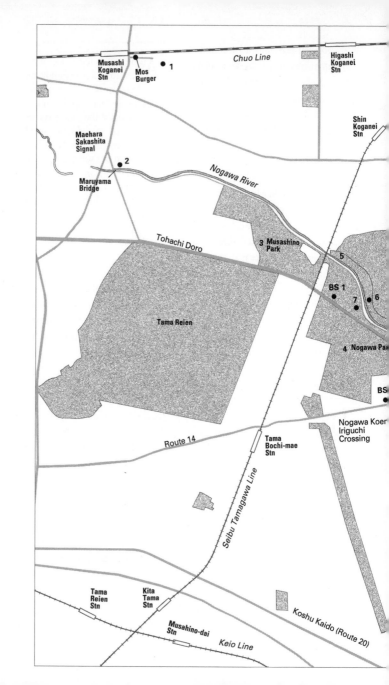

Chuo Line

Musashi
Koganei
Stn

Mos
Burger

● 1

Higashi
Koganei
Stn

Shin
Koganei
Stn

Maehara
Sakashita
Signal

● 2

Maruyama
Bridge

Nogawa River

Tohachi Doro

3 Musashino
Park

5

BS 1
●

7
●

● 6

Tama Reien

4 Nogawa Pa

BS

Nogawa Koen
Iriguchi
Crossing

Route 14

Tama
Bochi-mae
Stn

Seibu Tamagawa Line

Koshu Kaido (Route 20)

Tama
Reien
Stn

Kita
Tama
Stn

Musahino-dai
Stn

Keio Line

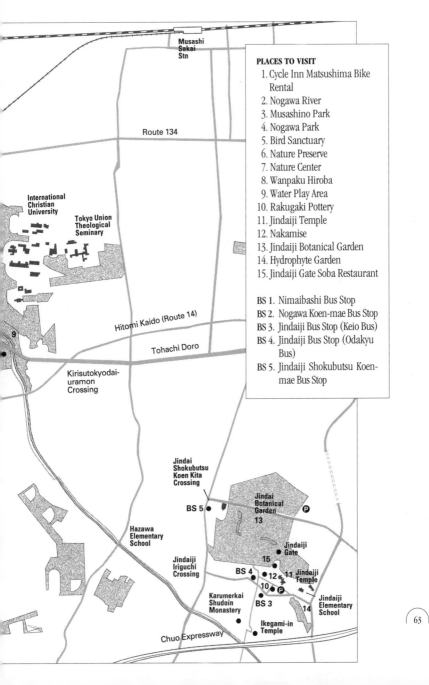

PLACES TO VISIT

1. Cycle Inn Matsushima Bike Rental
2. Nogawa River
3. Musashino Park
4. Nogawa Park
5. Bird Sanctuary
6. Nature Preserve
7. Nature Center
8. Wanpaku Hiroba
9. Water Play Area
10. Rakugaki Pottery
11. Jindaiji Temple
12. Nakamise
13. Jindaiji Botanical Garden
14. Hydrophyte Garden
15. Jindaiji Gate Soba Restaurant

BS 1. Nimaibashi Bus Stop
BS 2. Nogawa Koen-mae Bus Stop
BS 3. Jindaiji Bus Stop (Keio Bus)
BS 4. Jindaiji Bus Stop (Odakyu Bus)
BS 5. Jindaiji Shokubutsu Koen-mae Bus Stop

Musashi Sakai Stn

Route 134

International Christian University

Tokyo Union Theological Seminary

Hitomi Kaido (Route 14)

Tohachi Doro

Kirisutokyodai-uramon Crossing

Jindai Shokubutsu Koen Kita Crossing

BS 5

Hazawa Elementary School

Jindai Botanical Garden
13

Jindaiji Iriguchi Crossing

BS 4

15

12
10
11 Jindaiji Temple

Jindaiji Gate

Karumerkai Shudoin Monastery

BS 3

14

Jindaiji Elementary School

Ikegami-in Temple

Chuo Expressway

63

has no entrance charge. Ask for an English map at the ticket window. The gardens and lawns cover over 350,000 square meters and contain 3,500 varieties of plants, so you'll need several hours if you want to see everything. Once you leave the garden you cannot reenter without paying another entrance fee, so time your visit to fall before or after lunch. Also, you cannot take a bicycle into the gardens, but there is bike parking near the Jindaiji temple gates and the main entrance to the botanical garden.

EATING OPTIONS

Restaurants The area around Jindaiji is crowded with eateries in every price range, all specializing in one type of food: *soba*. Sample the local delicacy at colorful, cheap outdoor eateries or traditionally decorated restaurants. If you've ordered cold noodles, ask for *soba-no-yu*, the hot water used to cook the noodles. Mix it with the *soba* sauce left in your dipping cup for a different kind of after-lunch "tea." Near the Jindaiji Gate to the botanical garden, several *soba* restaurants with open terraces light small bonfires in the winter to warm guests while they slurp noodles.

Picnic Possibilities Plop down on a bench in Musashino or Nogawa Park or spread your feast on a picnic blanket. The lawns in the botanical garden also make a nice picnic spot. Kiosks inside the garden sell drinks, ice cream, crackers, and snacks.

FOR INFANTS AND TODDLERS

We don't suggest the bike ride for any child under seven, but robust parents can carry children up to age six on their bike in a kid's seat. The bike rental shop can arrange the seat for you, but bring your own cycle helmets. There are no diaper-changing or nursing facilities on the tour route, but you will find lots of park benches and quiet spots to use for infant care.

WHERE & WHEN

Cycle Inn Matsushima
サイクルイン松島
1–18–14 Honcho, Koganei-shi, Tokyo 184–0004
☎ (0423) 81–2078
東京都小金井市本町1-18-14　〒184-0004
OPEN: 10 A.M. to 7 P.M.
CLOSED: Sun. The shop also closes during New

Year's hols and for Obon (mid-Aug), but you are usually able to reserve a bike in advance for use during these periods and on Sundays.
FEES: ¥300/hour or ¥800/day, after 12 P.M. ¥500/day
DIRECTIONS: a 2-minute walk from the south exit of Musashi-Koganei station on the JR Chuo line.

PARKING: none

COMMENTS: all ages, no English, reservations required

Musashino Park

武蔵野公園 (Musashino Koen)

2–24–1 Tama-cho, Fuchu-shi, Tokyo 183–0002

☎ (0423) 61–6861

東京都府中市多磨町2-24-1　〒183-0002

OPEN: 24 hours

DIRECTIONS: take Keio bus #91 from Chofu station (Keio line) or JR Musashi-Koganei station and get off at Tamacho 2-chome. By car take Tohachi Doro toward Kunitachi-shi. The park is next to the Driver's Office.

PARKING: free, 24 spaces

COMMENTS: all ages, no English

Nogawa Park

野川公園 (Nogawa Koen)

6–4–1 Osawa, Mitaka-shi, Tokyo 181–0015

☎ (0422) 31–6457

東京都三鷹市大沢6-4-1　〒181-0015

OPEN: park is always open. Nature Preserve is open 8:30 A.M. to 5 P.M.

CLOSED: Nature Center and Nature Preserve closed Mon and Dec 29 to Jan 3

DIRECTIONS: take bus #8 bound for Asahi Machi or Kuruma Gaeshi Danchi from the south exit of Mitaka station (JR Chuo line) and get off at Nogawa Koen Iriguchi. Or take Odakyu bus #52 from the south exit of Mitaka station or the north exit of Chofu station (Keio line). By car, take route 246 to Osawa intersection and turn south on Hitomi Kaido (Route 14). Drive uphill for about 1 km and you will see the park on your right.

PARKING: 240 spaces, hourly rate

COMMENTS: all ages, no English

Rakuyaki Pottery

深大寺がま（楽焼）(Jindaiji-gama)

5–13–6 Jindaiji Motomachi, Chofu-shi, Tokyo 182–0017

☎ (0424) 83–7441

東京都調布市深大寺元町5-13-6　〒182-0017

OPEN: daily 9 A.M. to 5 P.M. (enter by 4:30)

FEES: pottery ¥300 to ¥2,500

DIRECTIONS: see Jindaiji temple

COMMENTS: 5 and up, no English

Jindaiji Temple

深大寺

5–15–1 Jindaiji Motomachi, Chofu-shi, Tokyo 182–0017

☎ (0424) 86–5511

東京都調布市深大寺元町5-15-1　〒182-0017

OPEN: daily 6 A.M. to 6 P.M.

DIRECTIONS: 15 minutes by Keio bus #21, which runs about every 10 minutes from Tsutsujiga-oka station on the Keio line; get off at Jindaiji-mae bus stop. From Kichijoji station take Odakyu bus #4 bound for Jindaiji from bus stop #6 and get off at Jindaiji Iriguchi. From the north exit of Chofu station take Keio bus #34 from stop #14. The bus goes to Jindaiji and loops back to the station. By car from central Tokyo, take Koshu Kaido. At Kojimachi crossing turn right and follow the road to Musashi-sakai Dori. Turn right at Jindaiji Iriguchi crossing. From Nogawa Park, turn right at Nozaki onto Musashi-sakai Dori and continue to Jindaiji Iriguchi crossing.

PARKING: parking lots near the shopping streets, many with daily rates

COMMENTS: all ages, no English

Jindai Botanical Garden

神代植物公園 (Jindai Shokubutsu Koen)

5–31–10 Jindaiji Motomachi, Chofu-shi, Tokyo 182–0017

☎ (0424) 83–2300

調布市深大寺元町5-31-10　〒182-0017

OPEN: 9:30 A.M. to 4:30 P.M., ticket window and greenhouse close at 4

CLOSED: Mon (Tues if Mon is a hol), Dec 29 to Jan 3

FEES: adults ¥500, junior high school students ¥200, younger children and adults over 65 free

OLD JAPAN FOR THE YOUNG   Tour 6

DIRECTIONS: see Jindaiji temple. By car from the temple area continue on Musashi-sakai Dori to Shokubutsu Koen-mae. Parking is located on the other side of the park.

PARKING: hourly rate

COMMENTS: all ages, English pamphlet

Hydrophyte Garden of the Jindai Botanical Garden

水生植物公園 (Suisei Shokubutsu-en)

2–15 Jindaiji Motomachi, Chofu-shi, Tokyo 182-0017

☎ see Jindai Botanical Garden

調布市神代寺元町2-15　〒182-0017

OPEN: same as Jindai Botanical garden

DIRECTIONS: see Jindaiji temple. Garden is opposite temple.

COMMENTS: all ages, no English

7

Kamakura with Kids

**Great Buddha • Hasedera Kannon Temple • Waka-
miya Oji Dori • Komachi Dori Shopping Street •
Tsurugaoka Hachiman Shrine • Kamakura
Museum of Modern Art • Kenchoji Temple •
Hansobo Temple**

Rolling green hills, ancient temples, and ocean views make Kamakura an excellent escape from the noise and bustle of the city. Most kids won't stand for a day of visiting temple after temple, but we've put together a route rich in history, with kid-pleasing features like secret gardens, mysterious paths, and squirrels that eat out of your hand. This is a full day. Go at your own pace and don't worry if you can't get to every stop before 5 P.M., when the temples close. You can always come back; it's only an hour away from Tokyo.

We suggest you come by train, especially on weekends when the population of the city triples and roads jam with traffic. Weekdays the town is peaceful and quiet. Start your day with a bus ride from JR Kamakura station to the

Kamakura is a beautiful, peaceful town that once was much more —the seat of the shogun's power and the most important city in Japan. While the emperor ostensibly ruled the country, from 1192 the power resided with Minomoto Yoritomo, the first reigning shogun, who established his seat in his ancestral home of Kamakura. Mountains on one side, the sea on the other, it was a very defensible fortress and for a time its distance from the pleasures of the Kyoto court served to keep the *bakufu,* Japan's military government, disciplined. Under Yoritomo and his

Great Buddha, or Daibutsu, Kamakura's main attraction and a national treasure. The Buddha, completed in 1252, was originally gilded and enclosed in a large temple. Terrible storms wrecked the building in 1335 and 1368, and in 1495 a tidal wave plowed through the Hase Valley and destroyed the structure. Since then, the awe-inspiring Buddha has remained seated alfresco with the Goko-san mountain as its backdrop. During the Great Kanto Earthquake of 1923, it moved about 50 centimeters and suffered slight damage on one cheek. The statue ranks as Japan's second-largest bronze Buddha; the largest one is in Nara, but the Kamakura Buddha is considered a finer piece of work. It weighs 124,478 kilograms, stands 11.25 meters high, and has ears more than 1.8 meters long. As is customary with Buddhas of this type, the head is covered with 656 curls, and a silver boss centered in the forehead is supposed to be the source of the light that will fulfill Buddha's mission of illuminating the world. For a small fee, you may enter the statue to have a look inside.

Behind the walls that enclose the serene Buddha lies a small wooded area with large, flat rocks perfect for taking a rest. The resident squirrels have grown accustomed to the tourists who flock here and will timidly eat nuts right out of your hand. When you are ready to move on, the next stop is only a few hundred meters down the road toward the sea.

successors, priests and monks flocked to Kamakura to build temples, including many dedicated to Zen Buddhism, well-suited to the spartan samurai code.

Yoritomo controlled all of Japan from Kamakura, and in many respects his reign was just and popular—but there was plenty of bloodshed. When Yoritomo himself was thrown from a horse and died in 1199, his strong-willed wife Masako and her father took control of the country, ruling through her eighteen-year-old son Yoriie. The Hojo family craftily eliminated any other clans than might be contenders for power, massacring hundreds. Under the title of regents to the shogun, the Hojo would rule Japan until 1333, when forces stormed into Kamakura under the flag of the emperor. After five days of fighting, the imperial troops were in control. Their doom certain, the regent and hundreds of followers committed mass suicide rather than surrender.

Kamakura didn't immediately sink into obscurity, but by the 1500s Odawara and Edo had eclipsed this once-great city, and it became again a sleepy fishing village. The train revived Kamakura's fortunes. As early as the late 1800s, its temples and lovely landscape made it a popular tourist spot. Today's visitors include wealthy Tokyoites with elegant second homes in the neighborhood, California-style surfers who crowd the beaches, and Zen priests mingling in the temples with tourists from around the world.

Hasedera, one of eastern Japan's most popular temples, houses an ancient gilded Kannon. This artists' rendering of the Buddhist goddess of mercy is reputed to be the tallest wooden statue in the country. As you climb the stairs leading to the main hall you will see thousands of little statues of Misuko Jizo in memory of babies who died before birth. Kyozo, the temple sutra repository positioned to the left of the main hall, has a revolving bookcase called a prayer wheel that contains the temple's important scriptures. According to tradition, rotating the wheel once carries the same benefit as chanting a Buddhist sutra.

The temple has a commanding view of the houses in the valley, the Zaimokuza coast, and the Miura peninsula. Relax at one of several outdoor tables and take a few moments to watch boats pass. Then venture down to the garden where you'll find a pond full of carp and turtles, a waterfall, and a cave to explore. On weekends and holidays from 9:30 A.M. to 4 P.M. you can have tea prepared by an expert in the Japanese tea ceremony in a building near the pond for ¥1,000.

Next, walk a few minutes south to Hase station on the Enoden line and take the train back three stops to Kamakura station. From there either rent a bike at **Kamakura Rent-a-Cycle** or walk to Tsurugaoka Hachiman Shrine. If your children are not practiced cyclists, you might find the curving narrow sidewalks too dangerous for pedaling. There are two routes: the scenic one is **Wakamiya Oji Dori,** built for the *omiya mairi* (a Shinto ceremony akin to a christening) of the shogun Yoritomo's first son. The peaceful lane, lined with cherry trees, makes a very pleasant stroll when the blossoms open in April. As you approach the shrine you will see shops on both sides of the street selling Kamakura Bori, a distinctive type of laquerware with intricate carvings. Originally used to make religious art for the thriving temples of old Kamakura, nowadays this technique is more likely to be associated with more practical works of art, like fine housewares and exquisite fashion accessories.

The other route to the shrine is **Komachi Dori**, Kamakura's main shopping street. Here you will find a plethora of restaurants, coffee shops, handicraft boutiques, and souvenir shops selling local delicacies. On the west side of the street, **Shato**, an elegant Japanese paper store, carries stationery and paper dolls. Down further on the opposite side of the street, **Kitotenkundo** is our favorite place to buy incense. The store also carries high-priced ceramic incense burners and other breakables, so you may want to skip it if your kids are going through one of the gangbuster stages. Walk past the shopping area till you come to the main thoroughfare, Kamakura Kaido, and turn right. The vermilion *torii* gate of **Tsurugaoka Hachiman Shrine** will appear on your left in a few minutes.

When Yoritomo chose Kamakura for his headquarters, he moved his ancestral shrine to the Tsurugaoka hills. In keeping with family tradition, the shrine was dedicated to Hachiman, god of war and the tutelary deity of the Minamoto clan. The red drum bridge in front of the shrine was used only by the shogun. At his wife Masako's suggestion, Yoritomo had a lotus pond constructed on the premises. The east side has three islands; the west has four. In Japanese, three is a homonym for birth and prosperity while four is a homonym for death. Therefore, the east part of the pond symbolized hopes for the prosperity of the Minamoto clan while the west side represented defeat for their archenemies the Taira. The lilies on the east were white, the color of the Minamoto, while the red of the Taira bloomed to the west.

Beyond the pond on the east side of the complex, you will find the Kokuhokan, a museum of national treasures. Of more interest to parents than children, the museum contains many important pieces of art from Kamakura's temples and shrines. Pigeons flock near the Maiden Hall in the middle of the complex, where you can buy food to feed them. Older kids enjoy this because the birds will land on your arms to get the food, but their aggressive behavior can be frightening for toddlers.

On the left side of the steps leading to the shrine's main buildings is a massive old ginkgo tree. Sanetomo, Yoritomo's second son and the third shogun, was killed in the winter of 1219 by an assassin who hid behind this tree. The murderer was his own nephew, who had been tricked by the Hojo clan into believing he was avenging his father's death.

Climb the steps up to the main

> The Maiden Hall has a poignant history. Yoritomo grew suspicious of his brother Yoshitsune because of the imperial honors he received for military success, and sent soldiers to murder him. Yoshitsune's prolonged flight and final suicide are a favorite theme of Noh and Kabuki plays. While Yoshitsune was still a fugitive, his mistress, Shizuka Gozen, an accomplished Kyoto dancer, was taken prisoner and brought to Kamakura. Yoritomo ordered her to dance in the Maiden Hall, but to spite him she danced an ode of love to Yoshitsune, father of the child in her womb. Yoritomo became enraged and ordered the dancer killed, but his wife Masako convinced him to spare her life. Instead, he ordered the woman's child to be killed should it be born a boy. Unfortunately, Shizuka gave birth to a boy who was, as ordered, executed on Yugihama beach.

shrine for a look at Yadaijin and Sadaijin, two guardian deities. Once upon a time, the shrine was classified as *ryobu shinto,* a sort of compromise between Buddhism and Shintoism that operated on the belief that Shinto gods were incarnations of

Buddhist divinities. In shrines like Tsurugaoka Hachiman the austerity of Shintoism merged with the decorative splendor of Buddhism. The fall of the shogunate and restoration of imperial power in 1868 led to the return of Shintoism and the decline of Buddhism. Much of the ornamentation of the shrine was removed, and it became the unembellished structure it is today. One important warning: consider carefully before coming to this shrine around New Year's. The shrine and streets leading to it are as packed as a Tokyo subway during rush hour.

Opposite the Kokuhokan on the edge of the shrine grounds is the main building of the **Kamakura Museum of Modern Art**. Check the exhibit to see if it interests you; we are occasionally delighted by the quality of the shows here. The annex building a few minutes' walk from the rear side gate of the shrine displays the museum's permanent collection.

Whether you exit the shrine at the main front gate or the rear side gate, you will come to Kamakura Kaido. Buses run along this historic avenue from Kamakura station to Kita Kamakura station and beyond. You can walk, cycle, or just jump on a bus to get to **Kenchoji** temple. Ranked first among Kamakura's five great Zen temples, Kenchoji is the oldest Zen training monastery in Japan. An avenue of cherry trees leads to the complex. The juniper trees beyond the main gate to the left of the central path were brought to Japan as seedlings by the temple's first abbot, who came from China over seven hundred years ago.

> Kenchoji is built on a former execution ground called the "Valley of Hell." Here a man destined to be executed was once saved by a small statue of Jizo. The man, Saita Kingo, hid the effigy in his topknot. The executioner struck two blows, but neither decapitated Saita. When the authorities examined him they found the statue with a crack where the sword had fallen, and claiming divine intervention they let him go. The small statue lies inside a bigger statue of Jizo in the Butsuden on the temple grounds.

A garden behind the main hall was designed by Zen master Muso Kokushi in the shape of the Chinese character *kokoro,* meaning the heart and spirit. Follow the path to the left and continue straight beyond the Kenchoji grounds till you come to the many flights of stairs that lead to **Hansobo**, the protecting shrine of Kenchoji. Race up the 248 steps to reach the shrine and its panoramic view of the valley, with layers of verdant hues in summer and beautiful reds and oranges in fall. Eleven long-nosed mountain goblins called *tengu* greet you at the top. Small *tengu* festivals are held the seventeenth and eighteenth of every month.

When you've finished with Hansobo, go back to Kamakura Kaido. If you have rented bikes, return them to the Rent-a-Cycle shop near Kamakura station. If not, head to Kita Kamakura station for an early dinner. It's a 15-minute walk or a short bus ride.

Other Things to Do in the Area

Just off Kamakura Kaido between Kenchoji and Kita Kamakura station are two temples with lovely gardens. **Meigetsu-in**, also called Ajisai-dera, is well known for its hydrangeas. Japanese flock here on the June weekends when this flower is in bloom, so try to come on a weekday. The rest of the year the temple is quiet, but you can still enjoy the gorgeous flowers: azalea, iris, lily of the valley, forsythia, and narcissus. The temple has a Zen rock garden across from its main hall. At the main hall, called the Hondo, you can drink frothy *matcha* (Japanese ceremonial tea) served with a sweet for ¥600.

Not far away lies **Tokeiji**, or "divorce temple." Long ago only men had the right to divorce their spouses. The only escape for an unhappy wife was three years of seclusion with the nuns at Tokeiji. If a woman reached the temple gates or even threw a shoe over the walls she was considered safe and could not be forced to leave. Once their time was completed they were considered divorced. Locals were always helping women who sought sanctuary in the temple—if they saw a woman running in the area, they would automatically assume she was being pursued by an abusive husband and call out directions to Tokeiji. The temple also offered marriage counseling in an effort to reconcile couples, but today it is a temple of the Rinzai sect with only men in residence. The temple grounds are at their best in February and March when the plum groves blossom and in summer when several species of iris are in bloom. The back of the grounds is like a secret garden, with soft mosses covering ancient steps and monuments, and towering bamboo that blocks out the sun—a peaceful place to cool down on a hot summer day.

Festivals and important dates for spots on this tour

- **January 1–3**
  New Year's Hatsumode (first visit to the shrine in the New Year) at Tsurugaoka Hachiman Shrine. Avoid this with children—two million people participate and the crowds are unbearable.
- **February 3**
  Setsubun (bean-throwing festival) at Tsurugaoka Hachiman Shrine
- **Second or third Sunday in April**
  Kamakura festival

- August 7–9
  Bonbori (paper lantern festival) at Tsurugaoka Hachiman Shrine
- September 15
  Tsurugaoka Hachiman Shrine festival
- September 16
  Yabusame (horseback archery) at Tsurugaoka Hachiman Shrine
- Early November
  Chrysanthemum Blossom Festival at Tsurugaoka Hachiman Shrine
- December 31
  Joyano-kane, New Year's bell ringing at Kenchoji temple

EATING OPTIONS

Restaurants There is everything from Zen cuisine to fast food along the tour. Our recommendations near Hasedera are either Sometaro Okonomiyaki shop, where you whip up your own savory Japanese pancakes and *yakisoba* (fried noodles) on a grill at your table, or Issa An *soba* shop, which serves handmade noodles, just a 2-minute walk along Kamakura Kaido from Tsurugaoka Hachiman Shrine. If you are into health food, you might want to try Kamakura Sasa no Ha near Kita Kamakura station for vegetarian meals and brown rice.

Picnic Possibilities Hasedera has a little shop selling snacks and light meals that you can eat on picnic tables overlooking the ocean, and there is a nice wooded spot behind the Daibutsu where you can eat. Several of the temples, like Meigetsu-in, prohibit bringing food and drinks into the temple grounds.

FOR INFANTS AND TODDLERS

None of the temples or shops we found had facilities for diaper changing or nursing. You'll have to search for quiet spots to make do—sometimes a challenge on weekends when the temples fill with tourists. Kamakura Rent-a-Cycle has bikes for kids but no infant or toddler seats that fasten to an adult's bike. You will definitely want your stroller on this tour even though all of the temples have some stairs. At Hasedera, park your stroller near the entrance gate, as there are too many stairs to make the stroller useful.

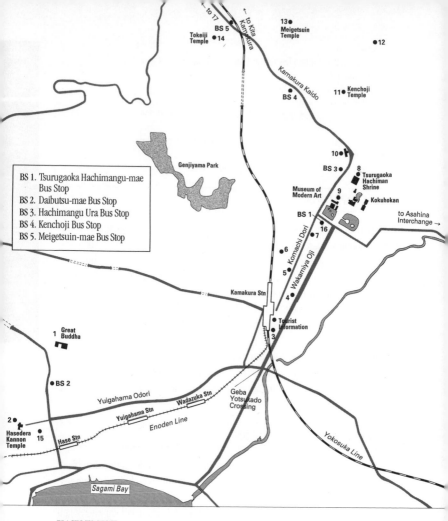

BS 1. Tsurugaoka Hachimangu-mae Bus Stop
BS 2. Daibutsu-mae Bus Stop
BS 3. Hachimangu Ura Bus Stop
BS 4. Kenchoji Bus Stop
BS 5. Meigetsuin-mae Bus Stop

PLACES TO VISIT

1. Great Buddha
2. Hasedera Kannon Temple
3. Kamakura Rent-a-Cycle
4. Wakamiya Oji Dori
5. Komachi Dori Shopping Street
6. Shato Japanese Paper Shop
7. Kitotenkundo Incense Shop
8. Tsurugaoka Hachiman Shrine
9. Kamakura Museum of Modern Art

10. Museum Annex
11. Kenchoji Temple
12. Hansobo
13. Meigetsu-in Temple
14. Tokeiji Temple
15. Sometaro Okonomiyaki Shop
16. Issa An Soba Shop
17. Kamakura Sasa-no-Ha

Great Buddha—Kotokuin Temple
大仏 (Daibutsu) – 高徳院
4–2–28 Hase, Kamakura-shi, Kanagawa-ken 248–0016
☎ (0467) 22–0703
神奈川県鎌倉市長谷4-2-28　〒248-0016
OPEN: daily 7 A.M. to 6 P.M. (summer), 7 A.M. to 5:30 P.M. (winter)
FEES: adults ¥200, children 6 to 12 ¥150
DIRECTIONS: from Tokyo, Shinagawa, or Yokohama stations take the JR Yokosuka line bound for Zushi and get out at Kamakura station. From the east exit of Kamakura station take either the Keihin Electric Express Railway, an old-style tourist bus that runs once or twice an hour, or a regular Keihin bus (these run at least 5 times an hour) from bus stop #2; get out at the Daibutsu-mae bus stop. Or, take the Enoden line (near the west exit of Kamakura station) to Hase station and walk about 8 minutes up the hill following the signs to the Daibutsu. By car from Tokyo take Yokohama Yokosuka Doro Toll Road and exit at Asahina interchange. Follow road signs in English to Kamakura Kaido (this street has many of the spots of interest on this tour) and take it to Tsurugaoka Hachiman Shrine. Turn right onto Wakamiya Oji and travel toward the sea. At Geba Yotsukado crossing turn right, go to the end of the street, and turn right again. The Great Buddha will be up the street a few hundred meters on your right.
PARKING: no related parking, although you may find an expensive lot in the area; most parking space in this neighborhood is reserved for buses
COMMENTS: all ages, adequate English

Hasedera Kannon Temple
長谷寺 (Hasedera)
3–11–2 Hase, Kamakura-shi, Kanagawa-ken 248–0016
☎ (0467) 22–6300
神奈川県鎌倉市長谷3-11-2　〒248-0016
OPEN: daily 8 A.M. to 5 P.M. (summer), 8 A.M. to 4:30 P.M. (winter)
FEES: adults ¥300, children 6 to 11 ¥100
DIRECTIONS: 300 meters south of the Great Buddha; see directions for Great Buddha. From Kamakura station's east exit take the bus from stop #2 and get out at Hase Kannon stop. A 5-minute walk from Hase station (Enoden line).
PARKING: 15 spaces; ¥300/30 minutes
COMMENTS: all ages, some English

Kamakura Rent-a-Cycle
鎌倉レンタルサイクル
1–1 Komachi, Kamakura-shi, Kanagawa-ken 248–0006
☎ (0467) 24–2319
神奈川県鎌倉市小町1-1　〒248-0006
OPEN: daily 8:30 A.M. to 5 P.M.
FEES: ¥500/hour, ¥250 each additional hour, ¥1,500/day
DIRECTIONS: on the left as you exit from the east side of JR Kamakura station
COMMENTS: 5 and up, no English

Shato Japanese Paper Shop
和紙専門店社頭
2–7 Komachi, Kamakura-shi, Kanagawa-ken 248–0006
☎ (0467) 22–2601
神奈川県鎌倉市小町2-7　〒248-0006
OPEN: 10 A.M. to 6 P.M.
CLOSED: Thurs
DIRECTIONS: on the west side of Komachi Dori, a 5-minute walk from the east exit of JR Kamakura station

Kitotenkundo Incense Shop
鬼頭天薫堂

1–7–5 Yukinoshita, Kamakura-shi, Kanagawa-ken 248–0005

☎ (0467) 22–1081

神奈川県鎌倉市雪ノ下1-7-5   〒248-0005

OPEN: daily 10 A.M. to 6 P.M.

DIRECTIONS: on the east side of Komachi Dori, a 10-minute walk from the east exit of JR Kamakura station

Tsurugaoka Hachiman Shrine
鶴ヶ岡八幡宮

2–1–31 Yukinoshita, Kamakura-shi, Kanagawa-ken 248–0005

☎ (0467) 22–0315

神奈川県鎌倉市雪ノ下2-1-31   〒248-0005

OPEN: 24 hours

DIRECTIONS: 15 minutes on foot from JR Kamakura station's east exit. Or, take a bus from stop #8 in front of the east exit and get out at Tsurugaoka Hachimangu-mae or Tsurugaoka Hachimangu Ura. By car, see directions for Great Buddha.

PARKING: none, but several lots in the area

COMMENTS: all ages, some English

Kamakura Museum of Modern Art
神奈川県立近代美術館 (Kanagawa-ken-ritsu Kindai Bijutsu-kan)

MAIN BUILDING: 2–1–53 Yukinoshita, Kamakura-shi, Kanagawa-ken 248–0005

☎ (0467) 22–5000

神奈川県鎌倉市雪ノ下2-1-53   〒248-0005

ANNEX: 2–8–1 Yukinoshita, Kamakura-shi, Kanagawa-ken 248–0005

☎ (0467) 22–7718

神奈川県鎌倉市雪ノ下2-8-1   〒248-0005

OPEN: 9:30 A.M. to 5 P.M. (enter by 4:30)

CLOSED: Mon, days following national hols, New Year's hols

FEES: adults ¥800/¥1,000, high school student ¥650/¥850, seniors over 65 and all others free

DIRECTIONS: for main building, see directions to Tsurugaoka Hachiman Shrine. Annex is on the west side of Kamakura Kaido a few meters from the rear exit of the shrine.

PARKING: 10 free spaces at main building; no parking at annex

COMMENTS: all ages, no English

Kenchoji Temple
建長寺

8 Yamanouchi, Kamakura-shi, Kanagawa-ken 247–0062

☎ (0467) 22–0981

神奈川県鎌倉市山ノ内8   〒247-0062

OPEN: daily 8:30 A.M. to 4:30 P.M. (admission until 4:30)

FEES: adults ¥300, high school students ¥200, junior high/elementary students ¥100

DIRECTIONS: a 20-minute walk from east exit of Kamakura station; a 15-minute walk from Kita Kamakura station. Or take a bus from stop #8 in front of the east exit of Kamakura station and get off at Kenchoji. By car, see directions for Great Buddha. Kenchoji is on Kamakura Kaido about 1 km before you reach Tsurugaoka Hachimangu Shrine.

PARKING: 25 spaces; hourly rate

COMMENTS: all ages, some English

Meigetsu-in Temple
明月院

189 Yamanouchi, Kamakura-shi, Kanagawa-ken 247–0062

☎ (0467) 24–3437

神奈川県鎌倉市山ノ内189   〒247-0062

OPEN: daily 8 A.M. to 5 P.M. in June for hydrangeas, 9 A.M. to 4 P.M. other seasons

FEES: adults and school children ¥300; free for preschoolers

DIRECTIONS: an 8-minute walk from Kita Kamakura station (Yokosuka line). From Kamakura station's east exit, take a bus from stop #8 and get out at Meigetsu-In-mae. Go back over the railroad tracks and cross the street to Meigetsu Dori, which leads to the temple. By car, see directions to Great Buddha. Meigetsu-In is on Meigetsu Dori, a little street accessible from Kamakura Kaido. It's on the east side of Kamakura Kaido shortly after you pass Kita Kamakura station.

PARKING: none. Try the lots at Engakuji temple just south of Kita Kamakura station or Kenchoji temple.

COMMENTS: all ages, some English

Tokeiji Temple
東慶寺

1367 Yamanouchi, Kamakura-shi, Kanagawa-ken 247–0062

☎ (0467) 22–1663

神奈川県鎌倉市山ノ内1367　〒247-0062

OPEN: daily 8:30 A.M. to 5 P.M.; Nov to March 8:30 A.M. to 4 P.M.

FEES: adults and students ¥100

DIRECTIONS: a 5-minute walk from Kita Kamakura station. From Kamakura station's east exit, take a bus from stop #8 and get out at Meigetsu-In-mae. Walk to the corner and the path to Tokeiji will be on your left. By car, see directions for Great Buddha. Tokeiji is on the west side of Kamakura Kaido a few hundred meters south of Kita Kamakura station.

COMMENTS: all ages, no English

Kamakura Sasa-no-Ha
笹の葉

499 Yamanouchi, Kamakura-shi, Kanagawa-ken 247–0062

☎ (0467) 23–2068

神奈川県鎌倉市山ノ内499　〒247-0062

OPEN: 11:30 A.M. to 7 P.M. Reservations needed after 4.

CLOSED: Mon and New Year's hols

DIRECTIONS: a 2-minute walk from Kita Kamakura station. By car, on Kamakura Kaido just north of Kita Kamakura station. Turn east at the Three F convenience store and it's on the right at the end of the little street.

PARKING: none

Sometaro Okonomiyaki Shop
染太郎

3–12–11 Hase, Kamakura-shi, Kanagawa-ken 248–0016

☎ (0467) 22–8694

神奈川県鎌倉市長谷3-12-11　〒248-0016

OPEN: daily 11:30 A.M. to 9 P.M.

CLOSED: irregularly

DIRECTIONS: on the south side of Kannon Dori, the street that leads to Hase Kannon Temple, just a 1-minute walk from the temple

PARKING: none

COMMENTS: English menu

Issa An Soba Shop
一茶庵

1–8–24 Yukinoshita, Kamakura-shi, Kanagawa-ken 248–0005

☎ (0467) 22–3556

神奈川県鎌倉市雪ノ下1-8-24　〒248-0005

OPEN: 11 A.M. to 7:30 P.M.

CLOSED: Thurs

DIRECTIONS: on Kamakura Kaido, a few minutes west of the main entrance to Tsurugaoka Hachiman Shrine

PARKING: free, but only 4 spaces

A Day with a Theme

Take advantage of the fact that certain parts of Tokyo and Yokohama have concentrations of places where you can learn about a special interest area—all offering firsthand experience in culture, commerce, or technology.

*Bring your family to **Otemachi** to learn about the history of communications and play with the latest technology, then tour the operations of the world's most widely read newspaper. Learn about currencies and stocks in Tokyo's financial district, where both the **Bank of Japan** and the **Tokyo Stock Exchange** have created marvelous exhibit halls to teach visitors young and old about their roles. You can watch stock traders in action and try your hand at buying and selling stocks with a computer simulation.*

*For a real port experience, take a cruise across Yokohama's harbor to Yamashita Park and the retired luxury liner Hikawa Maru. Walk through the red lacquer gates of **Chinatown** and get a taste of another Asian culture. We suggest coming back to Yokohama another day for a look at the whimsical figurines and antique toys from around the world in our **Yesterday's Toys** tour. We also take you to fashionable Motomachi shopping street, and the bluff area, where many of Japan's first Western residents lived.*

Children age ten or older will get the most out of the thematic tours in Tokyo, while those in Yokohama are suitable for all ages.

Media Mecca Otemachi

Communications Museum • Tour of Yomiuri Shimbun• Ninomaru Imperial Gardens

It's a bit of modern magic. Information exchange today is so advanced it's become simple: you just drop a letter in the mail, pick up the telephone, plug into the Internet, switch on the TV, or open a newspaper. But how much do you know about what goes on behind the scenes? Where did all this technology come from, and where is it going? With plenty of interactive displays, Otemachi's Communications Museum turns out to be one of the best in town. We've paired it with a tour of the world's most-read newspaper, the *Yomiuri Shimbun,* and for some contrast added a visit to a serene Japanese garden within the walls of the imperial moat.

At the **Communications Museum**, four powerful Japanese communications organizations have joined together: the Japanese postal system, KDD (an international telecommunications firm), NTT (the national telephone system), and NHK (the national radio and television broadcasting system). Start your tour on the third floor to see how communication has changed over the centuries. A bell relay system set up in 645 A.D. was an early way of transmitting information in Japan. The upper classes sent letters to each other by special messenger for centuries, but it wasn't until the Edo period (1603–1867) that the express messenger system was created, making it possible for the common people to communicate in writing. This early postal service was a lot like the American Pony Express, without the horses. Strong, swift men ran relays along regular routes that connected the country's main towns. The modern Japanese postal system was born in 1871; international mail service followed within the decade. Excellent displays tell this story vividly. You can also get a good look at a large letter-sorting machine, or compare post boxes from around the world.

One of the highlights is a driving simulator that lets you take a turn delivering the mail on one of those ubiquitous orange scooters, testing your ability to follow road safety rules. As in many other countries, Japan's postal system offers insurance policies and higher yielding savings accounts. To illustrate these financial products, there are several computer quizzes on personal finance in Japanese as well as a collection of piggy banks from countries all over the world.

Whether your interest in stamps is casual or passionate, you'll enjoy looking at the museum's gigantic collection. Displays along the wall show some of the most famous and valuable stamps in the more than 230,000-piece collection, and illustrate the history of stamps in Japan. Budding philatelists can pull out large panels arranged by country to examine stamps from around the world. Souvenirs are on sale in the Philately Shop, and there are also outstanding special exhibitions on the first floor.

The history of telecommunications in Japan is also on the third floor. Take a look at the telegraph machine Admiral Perry brought in 1854 to introduce the Japanese shogunate to modern technology, or read the introduction to Alexander Graham Bell's first paper on inventing the telephone. In the NTT Telecommunications Gallery, you can follow the development of modern communications equipment by examining historically significant telephone and telegraph models arranged in the order in which they appeared.

When you're finished, head down the escalator. In KDD World Communications Plaza on the second floor, you can call for weather information in New York or Paris, and learn about satellite communication. Sit down for a spell and check out the Hi-Vision Theater, which showcases NHK's version of high-definition television on a 110-inch screen. Clips from Japanese television dramas and a collection of television images from the Showa period (1926–1989) entertain visitors in the nearby Video Library Corner. Kids can learn the basics of satellite broadcasting with an exhibit that follows the weather report from a model broadcasting studio through a transmitter, satellite, and receiving dish, and finally into the home.

Around the corner you can try out communications equipment—from a model of Bell's first telephone to a terminal for surfing the Internet. All displays are hands-on, and while there is not much English, you may find an attendant who speaks enough to help you. Operate an old-time switchboard or send a message by telex. Learn about fiber optics, how a fax machine works, and the structure of a telephone number. Sit in front of videophone 1 and talk to a friend at videophone 2. You can also use a data base, shop by computer, and sample interactive videos and video-on-demand. There is a roomful of computers where you can try out Japanese educational software. The museum holds classes on personal computers for kids in fourth grade or older on the second and fourth Saturdays of the month, Sundays, and national holidays. Workshops on video conference systems follow the same schedule.

Displays on both the floors are clear, bold, and appealing. You'll find time slips by rather quickly, so be sure to schedule at least an hour and a half to go through the museum, if not longer.

You'll need about an hour for the next activity, a tour of the **Yomiuri Shimbun**. Make reservations in Japanese at least one week in advance. The tours are often full from October to March, so you might have to wait several weeks for a time slot. The tour starts with a 20-minute video that you can request to see in English when you make your reservations. At the end of the film, kids line up on benches in the back of the theater for a keepsake picture. For the rest of the tour you may want to bring along a friend who understands Japanese, or an interpreter. You'll spend 25 minutes learning about the work of reporters, editors, and graphic designers. You'll see computer scanners and picture trimmers. (If your timing is good, you may even get a paste-up of a weather map or some other illustration from the day's paper as a souvenir.) The tour guide will explain how the news goes from computer to negative to printing plate. Next you are off to the plant to see giant rolls of paper so heavy they can only be moved by machine. Watch the presses roll and see the day's edition packaged for distribution across the country. When the tour is over, you will receive a laminated copy of your keepsake photo printed on a mini sheet of newsprint.

On weekdays, you may also tour the **Imperial Palace's Inner Garden**, if you don't mind applying in advance. First call the Visitor's Office of the Imperial Household Agency (*Sankan-gakari*) to book the day for your tour; dial 3213–1111, ask for extension 485 (*naisen yon-hachi-go*), and you will be connected to an English-speaking receptionist. Then bring your alien registration or passport to the Imperial Household Agency on the palace grounds to apply for a visitor's permit; you will need to know the number of people in your party as well as everyone's name, age, address in Japan, employer, and passport number. Non-Japanese may submit an application as late as the day before the tour. Japanese and parties of ten or more regardless of nationality must apply at least ten days in advance. The 90-minute Japanese tour (English pamphlet available) starts at the Kikyomon gate and includes the remains of Edo castle and the former House of Lords. Tours start at 10 A.M. and 1:30 P.M. and are not available on weekends, the New Year's holiday season, and during imperial court functions.

Fresh air and flowers are a good way to clear your head after the intensity of the museum and newspaper tour; you'll find both at **Ninomaru Garden**, a 10-minute walk past the head offices of some of the world's largest banks and through the East Imperial Garden. Stop and admire the graceful swans in the palace moat, then follow our map to one of the most beautiful Japanese-style gardens in Tokyo. The route twists and turns, but you'll find this quiet spot well worth the walk. In every season, carp ponds, waterfalls, meticulously trimmed bushes, and gorgeous flowers delight guests of all ages. Quiet benches offer a relaxing respite from the city. The sights and scents are especially lovely in May, when the wisteria and other spring flowers are out. The garden is free, but you must pick up a visitor's pass at the gate and return it when you exit.

More Media Museums

People who are interested in stamps may want to visit the **Printing Bureau Memorial Museum** a few stops away. The bureau is responsible for producing both stamps and money and has displays of collector's items and a few videos on related subjects in English. To get there from Otemachi by subway, take the Tozai line to Iidabashi, transfer to the Yurakucho line, and go one stop to Ichigaya station. (Also described in Tour 9.)

The *Pacific Stars and Stripes*, the U.S. military newspaper, offers English tours of its facility in Roppongi. This makes a good option for those who don't understand Japanese and don't want to bother getting a translator, but you must be over ten years old to take the tour. (The *Yomiuri* has no age restrictions.)

EATING OPTIONS

Restaurants There is a restaurant and a coffee shop in the Communications Museum building, but the most popular spot with the foreign crowd is across the street in the basement of the Urbannet Otemachi Building. The Day and Night cafeteria, open for lunch from 11 A.M. to 2 P.M., is always packed at noon, but if you come a little later or earlier you can choose from a variety of dishes, including Indian curry, Japanese noodles, California-style sandwiches on whole wheat bread, and Chinese dishes. Like Urbannet, most Otemachi buildings have a variety of restaurants in different price ranges. You won't see them from the street, however; most are located on the basement level.

Picnic Possibilities You can eat your lunch in the large rest area on the first floor of the Communications Museum, or take it to the Imperial Gardens. A gift shop

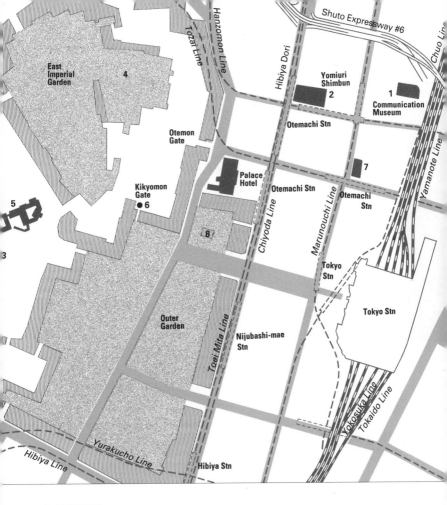

PLACES TO VISIT

1. Communications Museum
2. *Yomiuri Shimbun*
3. Imperial Palace's Inner Garden
4. Ninomaru Garden

5. Imperial Household Agency
6. Kikyomon Gate
7. Urbannet Otemachi Building
8. Fountain Park

in the gardens sells drinks and ice cream. You cannot throw away any trash from your lunch in the gardens. If the gardens are closed, the next best place is a small fountain park just south of the Palace Hotel. *Obento* boxed lunches are sold in a number of places in the neighborhood of the Communications Museum, including the basement of the Urbannet Otemachi Building across the street to the south.

FOR INFANTS AND TODDLERS

Bringing a stroller is probably a good idea, since the walk to the garden is several blocks and the entire route is stroller-friendly. A crib for diaper changing is located in front of the first-floor bathroom at the Communications Museum. Unlike the *Pacific Stars and Stripes,* the *Yomiuri* welcomes small children and infants on its tours, but visit the bathroom before you leave the Communications Museum. You cannot use the restrooms at the newspaper. The East Imperial Gardens also have no infant and toddler care facilities, but little ones are always fascinated by the colorful carp in the pond, while parents like the smooth, stroller-friendly paths.

WHERE & WHEN

Communications Museum

逓信総合博物館 (Teishin Sogo Hakubutsu-kan)

2–3–1 Otemachi, Chiyoda-ku, Tokyo 100–0004

☎ (03) 3244–6811

東京都千代田区大手町2-3-1 〒100-0004

OPEN: 9 A.M. to 4:30 P.M. (until 6:30 on Fri). Admission until 30 minutes before closing.

CLOSED: Mon (Tues if Mon is a hol), Dec 29 to Jan 3

FEES: adults ¥110, children under 12 years old ¥50 on normal days; students free on Sun and national hols

DIRECTIONS: a 1-minute walk from exit A4 or A5 of Otemachi station (Marunouchi, Tozai, Hanzomon, Chiyoda, and Toei Mita subway lines); a 10-minute walk from the Marunouchi north exit of Tokyo station (JR Yamanote, Tokaido, Chuo, Yokosuka, Keihin Tohoku, and Keio train lines and Marunouchi subway line). By car, take expressway #6 to Kanda-bashi ramp and go south on Hibiya Dori.

Take the 2nd left and the museum will be one block down on the right.

PARKING: no lot but there is some parking on the streets around the building

COMMENTS: 5 and up, English pamphlet

Yomiuri Shimbun (Yomiuri Newspaper)

読売新聞社

1–7–1 Otemachi, Chiyoda-ku, Tokyo 100–0004

☎ (03) 3217–8399

東京都千代田区大手町1-7-1 〒100-0004

OPEN: tours scheduled for 11 A.M., noon, 1 P.M., and 2 P.M. Mon through Fri

CLOSED: weekends, national hols, New Year's hols

FEES: none

DIRECTIONS: see Communications Museum. Newspaper is one block east of museum on the same side of the street.

PARKING: none

COMMENTS: 5 and up, reservations required

Ninomaru Garden

皇居東御苑二の丸 (Kokyo Higashi-Gyoen Ninomaru)

Kokyo Higashi-Gyoen Chiyoda, Chiyoda-ku, Tokyo 100–0001

☎ (03) 3213–2050

東京都千代田区千代田皇居東御苑　〒100-0001

OPEN: 9:30 A.M. to 3 P.M.

CLOSED: Mon and Fri, Dec 23 for the Emperor's Birthday, Dec 25 to Jan 3; also closed during Imperial Court functions

FEES: none

DIRECTIONS: a 10-minute walk from Yomiuri Newspaper or a few minutes on foot from exit C13b of Otemachi station (Marunouchi, Tozai, Hanzomon, Chiyoda, and Mita subway lines). An 8-minute walk from the Marunouchi exit of Tokyo station (JR Yamanote, Chuo, Yokosuka, Keihin Tohoku, Tokaido, and Keio train lines and Marunouchi subway line).

PARKING: none

COMMENTS: all ages, English pamphlet on sale

Imperial Household Agency

宮内庁参観係 (Kunaicho)

Visitor's Office, Ground Floor

1–1 Chiyoda, Chiyoda-ku, Tokyo 100–0001

☎ (03) 3213–1111, ext. 485 or 486

東京都千代田区千代田1-1　〒100-0001

OPEN: 9 A.M. to 4:30 P.M.

CLOSED: weekends, national hols, and Dec 25 to Jan 6

DIRECTIONS: inside the Imperial Palace Grounds, a 1-minute walk from Sakashitamon gate; pass through the gate and head slightly to the right. The Sakashitamon gate is a 10-minute walk from Nijubashi-mae station (Chiyoda line, exit 6) or Otemachi station (Marunouchi, Tozai, Hanzomon, and Mita lines, exit D2), or a 15-minute walk from JR Tokyo station, Marunouchi central exit.

PARKING: none

COMMENTS: make reservations here to visit the Imperial Palace's Inner Garden

Pacific Stars and Stripes

星条旗新聞社 (Seijoki Shinbunsha)

7–23–17 Roppongi, Minato-ku, Tokyo 106–0032

☎ (03) 5410–1984, (03) 3401–8935 (Tour Reservations)

東京都港区六本木7-23-17　〒106-0032

OPEN: most tours start at 11 A.M. but can be scheduled a little earlier or later

CLOSED: weekends and U.S. national hols

FEES: none

DIRECTIONS: a 5-minute walk from Aoyama Bochi (cemetery) exit of Nogizaka station (Chiyoda subway line). A 5-minute walk from exit 2 of Roppongi station (Hibiya subway line). By car, just northeast of where Gaien-Nishi Dori and Gaien-Higashi Dori fork.

PARKING: ample and free

COMMENTS: 10 and up, ample English, reservation required

9

Kabutocho Money Market Tour

Currency Museum • Tokyo Stock Exchange • Kabuto Shrine

No textbook can show how the world of business works as clearly as a trip to the stock exchange, and learning about money and markets is surprisingly intriguing for people of all ages. Find out how the currency designers foil counterfeiters at the Bank of Japan's Currency Museum, and learn the language and hand signals of traders at the Tokyo Stock Exchange. While you can watch the action on the stock floor and try the many interactive displays on the spur of the moment, if you want to take the English guided tour offered Monday to Friday starting at 1:30 P.M. you must make reservations by phone. Just say *"kengaku no tanto onegaishimasu,"* and the receptionist will connect you to an English-speaking tour guide.

Set out in the morning on the day of your appointment and give yourself time to learn about the history of money in Japan and around the world at the **Currency Museum** in Nihonbashi. Want to see the largest minted gold coin in the world? Leather coins from Siberia, pearl and stone money from the Yap Islands, or porcelain coins from Siam? The museum focuses on the development of currency in Japan but also has exhibits on currencies from both current and ancient civilizations elsewhere.

Rice and silk were the earliest mediums of exchange in Japan, but in 708 A.D. the government minted a large supply of copper coins similar to those that had been in use in China for several centuries. You can examine these early doughnut-shaped coins, as well as some interesting earlier Chinese money shaped like hoes or knives. As you walk through the exhibits, follow along in the small English booklet available in the museum. Entitled "A Brief History of Money in Japan," this publication provides excellent, detailed explanations of the main themes described in English on the cylindrical exhibit cases, although the terminology is occasionally different.

An exhibit called "Foreign Currencies Today" lets you look at money from around the world on numbered panels. You can also see notes used during the military occupations of Manchuria, Malaysia, Burma, and the Philippines, as well as bills used during the U.S. occupation of Japan. Learn tricks to frustrate counterfeiters, find out how bills are marked for the blind, and examine the currency curiosities in the collection, which includes Japanese notes and coins that were never issued. The museum occupies only one floor, but give yourself an hour or two to look at the displays and watch the English video on the Bank of Japan (BOJ) just in front of the exhibit room. The museum is located in the same building as part of the BOJ, which as Japan's central bank is the only note-issuing bank in the country and functions as the lender of last resort to the banking system and as treasurer of the government.

The **Tokyo Stock Exchange** (TSE) is only one stop away on the Ginza line. Use the side entrance to check in with the receptionist and meet your guide, then head up the escalator to the second floor. An informative 15-minute film explaining the international stock market, the Tokyo exchange, and stock transactions in general starts off the tour. Slide into a chair and find out how stock buyers are connected with sellers. Younger children may find parts of the film a little too advanced, but the explanation of how stock transactions occur is interesting and helpful in understanding what's happening when you move on to the trading floor.

Once you understand the rules of the game, trading floor activity can be as fun to watch as any spectator sport. Men and women in color-coded jackets flash cryptic hand signals back and forth. Suddenly, a frantically waving trader runs out of his booth and over to a trading counter. A stock price display board flickers while its numbers change and the room breaks into a round of applause—a big trade is always treated like a hole-in-one. Your tour guide and handy multilingual phone guides will explain the activity on the floor and the participants' roles. Phone guides provide explanations in seven languages: English, Japanese, French, Chinese, and Korean are marked on buttons one through five, and if you'd like Spanish or German, ask the tour guide to put it on button six for you.

Both adults and kids will enjoy learning a few hand signals for the names of listed companies. Many of them are a play on words. For example, to make the signal for Tokyo Gas, pinch your nose. For Nissan Motors, hold up two fingers, then three, then pretend to drive. (Two, three is *ni, san* in Japanese.) At the end of the trading day a bell rings and the letter E, for end, flashes across the display boards.

The tour guide can also take you up three floors to level five for a look at computer-aided stock transactions and the futures and options markets, where men seated at computers handle the market activity. This is not nearly as exciting, so unless you are particularly interested in this area we suggest you skip it and move to the next attraction.

While the TSE building generally looks a bit staid, the pink and blue neon of the Exhibition Plaza on its second floor is alluring. All but two small exhibits are in both English and Japanese, and a few are in other languages, too. Mechanical mannequins in the Kabuto Theater use easy words to explain the role and function of governments and corporations, and how they get the money to pay for their activities. A robot demonstrates hand signals used on the trading floor for numbers, buy and sell orders, and various company names. The Air Vision Theater provides a three-dimensional picture of trading. You can also check out the action on the world's other major stock exchanges via large TV screens.

Other exhibits include a computer simulator that allows you to try your hand at buying and selling stocks, and a "Terminology Box" that helps you get a handle on the trading lingo. If you are interested in the TSE's past, take a look at the small historical museum on the first floor. Titles of the exhibits are in both English and Japanese, as is an interactive video that tests how much history you've learned.

When you're finished, step out into one of the world's most powerful financial districts, its buildings emblazoned with the names of prestigious banks and investment houses. In Japan, Kabuto-cho conjures up the same images as Wall Street in America, or the City in the U.K. A *kabuto* is actually a warrior's helmet, and Kabuto-cho takes its name from **Kabuto Jinja**, a Shinto shrine located kitty-corner from the TSE.

The tiny shrine with its vermilion *torii* gate stands out among the gray office buildings like a plump red *umeboshi* (pickled plum) on a bowl of white rice. It was founded in 1878 by businessmen with dealings in the stock exchange—the main deity of the shrine is the god of commerce.

A historical rock called Kabuto Iwa, or helmet rock, is housed inside Kabuto Jinja. According to legend, a member of the powerful Minamoto clan received divine assistance after he put his helmet on this rock and prayed for victory in battle against other Japanese nobles (see Tour 7 for more on the Minamoto clan).

Unsurprisingly, the location and size of the shrine have changed several times over the last century to make way for new roads and buildings. Its festival is on April 1.

Other Things to Do in the Area

The shrine takes only a minute to see. If you are walking back to Nihonbashi station, you may want to stop at **Maruzen Bookstore**, which carries books in English and other foreign languages. On the second floor is a large selection of hardcover foreign books on a variety of subjects. You'll also find racks of books on Japan, paperback novels, magazines, and nonfiction. Foreign cookbooks and children's picture books are on the fourth floor.

Near the Currency Museum, **Mitsukoshi Department Store's flagship branch** makes for an opulent shopping experience. A five-hundred-year-old piece of Japanese cypress carved into the image of the goddess of sincerity sets the tone. The giant figure, beautifully gilded and studded with jewels, sits in the central hall on the first floor. If you'd like a musical break, a pipe organ is played for customers on the second floor of the atrium at 10 A.M., noon, and 3 P.M.

More Currency Exhibits

The **Printing Bureau Memorial Museum** is a few stops away, but interesting examples of Japanese currency make it another good place to learn about money. Displays on the first floor explain various aspects of printing; there are several English and Japanese videos that answer common questions about Japanese currency and stamps. The second floor houses the museum's currency exhibition and stamp collection. Look for secret marks that can only be seen under ultraviolet light and letters too small to read without a microscope, features that make forgery more difficult.

EATING OPTIONS

Restaurants   The Landmark Café and Restaurant on the fourth floor of the Mitsukoshi Department Store has a large, varied menu featuring several cuisines and a few children's lunches. Tokyu and Takashimaya Department Stores have restaurants and there are more restaurants in their vicinity. Be aware that from 11:45 A.M. to 1 P.M. the choice spots are crowded with lunching office workers. A coffee shop on the second floor of the Printing Bureau serves light meals.

Picnic Possibilities   The only nearby park, Tokiwabashi Park across the street from the Currency Museum, is a haven for the homeless and you might have trouble finding a free bench. Your next closest bet, Hibiya Park, is a fairly long trek.

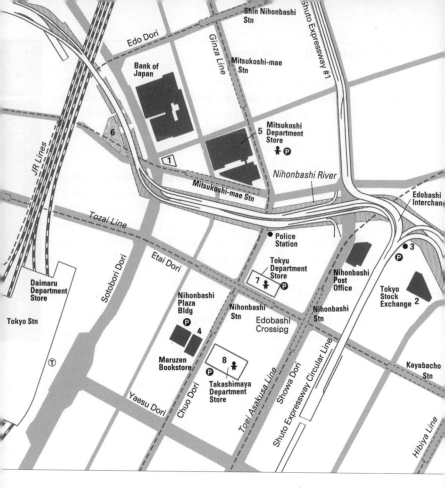

PLACES TO VISIT

1. Currency Museum
2. Tokyo Stock Exchange
3. Kabuto Shrine
4. Maruzen Bookstore
5. Mitsukoshi Department Store
6. Tokiwabashi Park

7. Tokyu Department Store (has restaurants)
8. Takashimaya Department Store (has restaurants)

Note: The Printing Bureau Museum is on the map for Tour 16.

FOR INFANTS AND TODDLERS

There are no diaper-changing or nursing facilities at the Currency Museum, TSE, or Printing Bureau Memorial Museum. If you want to make a full pit stop, try the baby room in the fourth-floor children's clothing section at the Mitsukoshi Department Store near the Currency Museum.

WHERE & WHEN

Currency Museum
貨幣博物館 (Kahei Hakubutsu-kan)
Bank of Japan's Annex Building
1–3–1 Nihonbashi-Hongokucho, Chuo-ku, Tokyo 103–8660
☎ (03) 3277–3037
東京都中央区日本橋本石町1-3-1　日本銀行分館　〒103-8660
OPEN: 9:30 A.M. to 4:30 P.M. (admission until 4) Mon to Fri, 2nd and 4th Sun
CLOSED: Sat, 1st and 3rd Sun, hols, Dec 29–31, Jan 1–4
FEES: none
DIRECTIONS: A 3-minute walk from exit A5 of Mitsukoshi-mae station on the Ginza line, a 1-minute walk from exit B1 of Mitsukoshi-mae station on the Hanzomon line, a 10-minute walk from the Nihonbashi exit or Yaesu central exit of JR Tokyo station. By car on Sotobori Dori near Tokiwabashi bridge. The museum is in the Bank of Japan Annex Building, next door to the bank offices.
PARKING: available only for tour buses
COMMENTS: 8 and up, ample English

Tokyo Stock Exchange
東京証券取引所
(Tokyo Shoken Torihikijo)
2–1 Nihonbashi, Kabuto-cho, Chuo-ku, Tokyo 103–8220
☎ (03) 3666–0141
東京都中央区日本橋兜町2-1　〒103-8220
OPEN: Exhibition Plaza 9 A.M. to 4 P.M.; trading hours 9 A.M. to 11 A.M. and 12:30 P.M. to 3 P.M.
CLOSED: Sat, Sun, hols
DIRECTIONS: a 5-minute walk from exit A2 of Nihonbashi station on the Ginza, Tozai, and Toei Asakusa lines. 5 minutes from exit 11 or 7 minutes from exit 7 of Kayabacho station on the Hibiya or Tozai lines. By car south of the Inner Circular line near Edobashi bridge.
PARKING: available only for tour buses
COMMENTS: 10 and up, ample English, reservations suggested for English tour

Kabuto Shrine
兜神社 (Kabuto Jinja)
2–8 Nihonbashi, Kabuto-cho, Chuo-ku, Tokyo 103–0026
東京都中央区日本橋兜町2-8　〒103-0026
OPEN: 24 hours
DIRECTIONS: see Tokyo Stock Exchange
PARKING: none
COMMENTS: all ages, no English, nursing room

Maruzen Bookstore
丸善
2–3–10 Nihonbashi, Chuo-ku, Tokyo 103–0027
☎ (03) 3272–7211
東京都中央区日本橋2-3-10　〒103-0027
OPEN: 10 A.M. to 7 P.M. Mon through Sat (until 6 on Sun and hols)
CLOSED: 1st and 3rd Sun of the month
DIRECTIONS: Connected to exit B3 of Nihonbashi station on the Ginza, Tozai, and Toei Asakusa lines. By car, on Chuo Dori directly across

from Takashimaya Department Store and between Yaesu Dori and Eitai Dori.

PARKING: Maruzen has no parking, but you may use the parking facility of the Nihonbashi Plaza Building next door or metered parking on the street

COMMENTS: all ages, English books available

Mitsukoshi Department Store (Main Store in Nihonbashi)
日本橋三越本店
1–4–1 Nihonbashi-muromachi, Chuo-ku, Tokyo 103–0022
☎ (03) 3241–3311
東京都中央区日本橋室町1-4-1　〒103-0022
OPEN: 10 A.M. to 7 P.M.
CLOSED: Mon
DIRECTIONS: follow the signs from Mitsukoshi-mae station on the Ginza and Hanzomon lines. A 12-minute walk from the Nihonbashi exit or Yaesu central exit of JR Tokyo station. By car, one street west of Chuo Dori south of Edo Dori crossing.
PARKING: free for the 1st 90 minutes with a purchase of ¥2,000 or more. Thereafter, ¥200

every 30 minutes. With no purchase, ¥250 for every 30 minutes.
COMMENTS: all ages, some English, nursing room

Printing Bureau Memorial Museum
大蔵省印刷局記念館 (Okura-sho Insatsu-kyoku Kinen-kan)
9–5 Ichigaya Honmuracho, Shinjuku-ku, Tokyo 162–0845
☎ (03) 3268–3271
東京都新宿区市ヶ谷本村町9-5　〒162-0845
OPEN: 9:30 A.M. to 4:30 P.M. (enter by 4 P.M.)
CLOSED: Mon
DIRECTIONS: a 15-minute walk from Ichigaya station on the JR Sobu line. A 10-minute walk from Ichigaya station on the Yurakucho line, exit 6. A 7-minute walk from Akebono-bashi station on the Toei Shinjuku line, exit A2. By car, take Gaien-Higashi Dori and turn east at Nakano-cho crossing. The museum is located on the right side of the street.
PARKING: free parking usually available in front of the museum
COMMENTS: 5 and up, some English

Yesterday's Toys

Kitahara Motion Figurines Display • Yokohama Doll Museum • Minato-no-Mieru Oka Park • Motomachi Shopping Street

Two toy museums and a tour through an old Western-style neighborhood offer insight into the history of Japan and her trading partners in the city where much of the world first came to Japan: the port of Yokohama. Moving figurines bring Mother Goose rhymes and well-known tales to life, and dolls from all over the world offer a chance to learn about different countries, including Japan.

Start your day with a display of antique mechanical figurines at the **Kitahara Motion Figurines Display**. The walrus chats with the carpenter, Humpty Dumpty tilts into his famous fall, royal flushes of hearts and diamonds play in a symphony, a mermaid accepts a diamond ring from her scuba-diving beau.

The collection is divided into different groupings, which are set in motion according to a schedule posted in both English and Japanese. It will take about 30 minutes to see all the pieces and watch the videos of the figurines in motion. The museum is located on the third floor of the Yokohama Marine Tower, which is famous for its bird's-eye view of the harbor, though you can see nearly the same thing from the hillside

All of the seventy or so pieces in the Kitahara collection share a diamond or jewelry theme. They were made by Baranger Studio of California between 1925 and 1969 for jewelry-shop window displays, then found their way into the hands of Teruhisa Kitahara. Kitahara, one of the world's foremost toy collectors, is a regular face on Japanese TV, and many of his toys are displayed at various locations around Japan.

park later in the tour. Buy a ticket to the top of the tower, which includes admission to the toy collection, or walk directly upstairs and buy a ticket for the toys only. When you are finished, the next spot on our tour, the **Yokohama Doll Museum**, is just two buildings away.

Dolls play an important role in Japanese culture. Families celebrate the Hina matsuri (Doll festival) on March 3 each year by displaying exquisitely attired figures representing the imperial court. At the Yokohama Doll Museum, collectors and casual visitors alike will marvel at beautiful Japanese dolls from every era. The displays also illustrate how the modern Doll Festival evolved. The large and varied collection of antique Western china dolls, bisque dolls, wax dolls, cloth dolls, and dolls in ethnic costume from around the world give visitors insight into the customs of many different cultures. Comparing the different types teaches quite a bit about the dollmaker's art and how it has changed over the years.

Small children will stand in awe watching revolving display cases where dolls in folk costumes are posed as if playing, dancing, or working. You can easily spend an hour or more examining the delicate features and intricate costumes of these dolls as you learn about their histories and how they are made. If possible, time either your arrival or departure from the Doll Museum for the hour or half hour so you can watch the Shoemaker and the Seven Elves. These mechanical dolls, installed outside on the second-story level of the wall near the main entrance, put on a delightful 5-minute show. A theater on the fourth floor has puppet and other shows several Sundays each month. Call in Japanese for information and show times.

Follow the brick France bridge behind the Doll Museum to its end, then walk up to the bluff. Unless you have a stroller, take the stairs and paths that lead through French Hill. In the 1860s and 1870s French and British soldiers responsible for protecting the foreign community camped on this wooded spot. It was later the site of the French legation, a beautiful building that collapsed in the Great Kanto Earthquake. At the top of the hill is **Minato-no-Mieru Oka** or Harbor View Park, which has a lovely formal garden and an excellent view of the Yokohama Bay bridge. The Kawasaki Museum of Modern Literature and the British Center, a community event center originally built in 1937 as a home for the British consul, add European charm to the park. The more recent museum, added in 1985, has a tearoom with a lovely view, as does the restaurant across the garden. You can climb French Hill in about 15 minutes; if you don't stop to rest, it should take about half an hour to visit the park and look briefly at the flowers and harbor.

Cross the street and saunter toward Yamate Hon Dori. The bluff area was among the first spots in Japan to be settled by foreigners, and it is now home to a number of attractive restaurants and museums. Most of the buildings were destroyed by either the Great Kanto Earthquake of 1923 or the bombs of World War II, but several remain and have been turned into museums. As you walk toward Motomachi, on your left you'll see the site of the Gaiety Theater, where Yokohama's expatriate society gathered for amateur plays and parties, now home to the Iwasaki Museum. On the corner, the gracefully rebuilt Christ Church Yokohama catches your eye—it provided solace and social life for late-Victorian Anglicans. Japanese tourists come from around the country to read the tombstones in the Foreign Cemetery that covers much of the hillside.

> The Foreign Cemetery got its start as a resting spot for a sailor from Commander Perry's second voyage in 1854. He lies beside foreign residents from all over the world who have lived and died in Japan. Japanese law and tradition have long dictated cremation, so this is one of the few places where Westerners can be buried in accordance with their customs.

You'll pass close to the graveyard whether you take the cobblestoned street that curves around it or walk down the many stairs on the path through beautiful tree-filled Motomachi Park, which also has ruins, play equipment, outdoor swimming pools, and picnic tables.

At the bottom of the hill is **Motomachi Shopping Street**, historically important in establishing Western fashion trends in Japan. The country's first Louis Vuitton boutique, opened in the 1920s, still stands on this beautiful stone-lined boulevard crowded with attractive shops. High-class jewelry stores and designer boutiques mix with shops selling casual clothes for young teens, an American furniture store, and a grocer that specializes in imported foods. Prices are often surprisingly reasonable, and tempting little cafés and restaurants are everywhere. If your children were inspired by the museums you visited earlier, you may want to stop at **Familiar**, which has high-quality toys and clothing for children, along with plenty of things to distract the kids while you shop. For jewelry, try **ShiMaMine**, which sells accessories starting at ¥100. Girls will like their inexpensive but stylish gold jewelry and cheap costume gems. The shopping area ends near Ishikawacho station.

Other Things to Do in the Area

Just around the corner from the Foreign Cemetery is the small **Toys Club Museum and Shop**, full of tin toys from the 1940s and 1950s. Alongside Betty Boop dolls are many cars, motorcycles, and robots. To the side is **Toy's Garage**, which sells adult clothes and a small collection of children's wear. And round back is the **Christmas Store**, where it's Christmas 365 days a year. All three shops feature toys collected by Teruhisa Kitahara. He also has museums in Sagamihara and Hokkaido, and a toy store on the third floor of the Landmark Plaza in Yokohama (see Tour 28).

Most of the area's other small museums are unlikely to interest children, but for historians we mention two of the better options. To learn more about the people buried in the graveyard, stop in at the tiny **Yamate Museum**, which has a few mementos from some of Yokohama's early foreign residents and describes their contributions to Japanese society. Quality levels fluctuate at the small but luxurious **Iwasaki Museum**, where historic memorabilia and old-fashioned furniture pay tribute to the Gaiety Theater. Glassware fills one hall, while another is rented out as a gallery to artists good and bad. The history of Western clothing is illustrated by thirty-two costumed mannequins just a meter tall. The lounge downstairs has self-service beverages for ¥300. At the photo studio you can dress up in gowns from past eras and have your picture taken for ¥1,000 to ¥4,000 (depending on the outfit), including the negative. Most of the dresses are a Japanese size nine (U.S. 6, French 36) and the selection varies depending on what is at the cleaner's.

For the best ocean view, cross the Bay bridge to Daikoku Pier and the **Sky Walk**. Boats pass right under your feet as you walk beneath a section of the graceful Bay bridge. You can also get an unobstructed look at the harbor skyline with Mount Fuji in the background (weather permitting), watch the Marine Tower flash signals to vessels passing by, and check out the action on Honmoku Pier. And if you are traveling by car your kids will get a kick out of F Cap, a boat turned floating parking lot, docked right outside the Sky Walk's Sky Tower.

EATING OPTIONS

Restaurants   The Planet on the first floor of the Star Hotel, a few doors down from the Marine Tower, serves three-course French lunches on the weekdays from about ¥900 to ¥2,000. On the weekends the lunch is a little fancier and the prices are higher. Colline Arrondie, located in Minatomieruoka Park, has an excellent view of the harbor and offers sandwiches for around ¥1,000. There are countless little restaurants in Motomachi. Chinatown, packed with Chinese eateries, is just 5 minutes to the left as you walk through Motomachi (see Tour 11).

Picnic Possibilities   If it isn't too crowded, you could enjoy your lunch along with the harbor view on one of the benches in Minatomieruoka Park. Yamashita

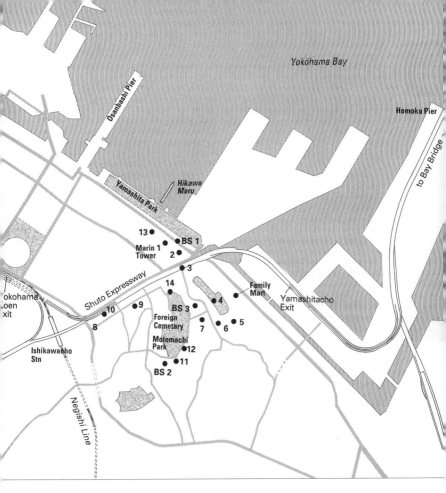

PLACES TO VISIT

1. Kitahara Motion Figurines Display
2. Yokohama Doll Museum
3. France Bridge
4. Minato-no-Mieru Oka Park
5. Kawasaki Museum of Modern Literature
6. British Center
7. Iwasaki Museum
8. Motomachi Shopping Street
9. Familiar

10. ShiMaMine
11. Toys Club Museum with Christmas Store and Toy's Garage
12. Yamate Museum
13. Star Hotel
14. Stroller-friendly Walk Way

BS 1. Yamashita Futo Iriguchi Bus Stop
BS 2. Motomachi Koen Bus Stop
BS 3. Minato-no-Mieru Oka Bus Stop

Park, across from the doll museum, is another option. Motomachi Park has plenty of benches, as well as picnic tables with an excellent view of the Marine Tower and Landmark Tower.

FOR INFANTS AND TODDLERS

The Marine Tower has a baby bed near the restaurants on the first floor. Familiar has everything you need for diapering, nursing, or bottle preparation.

Although French Hill is nice to walk through, there are many stairs requiring extra effort for parents pushing strollers, so you may want to follow the street along the edge of the park. The steep hills also pose a problem when you head back down. There are two ways to descend to Motomachi from the bluff area. Both have stairs, but one of them (indicated on the map) is much easier with a stroller.

WHERE & WHEN

Kitahara Motion Figurines Display
機械じかけのおもちゃ館 (Kikai Jikake no Omocha-kan)
Yokohama Marine Tower 3rd Floor
15 Yamashita-cho, Naka-ku, Yokohama-shi, Kanagawa-ken 231–0023
☎ (045) 641–1595
横浜市中区山下町15　マリンタワー3階
〒231–0023
OPEN: 10 A.M. to 7 P.M. (changes seasonally)
CLOSED: once a year for 7 days
FEES: adults ¥200, children ¥100, preschoolers ¥50; free with Tower entry ticket
DIRECTIONS: a 15-minute walk from JR Kannai or Ishikawacho stations (JR Keihin Tohoku and Negishi lines). By car, take the Shuto expressway, Yokohama Koen exit or Daini Keihin (also called Route 1), Sakuragicho exit.
PARKING: none
COMMENTS: all ages, adequate English

Yokohama Doll Museum
横浜人形の家 (Yokohama Ningyo no Ie)
18 Yamashita-cho, Naka-ku, Yokohama-shi, Kanagawa-ken

☎ (045) 671–9361
横浜市中区山下町18
OPEN: 10 A.M. to 5 P.M. (7 P.M. from the 3rd Sat of July through Aug)
CLOSED: Mon (Tues if Mon is a hol), Dec 29 to Jan 1
FEES: adults ¥300, junior high/elementary school students ¥150
DIRECTIONS: a 10-minute ride on bus #8 from Sakuragicho station (Tokyu Toyoko, JR Keihin Tohoku and Negishi lines); get off at Yamashita Futo Iriguchi. A 20-minute walk from Ishikawacho station (JR Keihin Tohoku and Negishi lines). From Yokohama station you can also take the ferry to Yamashita Park (see Tour 11). By car, take the Shuto expressway, Yokohama Koen exit or Daini Keihin, Sakuragicho exit.
PARKING: 24 hours, 20 spaces, hourly rate
COMMENTS: all ages, English

Minato-no-Mieru Oka Park (Harbor View Park
港見える丘公園 (Minato-no-Mieru Oka Koen)
114 Yamate-cho, Naka-ku, Yokohama, 231

☎ (045) 622–8244

神奈川県横浜市中区山手町114

OPEN: daily, 24 hours

FEES: none

DIRECTIONS: bus #11 from Sakuragicho station (Toyoko, JR Keihin Tohoku lines) or bus #20 from Yokohama station; get off at Minato-no-Mieru Oka; a 20-minute walk from Ishikawa-cho station (JR Keihin Tohoku line). By car, take the Shuto expressway, Yokohama Koen exit, or Daisan Keihin toward Sakuragicho from the end of the Daisan Keihin expressway.

PARKING: cheaper hourly rates than other area lots, but all 20 spaces are usually full.

Motomachi Shopping Street
元町商店街

DIRECTIONS: a 5-minute walk from Ishikawa-cho station (JR Keihin Tohoku and Negishi lines) or by car, take Daini Keihin to Yamashita-cho exit. Metered street parking available, but spaces go fast, especially on weekends.

• Familiar
ファミリア

2–89 Motomachi, Naka-ku, Yokohama-shi, Kanagawa-ken 231–0861

☎ (045) 662–3789

神奈川県横浜市中区元町2-89　〒231-0861

OPEN: 10:45 A.M. to 7 P.M.

CLOSED: 1st and 2nd Mon

COMMENTS: nursing room

• ShiMaMine
シマミネ

1–29 Motomachi, Naka-ku, Yokohama-shi, Kanagawa-ken 231–0861

☎ (045) 664–2780

神奈川県横浜市中区元町1-29　〒231-0861

OPEN: 10 A.M. to 8 P.M.

CLOSED: Jan 1

Toys Club Museum
ブリキの町おもちゃの博物館 (Buriki no Machi Omocha no Hakubutsu-kan)

239 Yamate-cho, Naka-ku, Yokohama-shi, Kanagawa-ken 231–0862

☎ (045) 621–8710

神奈川県横浜市中区山手町239　〒231-0862

OPEN: 9:30 A.M. to 7 P.M., (until 8 P.M. on weekends). Opens from noon during New Year's.

FEES: adults ¥200, junior high/elementary school students ¥100

DIRECTIONS: a 10-minute walk from Ishikawa-cho station or, from Sakuragicho station, take bus #11 bound for Hodogaya and get off at Motomachi Koen-mae stop.

PARKING: limited parking available

COMMENTS: all ages, no English

Sky Walk
スカイウォーク

1 Daikoku Futo Tsurumi-ku, Yokohama-shi, Kanagawa-ken 230–0054

神奈川県横浜市鶴見区大黒ふ頭1　〒230-0054

☎ (045) 506–0500

OPEN: April 1 to Sept 30, 9:30 A.M. to 8 P.M. (enter by 7:30); Oct 1 to March 31, 10 A.M. to 6 P.M. (enter by 5:30); Jan 1, 6 A.M. to noon

CLOSED: Tues

FEES: adults ¥600, junior high/elementary school students ¥300; children under 6 free

DIRECTIONS: from the Doll Museum take bus #109 from Yamashita-koen. You can also catch this bus from Sakuragicho station or the Blue line bus from Yokohama station. By car, take the Bayshore line expressway (Kosoku Wangansen) and exit at Daikoku Pier.

PARKING: Use the lot next to the Sky Walk. ¥500/one hour.

COMMENTS: all ages, English pamphlet

Yamate Museum

山手資料館 (Yamate Shiryo-kan)

Yamate Juban-kan

247 Yamate-cho, Naka-ku, Yokohama, Kanagawa-ken 231–0862

☎ (045) 622–1188

神奈川県横浜市中区山手町247　〒231-0862

OPEN: 11 A.M. to 4 P.M.

CLOSED: Dec 30 to Jan 2

FEES: adults ¥200, children ¥150, over 65 free; one child under age 12 free with a paying adult

DIRECTIONS: see Iwasaki Museum. Located around the corner, just across from the Foreign Cemetery.

PARKING: none

COMMENTS: 8 and up, adequate English

Iwasaki Museum

岩崎博物館 (Iwasaki Hakubutsu-kan)

254 Yamate-cho, Naka-ku, Yokohama-shi, Kanagawa-ken 231–0862

☎ (045) 623–2111

横浜市中区山手町254　〒231-0862

OPEN: 9:40 A.M. to 6 P.M. (enter by 5:30, photos until 5)

CLOSED: Mon (Tues if Mon is a hol); call for New Year's schedule

FEES: adults ¥300, elementary and middle school students ¥100

DIRECTIONS: bus #11 from Sakuragicho station (Toyoko, JR Keihin Tohoku lines) or bus #20 from Yokohama station; a 20-minute walk from Ishikawacho station (JR Keihin Tohoku line). By car, take the Shuto expressway, Yokohama Koen exit or toward Sakuragicho from the end of the Daisan Keihin expressway.

PARKING: limited parking available for hourly rate

COMMENTS: 8 and up, English pamphlet

11

A Slow Boat to Chinatown

Sea Bass Harbor Cruise • *Hikawa Maru*
Passenger Liner • Yamashita Park • Chinatown

Salty breezes, rusty ship hulls, sea gulls wheeling overhead … a harbor can be experienced most vividly from the water. Climb aboard a **Sea Bass shuttle** and set out on an excursion to the exotic side of Yokohama, one of the world's busiest ports.

Board the boat just outside Sogo Department Store, which is connected to Yokohama station by an underground passage lined with shops. Shuttles depart four times an hour; the trip itself takes about 15 minutes. Small, sleek, and modern, the boats ride close to the water and offer excellent views of the colossal Minato Mirai 21 complex and graceful Yokohama Bay bridge from both indoor and outdoor seats. These recently completed landmarks attract tourists from all over Japan; Minato Mirai boasts the country's tallest building. (See Tour 28 for more information on Minato Mirai.)

Drawing nearer to the historic center of Yokohama, visitors see the same elegant European-style buildings and green rolling hills that once welcomed passengers on the ***Hikawa Maru***, a retired liner permanently docked at the pier where the shuttle stops. Charlie Chaplin was among the nearly twenty-five thousand people who steamed across the Pacific aboard this ship, which traveled between Yokohama, Seattle, and Vancouver from 1930 to 1960. During the war years the *Hikawa Maru* was commandeered by the navy, serving as a hospital ship in Southeast Asia; it was one of the few boats to survive intact. In 1961 it became a floating museum as well as a popular spot for parties and a well-loved symbol of Yokohama.

Wandering the ship's decks and peering into cabins furnished as they were in the

Hikawa Maru's heyday, you get a strong feeling for the time when a slow steamer was the most common way to travel to the Orient. Stop to relax in one of the lounges, have a look in the engine room, visit a restaurant, or take a turn at the wheel. On the bridge, a lifelike robot dressed as the ship's captain spins sailor's yarns about past voyages, unfortunately in Japanese only. Beautiful Christmas decorations grace the ship during the holiday season.

A game room, rides for young ones, model ships, videos, and a 3-D picture collection are among the modern additions designed to entertain visitors. A play area for small children and an open-air café make the main deck an excellent place to sit on sunny days or after dark, when the ship is decorated with tiny lights that sparkle against the night sky. *Hikawa Maru* souvenirs are sold in a shop located in the bow's lower hold. If you're tempted to have your picture taken in a ball gown or captain's uniform in the nearby photo studio, be sure you are prepared for the price: ¥15,000.

When you're ready to disembark, stroll along the pier to **Yamashita Park**, Japan's oldest harbor park. With fountains, flowers, and smooth gray flagstones, Yamashita Park has a distinctly European atmosphere that owes much to Yokohama's early foreign residents. Stretching 1 kilometer along the harbor, the park offers a wonderful view of the water that attracts artists, sweethearts, musicians, and food vendors.

During the summer holidays in late July and early August, concerts

As you stroll the promenade, you'll see one of the most famous sights in Yamashita Park: a little statue of the girl in the old, sad song *Akai Kutsu* (Red Shoes), about a little girl in red shoes who is last seen with a foreigner. The song is vague as to what happened, but whether she was adopted, kidnapped, or something else, the singer remembers the little girl whenever she sees red shoes.

and other events are staged in and around the park, creating a carnival atmosphere. There are spectacular fireworks displays over the water on July 20 and August 1. December 31 is another popular time; all the ships docked in Yokohama blow their horns at midnight to celebrate the New Year. Be forewarned: almost every night of the year, Yamashita Park's romantic benches attract crowds of lovers.

It is only a short walk from Yamashita Park to the enormous red gate that marks the east entrance to **Chinatown**, where you'll find over five hundred restaurants and shops. With everything from tiny vegetable stands to opulent multistoried four-star restaurants, this thriving community is a reminder that the Chinese were among the first and most ambitious foreigners in Japan. Yokohama's Chinatown has also served as a base away from home for many historical figures, including Sun Yat-sen and Chiang Kai-shek.

Always crowded, the narrow streets of Chinatown seem a world away from suburban Tokyo. Shop windows are crammed with brightly colored satin dresses and cheap imported souvenirs, and everywhere you encounter red pillars and exotic smells. Food is the main attraction, but there are plenty of other things to do. Peer at Chinese herbs, buy thousand-year-old eggs and dragon fruit, visit a Chinese temple. Shop for everything from trinkets to traditional Chinese clothing and expensive gold jewelry, and learn a bit about Chinese culture.

While we have seldom had a bad meal in Chinatown, at some of the most famous restaurants we have found grumpy service and lines much too long for small, impatient, hungry stomachs. So when we come here with kids, our game plan is to eat on the perimeter, away from the well-known restaurants with lines out the door. There is something for every price range; see our recommendations in the restaurant listings for ideas. Even if you aren't hungry, stop into a bakery and check out the delicious Chinese sweets.

Take the road furthest to the left shortly after you pass through the East Gate. Entrepreneurs cashing in on Japan's new surging interest in Central and Southeast Asia have set up funky import shops along the street recently renamed Silk Road. Besides textile goods and housewares you will find attractive and inexpensive musical instruments and toys that make great presents, stocking stuffers, and party favors.

Walk to the end of the road for a closer look at the South Gate and then backtrack to Kanteibyo Dori. Kanteibyo Temple, the place of worship for most Chinese residents and starting point for many of the area's festivals, is further up the street on your right. The temple was originally built in 1887; the current structure was built after a fire in 1987 that damaged the building but not the statues inside. You may not enter, but you can buy a few sticks of incense to offer. From the temple, head east toward the Zenrinmon gate, a symbol of friendship between Chinese residents and the Japanese.

Especially exciting times to visit Chinatown are during the Chinese New Year festival in late January or early February, China's National Independence Day on October 1, and the Double Tenth Festival on October 10, when residents hold parades with dancing dragons and lions. Other festival dates include New Year's Day, May 2 and 3 for the Yokohama International Costume Parade, and the Kanteibyo Temple Festival, for which the date changes every year.

Chinatown's west gate is just a short walk from Ishikawacho station, where this tour ends. This is one of the few daytrips where all the attractions are open on Mondays and at New Year's. No matter when you visit, an outing to Yokohama is sure to be fun for toddlers, teenagers, or visiting relatives.

Other Things to Do in the Area

The **Silk Museum** on the second floor of the Silk Center is just the place for the clotheshorse in your family. It will also please budding entomologists who like to examine creepy-crawlies. The museum has a whole section of exhibits on silkworms, some of them alive and wiggling. A historical photographic fashion review starts with the days when bustles decorated gowns, ends with hot pants, and even includes Japanese flappers. Learn a bit about the Silk Road, check out a cocoon with a microscope, guess which mannequin is wearing real silk and which are dressed in fakes, and meander through a whole floor of Japanese costumes from prehistoric times to the Meiji period. Except for one display on natural dying materials every exhibit has a detailed English explanation.

When most international travelers hear the word "Customs" they groan at the memory of tax bills. But beyond tax collecting, customs authorities do a lot of good by discouraging the slaughter of endangered species and stemming the flow of contraband onto city streets. Though the **Customs Museum** is small, the exhibits inside inspire and impress school-age children. Plans are just now forming to revamp the museum and perhaps include explanations in several languages. For now, the white English-Japanese bilingual brochure titled "Yokohama Customs" will assist you in fielding the onslaught of questions your children will ask. Inquire at the little office in the back to receive it. The museum is a good place to spark discussions on trademarks and copyrights, imports and exports, and endangered species. Particularly striking exhibits include a stool made from an elephant's foot, a bag crafted so the face of a real alligator is part of its design, and a huge number of items made of ivory. Smuggling seems more real as you examine tables, statues, books, and other items hollowed out to hide contraband, and the drugs and guns found inside them.

Across the street from Yamashita Koen is the **Yokohama Marine Tower**, an observatory that is also the world's tallest lighthouse. In addition to excellent views of the harbor and, on exceptionally clear days, Mount Fuji, the tower has a collection of antique moving figurines (more fully described in Tour 10) and a collection of birds of the world. You can buy a ticket that allows you to enter both the tower and the *Hikawa Maru* if you are interested.

EATING OPTIONS

Restaurants From Sogo's nautical-theme dockside restaurant to the *Hikawa Maru*'s café and Chinatown's many eateries, the route is packed with reasonably priced food options. Western fare is also available in nearby Motomachi.

If you are visiting Chinatown with children, we offer a few suggestions. The owner of Minyan, Chinatown's only restaurant specializing in Hunan cuisine, dotes on children. Hunan dishes, prepared with vegetable oils instead of animal fats, taste less oily than most other Chinese cuisines, but the spicy dishes are very hot. If your kids are sensitive to spicy dishes you may want to order à la carte at this moderately priced restaurant. Yokaro Nanmonjo on Chinatown's Silk Road looks formal and caters elegant feasts for weddings and other occasions, but it also serves casual Beijing-style meals for drop-in guests. Look for the huge white building with the golden dragon between its staircase and escalator. This is the place to go for *shoronpu,* a soup served with dim sum, and there is usually a reasonably priced lunch special. Lai Shiang Song Shu-ka, in the large black building across from Kanteibyo Temple, serves Cantonese food and has an inexpensive all-you-can-eat lunch. The food isn't bad, you will like the view of the temple, and diners can park for free. Yokohama Daihanten's Hong Kong cooks serve delicious homemade noodles. Try the fried noodle dish called *roumin.*

Picnic Possibilities Yamashita Park is a great spot for outdoor eating; bring your own lunch, pick up something in Sogo Department Store's extensive deli, or visit a Motomachi bakery. Many shops in Chinatown have vendors outside selling steamed white buns stuffed with meat (*niku man*) and sweet bean paste (*an man*); these make a nice picnic option.

FOR INFANTS AND TODDLERS

Sogo Department Store, directly connected to Yokohama station, has a large children's department with a baby room on the fifth floor. There are no baby facilities in Chinatown or Yamashita Park, but check the options in our "Yesterday's Toys" tour in the same general area.

Stairs in the *Hikawa Maru* make a stroller more of a liability than an asset. Store yours at the reception area at the entrance to the boat. On the weekends, the crowded central streets of Chinatown can be dangerous for kids in strollers. Passersby may trip over the stroller or unknowingly knock your child's head with a purse or bag.

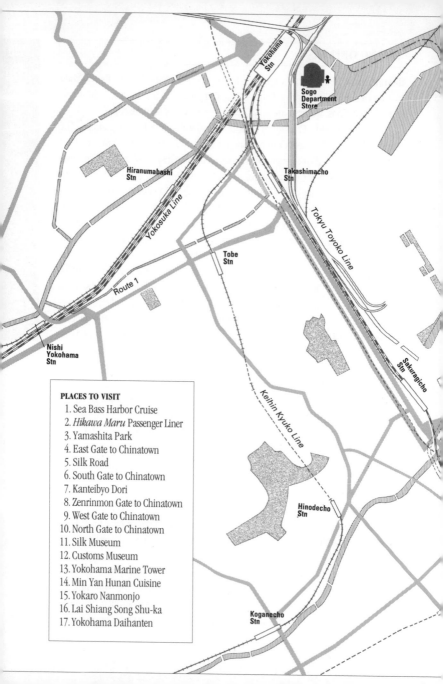

Yokohama Stn

Sogo Department Store

Hiranumabashi Stn

Takashimacho Stn

Yokosuka Line

Tokyu Toyoko Line

Tobe Stn

Route 1

Sakuragicho Stn

Nishi Yokohama Stn

Keihin Kyuko Line

Hinodecho Stn

PLACES TO VISIT
1. Sea Bass Harbor Cruise
2. *Hikawa Maru* Passenger Liner
3. Yamashita Park
4. East Gate to Chinatown
5. Silk Road
6. South Gate to Chinatown
7. Kanteibyo Dori
8. Zenrinmon Gate to Chinatown
9. West Gate to Chinatown
10. North Gate to Chinatown
11. Silk Museum
12. Customs Museum
13. Yokohama Marine Tower
14. Min Yan Hunan Cuisine
15. Yokaro Nanmonjo
16. Lai Shiang Song Shu-ka
17. Yokohama Daihanten

Koganecho Stn

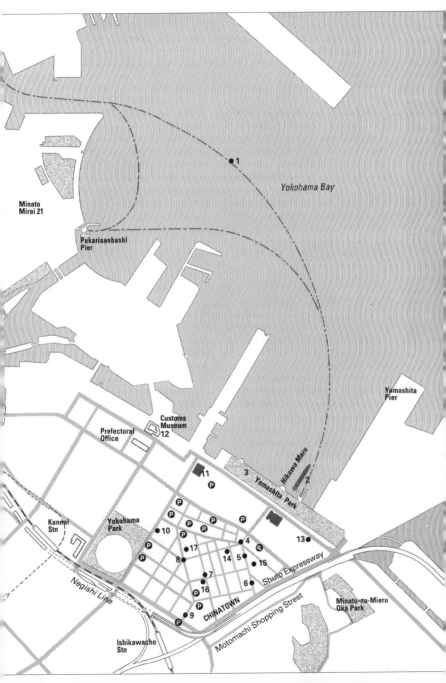

Minato
Mirai 21

Pukarisanbashi
Pier

Yokohama Bay

● 1

Yamashita
Pier

Customs
Museum
12

Prefectural
Office

● 11

3 *Yamashita Park*

Hikawa Maru
2

Kannai
Stn

Yokohama
Park

● 10

13 ●

● 17

● 4

Shuto Expressway

8 ●

14 5

15

Negishi
Line

● 7

● 16

6 ●

Shuto Expressway

● 9

CHINATOWN

Motomachi Shopping Street

Minato-no-Mieru
Oka Park

Ishikawacho
Stn

WHERE & WHEN

Sea Bass Harbor Cruise
ポートサービス シーバス

Yokohama Station, East Exit; Yamashita Park; Minato Mirai Pukari Sanbashi Pier
☎ (045) 453–7047

OPEN: 10 A.M. to 7:05 P.M. (Yokohama station to Yamashita Park; boats run every 15 minutes, alternate shuttles stop at Minato Mirai); 10 A.M. to 6:35 P.M. (Yamashita Koen to Yokohama station; boats run every 15 minutes, alternate shuttles stop at Minato Mirai)

CLOSED: no scheduled hols

DIRECTIONS: Yokohama station (JR Keihin Tohoku, JR Yokosuka, JR Tokaido, Tokyu Toyoko, Keihin Kyuko train lines, Yokohama subway line). Take the east exit and follow signs to Sogo Department Store; go to the 2nd floor and through the annex to the east (harbor) exit. The pier is across the covered bridge. By car, take expressway Yokohane, exit at Kinko interchange and go back to Sogo Department Store.

PARKING: you can use Sogo Department Store's lot; fees will depend on how long you stay and whether you make purchases above a certain amount.

Hikawa Maru Passenger Liner
氷川丸

Yamashita Koen, Yamashita-cho, Naka-ku, Yokohama-shi, Kanagawa-ken 231–0023
☎ (045) 641–4361
神奈川県横浜市中区山下町山下公園　〒231-0023

OPEN: 9:30 A.M. to 9 P.M.

FEES: adults ¥800, children ¥400, 3–5 years ¥300, under 3 years free; discount ticket including the Yokohama Marine Tower available

DIRECTIONS: a 15-minute walk from Ishikawa-cho station (JR Keihin Tohoku and Negishi lines); bus #8 or 26 from Sakuragicho station (Tokyu Toyoko, JR Keihin Tohoku and Negishi lines and Yokohama subway line); Sea Bass shuttle boat from Yokohama station. By car, take the Shuto expressway exit at the Yamashita ramp exit and it's a 5-minute drive.

PARKING: available in Yamashita Park

COMMENTS: all ages, no English

Yamashita Park
山下公園 (Yamashita Koen)

Yamashita Koen, Yamashita-cho, Naka-ku, Yokohama-shi, Kanagawa-ken 231–0023
☎ (045) 681–1860
神奈川県横浜市中区山下町山下公園
〒231-0023

OPEN: 24 hours

FEES: none

DIRECTIONS: see *Hikawa Maru* Passenger Liner

PARKING: parking lots on either side of park have space for 500 cars at an hourly rate

Chinatown
中華街 (Chukagai)

DIRECTIONS: a 15-minute walk from Ishikawa-cho station (JR Keihin Tohoku and Negishi line); a 10-minute walk from Kannai station (JR Keihin Tohoku and Negishi lines, and Yokohama subway line). By car, see directions for *Hikawa Maru*. Chinatown is just south of Yamashita Park.

Minyan Hunan Cuisine
中国湖南料理 明揚

192 Yamashita-cho, Naka-ku, Yokohama-shi, Kanagawa-ken 231–0023
☎ (045) 681–0231
神奈川県横浜市中区山下町192　〒231-0023

OPEN: 11 A.M. to 10:30 P.M.

DIRECTIONS: see Chinatown map

Yokaro Nanmonjo
陽華楼南門城

102 Yamashita-cho, Naka-ku, Yokohama, Kanagawa-ken 231–0023

☎ (045) 681–3466

神奈川県横浜市中区山下町102　〒231-0023

OPEN: 11 A.M. to 9 P.M.

DIRECTIONS: on Silk Road across from Tenchomon gate

Lai Shiang Song Shu-ka
荔香尊酒家 (Rai San Son Shuka)

166 Yamashita-cho, Naka-ku, Yokohama-shi, Kanagawa-ken 231–0023

☎ (045) 663–0800

神奈川県横浜市中区山下町166　〒231-0023

OPEN: 11:30 A.M. to 10 P.M.

DIRECTIONS: see Chinatown map. Across from Kanteibyo Temple.

PARKING: free for 30 cars

Yokohama Daihanten
横浜大飯店

218 Yamashita-cho, Naka-ku, Yokohama-shi, Kanagawa-ken 231–0023

☎ (045) 641–8283

神奈川県横浜市中区山下町218　〒231-0023

OPEN: 11 A.M. to 9 P.M.

DIRECTIONS: see Chinatown map

Silk Museum
シルク博物館

Silk Center, 2F

1 Yamashita-cho, Naka-ku, Yokohama, Kanagawa-ken 231–0023

☎ (045) 641–0841 (Silk Center)

神奈川県横浜市中区山下町1　シルクセンター2階　〒231-0023

OPEN: 9 A.M. to 4:30 P.M. (admission until 4)

CLOSED: Mon (if Mon is a hol, the next working day), Dec 28 to Jan 4.

FEES: adults ¥300, college/high school students ¥200, junior high/elementary school students ¥100

DIRECTIONS: short walk from Yamashita Park and Chinatown. A 15-minute walk from Sakuragicho or Kannai stations on the Negishi line. Or you can reach it by bus from Yokohama or Sakuragicho stations. By car, it is near the Yokohama Koen ramp on the Shuto expressway. Drive toward the bay and the Silk Center will be on your right.

PARKING: ample, hourly rates

COMMENTS: 5 and up, adequate English

Customs Museum
税関博物館 (Zeikan Hakubutsu-kan))

Customs Building, 1F

1–1 Kaigan Dori, Naka-ku, Yokohama-shi, Kanagawa-ken 231–0002

☎ (045) 212–6053

神奈川県横浜市中区海岸通り1-1　税関本館1階　〒231-0002

OPEN: Mon through Fri 10 A.M. to 4 P.M.

CLOSED: national hols and weekends

FEES: none

DIRECTIONS: a 10-minute walk from Kannai station, about 350 meters east of Yamashita Park. From the Shuto expressway take the MM21 exit; it's about a 5-minute drive from there.

PARKING: free but space is limited and the lot is almost always full

COMMENTS: older children, no English

Yokohama Marine Tower
横浜マリンタワー

15 Yamashita-cho, Naka-ku, Yokohama-shi, Kanagawa-ken 231–0023

☎ (045) 641–3902

神奈川県横浜市中区山下町15　〒231-0023

OPEN: 10 A.M. to 7 P.M.; hours extended to 9 P.M. during summer vacation, closes at 6 P.M. Dec–Feb

FEES: adults ¥700, children ¥350 (discount tickets combining the *Hikawa Maru* sold)

DIRECTIONS: see *Hikawa Maru* Passenger Liner

COMMENTS: all ages, no English

Sogo Department Store
そごうデパート

2–18 Takashima, Nishi-ku, Yokohama-shi,
Kanagawa-ken 220–0011

☎ (045) 465–2111

神奈川県横浜市西区高島2-18　〒220-0011

OPEN: 10 A.M. to 7:30 P.M.

CLOSED: Tues

DIRECTIONS: see Sea Bass Harbor Cruise

PARKING: parking available for an hourly fee but there are often long lines on the weekends

COMMENTS: nursing room

Uptown Tours

One of the great advantages of big city life is the tremendous variety of things to do. For those days when you feel like going uptown, we've put together four tours in different Tokyo neighborhoods, each with a distinctly different focus and flavor.

A green suburban center is where you'll find one of the best play spots around for babies and toddlers: **0123 Kichijoji**. Great play equipment and a shady outdoor pool will keep children under four entertained for hours. Nearby Inokashira Park has a pond with carp and boats, orchards of flowering trees, a zoo, an aquarium, and a small amusement park.

Trendy **Shibuya** can be surprisingly inexpensive when it's kids' fun you're looking for. Watch television shows in the making at NHK Studio Park, where visitors can take a turn playing news anchor and watch high-definition television. At the TEPCO Energy Museum, kids can play with computers and learn about how nuclear power plants work. Tokyo Metropolitan Children's Hall has plenty of educational fun, no matter how old your child is or what the weather's like—and it's free. You'll want to come back again and again.

Take your little princess to **Meguro** to visit an art deco palace-cum-art-museum with beautiful lawns and gardens. Admire a ball gown worn by the Meiji empress and follow the history of fashion at the Sugino Gakuin Museum of Clothing, then relax over afternoon tea at a very opulent and modern Japanese-style hotel.

Tokyo's fashion center, sophisticated **Aoyama**, is a great place for a family outing, especially on Sundays. We offer suggestions for brunch, then take you to the lovely Japanese garden at the Nezu Institute of Fine Arts. You can also take your young ones to the Children's Castle, one of the best-known and best-loved play spots in the city.

Little Princess Tour, Meguro

Tokyo Metropolitan Teien Art Museum • Sugino Gakuen Museum of Clothing • Meguro Gajoen Hotel

Visit fashionable Meguro when you want an elegant outing fit for a modern princess. Feel like royalty as you stroll through the garden and halls of a former palace, examine silk and lace gowns at a museum sponsored by a fashion school, then relax and enjoy afternoon tea surrounded by the opulence of a very Japanese hotel famous for its wedding and banquet facilities.

The Tokyo Metropolitan Teien Art Museum is a work of art itself. Marble stairs and red carpets, a dining room with an adjoining terrace, and beautiful garden views create an atmosphere of art deco luxury. The exquisite glass doors near the entrance and the chandeliers in the grand guest room and great dining hall were created by René Lalique, the greatest artist of the art deco movement working in the medium of glass. You won't find any art deco furniture in the palace, but it has been turned into a beautiful showcase for paintings and sculptures and attracts some extremely good shows. You can call for information or watch for interesting exhibitions in the *Tokyo Journal*, a local English newspaper, or visit Tokyo Q on the Internet (see Appendices).

Prince and Princess Asaka (the eighth son of Prince Kuni and the eighth daughter of Emperor Meiji) traveled to Paris in 1925, fell in love with the art deco style popular there at the time, and incorporated it into their home and gardens when they returned to Japan. French designer Henri Rapin was hired to assist with the interior of the couple's residence; when completed in 1933 the home combined unusual imported features with outstanding Japanese workmanship.

The grounds surrounding the former palace are also an aesthetic pleasure. Spacious lawns, tall trees, and understated flower beds make the Western-style gardens quite lovely, especially in the spring. White wrought-iron tables and chairs on the east lawn provide the perfect setting for an elegant picnic. Pick a day in early April to stretch out under a flowering cherry tree and watch the soft pink petals float gently on the wind. One section of the garden is Japanese-style; here, ducks swim and splash in a small pond surrounded by sculpted shrubs. Strolling through the gardens and looking through the parlors and private rooms of the palace should take you about an hour, two if you choose a more leisurely pace. When you're ready to move on, follow the map back to the station, beyond Sakura Bank, and down Dressmaker Dori to the **Sugino Gakuen Museum of Clothing**.

A little garden with palm trees lies outside the pillars of the weathered gray building housing the museum, part of Sugino Gakuen. The founder of this noted fashion design school, Yoshiko Sugino, made her mark on Japan's fashion industry by introducing clothing based on Western styles that suited the lives of Japanese women in the pre- and postwar years. When she died in 1978, she left the school as her legacy.

Entering the old-fashioned museum, you have the feeling of wandering into a musty attic filled with frills and fashions from bygone eras. Forty life-size mannequins model a variety of styles that together tell the history of Western clothing. Upstairs on the fourth floor you'll find many layers of kimono in the style of the Heian court, the era of Prince Genji, along with firefighters' *happi* coats, traditional costumes of Japan's indigenous people, the Ainu, and a variety of other ancient Japanese fashions. The embroidered violet gown with wisteria appliqué, now faded to gray, belonged to the Meiji empress. The motif was chosen because wisteria was part of her father's family crest.

On the third floor, the long, flowing skirts of medieval European noblewomen and bright-colored, leg-revealing men's breeches illustrate the way fashion trends have changed—and stayed the same. This hall is devoted to Western clothing from the mid-thirteenth century to the mid-1900s, and also includes several displays of the clothing popular among common folk. Audio-visual displays on this floor are fun to watch, although they're only in Japanese. If you are looking for a more detailed learning experience and understand the language, you may also want to inquire at the first-floor reception desk about the slide show on the second floor. Throughout the museum the English is sketchy, but costume lovers will be reasonably satisfied just to look at the ruffles and ribbons, prints, patterns, and pleats.

Some of the best displays, located on the first floor, illustrate how different the long skirts, leg-o'-mutton sleeves, and bustles of the 1900s are from the narrow, sleeveless, calf-length dresses of the 1920s.

For more modern interpretations of elegance, we refer you to the patrons of the nearby **Meguro Gajoen Hotel**. As you walk there you will descend a steep slope called Gyonin-zaka; in former times this was the main link between Edo and Meguro. The hotel, opened in 1931 as a three-story wooden building and rebuilt in 1991, is most commonly used as a wedding venue. The building itself is large and easy to spot. Inside, a distinctly Japanese atmosphere and an art museum set it apart from Tokyo's other expensive hotels. Parts of the original structure were used to decorate the new building; one good example is the elegant wood paneling on the ceiling of the museum shop. The walls near the museum souvenir shop are decorated with colorful murals of women in kimono. A small stream runs through the first floor, a spacious area filled with restaurants and greenery where you can enjoy an excellent view of the stream and a beautifully landscaped garden. Treat yourself to tea and cake for a price not too far above the average for Tokyo in an environment you won't soon forget. Afterward, take your little princess out into the garden.

Before going home, be sure to visit the most frequently televised part of the hotel: the ladies' room. With lacquer appointments, little rock gardens, and even a bridge, this has got to be one of the most decorative spots in the world to powder your nose.

Other Things to Do in the Area

While in the hotel, you may also want to visit the **Meguro Gajoen Museum of Art**, depending on what is showing. The permanent exhibit (not always on display) is worth seeing and includes mainly soft-colored paintings of women in kimono from the early twentieth century. The museum is on the third floor; to get there, take the elevator with the mother-of-pearl inlaid doors near the main entrance.

Next to the Teien museum is a 200,000-square-meter nature preserve with ponds, trees, and an insect house where you can see all kinds of bugs from 10–11 A.M. every Sunday from April to November. Wandering the paths through the thick woods of the **Institute for Nature Study of the National Science Museum**, you get a feel for what the ecosystem of the Musashino Plain must have been like before they filled it with concrete. Ducks and birds abound and there are tables and benches for picnickers. Kids can attend classes in Japanese on insects, plant identification, and more on the second Saturday of the month in the Visitors Hall.

The **Meguro Citizens' Center** complex has a children's hall that rivals the one in Shibuya. The Shibuya facility is larger, but if you include Meguro's gymnasium, indoor and outdoor swimming pools, and the Meguro Museum of Art, this one has more things to do. It's rarely crowded, and there is parking. Unfortunately, all information is written in Japanese only, and the place closes during the lunch hour. But you'll have no problem feeding the kids—in the center of the complex there is an inexpensive restaurant as well as a mini-park where you can eat a homemade lunch. The children's hall and art museum hold special events for kids during the Japanese school holidays. The children's hall also has a very good weekday program for latchkey children. Other amenities include a gymnasium that you can book for sporting events, the Dendo Fureai Kan citizens' hall, where you can reserve rooms for meetings and parties, and tennis courts you can sign up for by entering a lottery held two months in advance.

We've spent entire days in the children's hall, starting with active play and then winding down in the music room or the wood shop. Older kids like the billiards and ping-pong tables. Those who live nearby make this a regular haunt.

EATING OPTIONS

Restaurants   Just inside the Teien Art Museum is a café with indoor and outdoor seating that serves sandwiches, as well as cake and tea for about ¥300 each. Kaifu, a coffee shop in the Gajoen Hotel, has cake and tea sets for about ¥1,300, as well as a variety of sandwiches. The Meguro station building has half a dozen restaurants on the fifth floor, including Fujiya, the family restaurant small children adore because of its mascots Peko and Poko-chan. Fujiya also has a children's menu. At the Meguro Citizen's Center, Kumin Restaurant serves simple and inexpensive meals. Buy tickets for the items you want to order from the vending machine just inside the door.

Picnic Possibilities   Pack a box of goodies from home or stop at Kentucky Fried Chicken or McDonald's on your way to the art museum. Lovely tables and chairs in a wide grassy area make the garden an excellent place for a picnic. You can also eat inside in the costume museum; ask permission to use the classroom just off the second-floor landing to your right. At the Citizen's Center, use one of the benches in the Children's Play Park.

FOR INFANTS AND TODDLERS

At the costume museum, you may change diapers in the classroom just off the second-floor landing on the right side if you ask permission. Strollers cannot be used in either museum, but you'll probably want one for the walk between them. You'll find a diaper-changing table in the ladies' room between the third and fourth floors of Sun

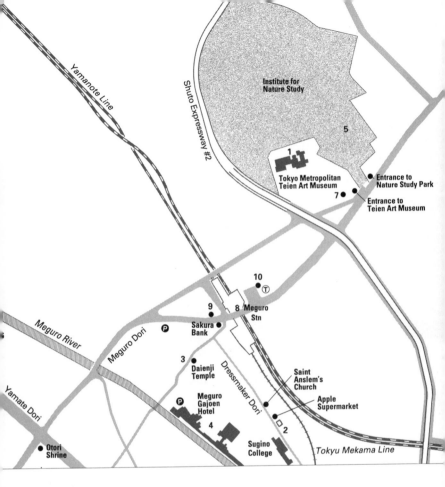

PLACES TO VISIT

1. Tokyo Metropolitan Teien Art Museum
2. Sugino Gakuen Museum of Clothing
3. Gyonin-zaka Slope
4. Meguro Gajoen Hotel and Museum of Art
5. The Institute for Nature Study, National Science Museum
6. Meguro Citizens' Center
7. Café Teien
8. Meguro Station, Sun Meguro Building (restaurants)
9. Kentucky Fried Chicken
10. McDonald's

Meguro, the station building, on the side opposite the elevators. You can also use one of the vanities in the ladies' room at the Gajoen Hotel. Each vanity is enclosed in a booth so you can nurse in relative privacy. There is a changing table on the basement floor of the Meguro Citizens' Center children's hall in the room just to the right of the staircase. While there is no private enclosure, many mothers nurse in the same room.

WHERE & WHEN

Tokyo Metropolitan Teien Art Museum

東京庭園美術館 (Tokyo Teien Bijutsu-kan)
5–21–9 Shiroganedai, Minato-ku, Tokyo 108–0071

☎ (03) 3443–0201

東京都港区白金台5-21-9　〒108-0071

OPEN: 10 A.M. to 6 P.M. (admittance until 5:30)
CLOSED: 2nd and 4th Wed of the month (Thur if Wed is hol), also during the New Year's hols and prior to new exhibitions
FEES: garden only—adults ¥100, school children ¥50; museum—varies according to the exhibit
DIRECTIONS: a 7-minute walk from the east exit of Meguro station (JR Yamanote line and Tokyu Mekama line). By car, it is at the intersection of Shuto expressway #2 and Meguro Dori.
PARKING: none
COMMENTS: all ages, English pamphlet

Sugino Gakuen Museum of Clothing

杉野学園衣裳博物館 (Sugino Gakuin Isho Hakubutsu-kan)
4–6–19 Kami-Osaki, Shinagawa-ku, Tokyo 141–8652

☎ (03) 3491–8151, ex 220

東京都品川区上大崎4-6-19　〒141-8652

OPEN: 10 A.M. to 4 P.M.
CLOSED: Sun, national hols, early Aug to early Sept, Dec 28 to Jan 9
FEES: adults ¥200, high school students ¥160, children ¥100

DIRECTIONS: a 5-minute walk from the west exit of Meguro station. By car, south of Meguro Dori on the east side of Dressmaker Dori.
PARKING: none
COMMENTS: 5 and up, no English

Meguro Gajoen Hotel and Museum of Art

目黒雅叙園美術館
1–8–1 Shimomeguro, Meguro-ku, Tokyo 153–0064

☎ (03) 3491–4111

東京都目黒区下目黒1-8-1　〒153-0064

OPEN: museum is open from 10:30 A.M. to 6 P.M. (admittance until 5:30)
CLOSED: museum is closed on Mon (Tues if Mon is a hol)
FEES: museum—adults ¥500, children ¥200
DIRECTIONS: a 5-minute walk from the west exit of Meguro station. By car, exit expressway #2 at the Meguro ramp and go west on Meguro Dori to Gyonin-zaka. The hotel is on the south side of Gyonin-zaka.
PARKING: free for the 1st 2 hours with a receipt from the coffee shop; overtime charges are calculated by the hour
COMMENTS: 5 and up, no English

Institute for Nature Study, National Science Museum

自然教育園 (Shizen Kyoiku-en)
5–21–5 Shiroganedai, Minato-ku, Tokyo 108–0072

☎ (03) 3441–7176

東京都港区白金台5-21-5　〒108-0072

OPEN: 9 A.M. to 4:30 P.M. (admittance until 4) Sept 1 to April 30; 9 A.M. to 5 P.M. (admittance until 4) May 1 to Aug 31

CLOSED: Mon (Tues if Mon is a hol), the day following a hol

FEES: adults ¥210, children ¥60

DIRECTIONS: see directions for Teien Art Museum. The entrance to the nature park is on Meguro Dori a few meters past the entrance to the art museum.

PARKING: none

COMMENTS: all ages, English pamphlet for sale

Meguro Citizens' Center

目黒区民センター (Meguro Kumin Center) 2–4–36 Meguro, Meguro-ku, Tokyo 153–0063

☎ (03) 3711–1121

東京都目黒区目黒2-4-36　〒153-0063

OPEN: *children's hall*, 9 A.M. to noon and 1 P.M. to 5 P.M.; *outdoor kiddie pool*, 10 A.M.–noon, 12:30–2:30 P.M., 3–5 P.M.; *outdoor 50 m pool*, 10 A.M.–noon, 1–3 P.M., 3:30–5:30 P.M., 6–8 P.M.; *indoor pool*, from July to Sept 10, 10:30 A.M.–12:30 P.M., 1:30–3:30 P.M., 4–6 P.M., 6:30–8:30 P.M.; from Sept 11 to end of June, 10 A.M.–noon, 1–3 P.M., 3:30–5:30 P.M., 6–8 P.M.; *museum*, 10 A.M. to 6 P.M.

CLOSED: Mon

FEES: children's hall is free. Pools, ¥200/2 hours. Museum often free but some exhibitions have entrance fees.

DIRECTIONS: a 10-minute walk from Meguro station (JR Yamanote line, Mekama line). By car, northeast of the intersection of Yamanote Dori and Meguro Dori.

PARKING: free for 60 cars from 9 A.M. to 8 P.M. Lot sometimes fills on summer weekends.

COMMENTS: all ages, no English

13

Shibuya on Pocket Change

NHK Studio Park • TEPCO Electric Energy Museum • Tokyo Metropolitan Children's Hall

Where can you watch the action of a live TV studio, build your own wooden birdhouse, and learn about energy while you play computer games? Rain or shine, Shibuya offers a hodgepodge of affordable fun with an educational twist. Two of the spots we highlight have no entrance charge and so much to do you'll want to come several times.

As you walk into **NHK Studio Park** you'll see your face on a 150-inch screen. Japan's public broadcasting system has always enjoyed great popularity, and exhibits take you through the country's television past with displays on a long-running children's show, a samurai drama set, a pictorial history of Japan's TV milestones, famous personalities, and TV coverage of disasters and historical events.

Japan's first satellite broadcast was to be a speech from then U.S. President John F. Kennedy. But that day in November 1963, when millions of Japanese excitedly turned on their sets, instead of the expected speech they got news of Kennedy's assassination.

Studio Park has plenty of fun for kids. Japanese-speaking youngsters can get a feel for what it is like to be a news anchorman in a real studio complete with sound room, cameras, and audience. On Sundays, preschoolers get a big kick out of looking down on the studio taping of *Okaasan to Issho* ("With Mothers"), a long-running educational program, aired on NHK 1 and 3. This is a much easier way to get a close-up view of the show's popular characters than trying to become a member of its studio audience. For that, you must apply by *ofuku* (return) postcard in Japanese. Participants are selected by monthly lotteries. Only three-year-olds are eligible and you can only send in one postcard per month.

Watch 3D Hi-Vision TV in a special theater and peek in on several live shows. Take a look at the future of multimedia: answer a videophone, use video on demand to call up a documentary on sea life, or browse through an audio catalog. Ask to see the high-definition television electronic newspaper; they can film a video image of you and print it in color with the rest of the news. Downstairs there is a space for special events and a shop selling character and educational videos and toys. For a reasonable price you can have your picture taken with a background like the *Okaa-san to Issho* characters or wild animals.

Aside from a Sesame Street display and some character merchandise, you will find no English at NHK Studio Park, and the nostalgia of several displays is lost on anyone new to the country. But for the small entrance fee there are plenty of novel experiences to register in young minds. Count on spending 30 minutes—longer if the people in your party speak Japanese well. Then follow the map for a look into electric power.

TEPCO's Electric Energy Museum has seven floors of exhibits in an imposing silver building with a colorful moving window display and domed roof. Here your kids can learn about pulse, frequency, the difference between alternating and direct currents, and much more. Walk through an underground conduit, manipulate a robot's arm to put pieces in a puzzle, and tally up watts of energy as you do a simulated tour of Shibuya on a stationary bike. A revolving theater with several stages shows how energy is created and used. Thermal, hydroelectric, and nuclear energy are all explained with colorful panoramas, games, and exhibits. There is even a model nuclear reactor (one-third actual size), and, since the museum is a showcase for the energy company, lots of explanations on the necessity of nuclear energy and the careful handling of nuclear waste. A small picture book library for younger kids holds slender volumes from all over the world. Non-Japanese speakers will appreciate the museum's thorough English brochure and English fliers on every floor.

TEPCO is a generous sponsor: entrance is free and they offer all kinds of cheap or free services. Check out the Monday Movie Theater, where you can see a different movie each week—most in English—for ¥100. Short courses on various cuisines are taught in a state-of-the-art kitchen, including some especially for kids or dads. They often have a class in English, but it is usually for students who want to learn the language more than new recipes. There are also science and handicraft classes in Japanese for school-aged kids and a science laboratory that teaches about topics from static electricity to superconductors. This place will even counsel you on the best lighting systems for your home. Check their monthly schedule to see what interests you. Inquisitive children can spend hours here and still not want to leave.

With seven floors for families to explore, the **Tokyo Metropolitan Children's Hall** is a good inducement to move on. Wander from the basement to the roof, encountering places to climb and play, quiet spots for story reading, as well as well-structured areas for scientific discovery and artistic expression. Built in 1964, the children's hall is the city's largest public facility for kids. Its primary function is to provide access to culture and recreation for children in a crowded metropolis where play space

Ask around; there's sure to be a children's hall in your neighborhood that can be used for play-group meetings, after-school activities, or just goofing off on a rainy afternoon. In fact, the authors of this book met at a play circle one of us had organized at a local children's hall. Each hall has different toys and facilities, but the best and biggest is the one in Shibuya.

diminishes in size and quality each year. It also provides support services and assistance to the nearly six hundred regional children's halls located throughout the city.

The second floor has a playroom with a jungle gym for active kids and an open play space for crawlers and toddlers. The third floor features a science craft area, displays on time and space, a room full of wireless radios, and a cluster of personal computers ready for you to log on. There is also a theater here showing cartoons and educational films and an old-style farmhouse to teach youngsters about Japan's cultural past. The fourth floor has a Music Amusement Room where you can tickle the ivories and try your hand at a variety of other instruments. There is also a fully equipped sound studio available by appointment for band practice. The roof opens for roller skating, rollerblading, and unicycling on fair-weather weekends and national holidays. The staff has a knack for getting beginners off on the right foot. For those who don't understand Japanese, body language goes a long way. Bring socks for rollerblading and shoes, not sandals, for roller-skating.

The Tokyo Metropolitan Children's Hall does a particularly good job with art projects like painting, clay modeling, and papercrafts. They hire graduates of local art colleges to teach crafts to children, performing a great support service to both kids and fledgling artists. There are crafts and fine arts centers on the fourth and fifth floors. You can try your hand at carpentry in the basement woodworking room—do one of the projects suggested by the hall or put together one of your own creations. Unfortunately, crafts and building instructions are in Japanese only. And be fore-

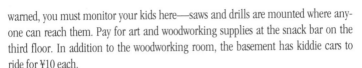
warned, you must monitor your kids here—saws and drills are mounted where any-one can reach them. Pay for art and woodworking supplies at the snack bar on the third floor. In addition to the woodworking room, the basement has kiddie cars to ride for ¥10 each.

There are performances, classes, and events scheduled weekly, monthly, and annually. Pick up a copy of the monthly event guides and facilities guide—both available in English—at the reception desk. You can even have your child's birthday party here if you book at least six months in advance.

Since it is publicly funded and constantly used by kids, the hall is not always in the best state of repair. Still, there is so much to do here and, except for the paltry fees charged for craft supplies and rides, it's free, so most patrons are repeat users. In fact, a survey of foreign kids who visit the Children's Hall posed the question: Which would you choose, Tokyo Metropolitan Children's Hall or Disneyland, if you had to go there every day? The overwhelming majority chose the Children's Hall because it requires more creativity and allows for more active discovery. Once your family experiences this wonderful play place, you'll find yourselves returning again and again.

Other Things to Do in the Area

Shibuya Top Circuit, outdoors on the roof of Tokyu Department Store's Shibuya station branch, has a 150-meter circuit for radio-controlled cars and two smaller circuits with ramps for the smaller battery-powered plastic models. Bring your own cars. Charges for the radio-controlled circuit go beyond our concept of "pocket change" even for Top Circuit club members, who get discounts, but you can run plas-tic models on the small tracks and watch the action on the large circuit for free. Tamiya-brand parts, cars, and accessories are sold on the premises, and some visitors even buy a small model, assemble it on one of the outdoor tables, and send it zipping around the tracks that same day. A plastic model car, motor, and battery cost around ¥1,500. (The radio-controlled cars cost at least ten times that much.) Friendly staff help with repairs and advice. Radio-controlled car races are held about once a month on the big circuit; call in Japanese for schedules and entry fees. This place isn't grand in terms of size or decor, but we know kids who would spend all day here—skipping meals—if their parents would let them.

Man's first clothes were fashioned from byproducts of his meals: cleaned and stretched animals skins and vegetable fiber too tough for human teeth to chew. Chiyo Tanaka, founder of a fashion college in Shibuya, was fascinated with why and how people clothed themselves. Starting in 1928, she traveled the globe, amassing a sizable collection of folk costumes; she then built an elegant little museum to display them. Exhibits rotate at the **Museum of World Folk Costumes**, but no doubt there will be rich tapestries, crude but intricate beading, the muted hues of natural dyes, time-consuming embroidery, and other embellishments from every part of the world. It's a 5-minute walk from the Tokyo Children's Hall, and you can see the whole museum in less than an hour.

EATING OPTIONS

Restaurants Both NHK Studio Park and TEPCO Electric Energy Museum have restaurants selling spaghetti, curry, snacks, and drinks. The third-floor snack bar in the children's hall serves food, but the pickings are slim. You would do much better with one of the restaurants in the area. Tokyu Department Store's ninth-floor collection of restaurants offers a wide variety but is crowded during lunchtime, especially on weekends. Maisen, perhaps Tokyo's best *tonkatsu* (fried pork cutlet) restaurant, has a branch here.

Picnic Possibilities NHK Studio Park is next to Yoyogi Park, which has many pleasant picnic spots as well as a place where kids can rent bicycles. At the Children's Hall eat your homemade lunch in the third-floor snack bar or the designated eating areas on the first and second floors. You can also buy something at the B1 food floor of Tokyu Department Store's Shibuya branch and eat it on one of the rooftop tables at Shibuya Top Circuit.

FOR INFANTS AND TODDLERS

There are three diaper-changing tables in and around the first-floor ladies' room and one near the exit at NHK's Studio Park. TEPCO has diaper-changing tables in the ladies' restrooms on the fourth and sixth floors. Tokyo Metropolitan Children's Hall has diaper-changing tables in front of the restrooms on every floor. They also have a nursing room on the second floor next to the play area; ask the floor attendant for a key to open the room. The Museum of World Folk Costumes has no diapering or nursing facilities. Tokyu Department Store has a well-appointed nursery on its sixth floor with diaper-changing and nursing facilities.

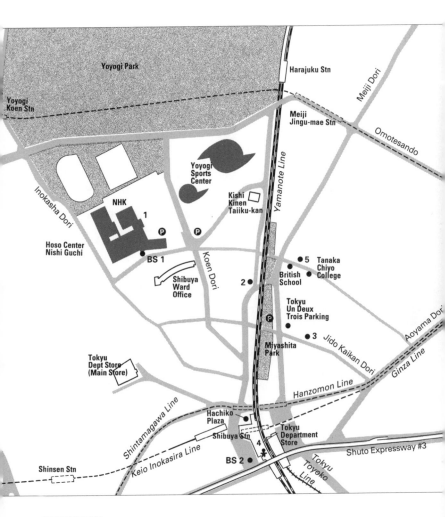

PLACES TO VISIT

1. NHK Studio Park
2. TEPCO Electric Energy Museum
3. Tokyo Metropolitan Children's Hall
4. Shibuya Top Circuit, Restaurants (Tokyu Department Store, Toyoko branch)

5. Museum of World Folk Costumes

BS 1. Shibuya Kuyakusho Bus Stop
BS 2. South Exit Bus Terminal

WHERE & WHEN

NHK Studio Park

NHK　スタジオパーク

2–2–1 Jinnan, Shibuya-ku, Tokyo 150–0041

☎ (03) 3485–8034

東京都渋谷区神南2-2-1　〒150-0041

OPEN: 10 A.M. to 6 P.M. (admission until 5 P.M.)

CLOSED: 2nd Mon of the month except when that day falls on a hol or in Aug

FEES: adults ¥200, junior/senior high school students ¥150, under 12 years old free

DIRECTIONS: a 10-minute walk from Shibuya station (JR Yamanote, Tokyu Toyoko, Shin-tamagawa, and Inokashira train lines and Ginza and Hanzomon subway lines) or from the south exit at Shibuya station take Keio bus #63 from stop #13, bus #64 from stop #11, or bus #51 from stop #14 and get off at Shibuya Kuyakusho. Or take Keio bus #66 from stop #15 or Tokyu bus #61 from stop #16 and get off at Hoso Center Nishi Guchi. Also a 10-minute walk from Harajuku station (JR Yamanote line) and either Meiji Jingu-mae or Yoyogi Koen stations (Chiyoda subway line). By car, between Yamate Dori and Meiji Dori just south of the intersection of Inokashira Dori and Koen Dori.

PARKING: no parking available at NHK Studio Park, but you may find a space at the Shibuya Ward office lot on the same side of the street. They give a discount to visitors of NHK Studio Park. There is also parking at the Kishi Memorial Hall (Kishi Kinen Taiiku Kan) nearby.

COMMENTS: all ages, no English

TEPCO Electric Energy Museum

テプコ電力館 (TEPCO Denryoku-kan)

1–12–10 Jinnan, Shibuya-ku, Tokyo 150–0041

☎ (03) 3477–1191

東京都渋谷区神南1-12-10　〒150-0041

OPEN: 10:30 A.M. to 6:30 P.M.

CLOSED: Wed and New Year's hols

FEES: none

DIRECTIONS: a 7-minute walk from Shibuya station (JR Yamanote, Tokyu Toyoko, Shin-tamagawa, and Inokashira train lines, and Ginza and Hanzomon subway lines). By car, a few blocks north of Shibuya station one street west of Meiji Dori.

PARKING: none

COMMENTS: 5 and up, English pamphlets

Tokyo Metropolitan Children's Hall

東京都児童会館 (Tokyo-to Jido Kaikan)

1–18–24 Shibuya, Shibuya-ku, Tokyo 150–0002

☎ (03) 3409–6361

東京都渋谷区渋谷1-18-24　〒150-0002

OPEN: 9 A.M. to 5 P.M. (admission until 4 P.M.)

CLOSED: generally closed 2nd and 4th Mon of the month, occasionally closed on other days for preparation, repairs, etc. Also closed for New Year's hols.

FEES: none

DIRECTIONS: a 7-minute walk from Shibuya station (JR Yamanote, Tokyu Toyoko, Shin-tamagawa, and Inokashira train lines, and Ginza and Hanzomon subway lines). By car, on Jido Kaikan Dori between Meiji Dori and Aoyama Dori.

PARKING: free for 12 cars

COMMENTS: all ages, English pamphlets, nursing room

Shibuya Top Circuit

シブヤ・トップ・サーキット

Tokyu Department Store, West Annex Roof Garden

2–24–1 Shibuya, Shibuya-ku, Tokyo 150– 0002

東京都渋谷区渋谷2-24-1　東急デパート西館屋上　〒150-0002

☎ (03) 3477–4103

OPEN: 10 A.M. to 9 P.M.

CLOSED: one or two Thurs per month

FEES: none for the small battery-operated cars; to race the radio-controlled cars you must become a member (¥5,000 plus the price of the car), then pay additional fees for use of the track.

DIRECTIONS: on the roof of the Tokyu Department Store (Toyoko branch) connected to Shibuya station (JR Yamanote, Tokyu Toyoko, and Inokashira train lines, Ginza, Hanzomon, and Chiyoda subway lines). By car, near the intersection of expressway #3 and Meiji Dori.

PARKING: the closest parking lot is at Miyashita Park or the Tokyu Un Deux Trois Building

COMMENTS: 5 and up, no English, nursing room

Museum of World Folk Costumes

田中千代学園民族衣装館 (Tanaka Chiyo Gakuen Minzoku Isho-kan)

5–30–1 Jingu-mae, Shibuya-ku, Tokyo 150–0001

☎ (03) 3400–9777

東京都渋谷区神宮前5-30-1　〒150-0001

OPEN: 10 A.M. to 4 P.M. (admission until 3:30 P.M.)

CLOSED: Sun, hols, the month of Aug, Dec 26 to Jan 10 and when preparing for exhibits

FEES: adults ¥300, students ¥200

DIRECTIONS: an 8-minute walk from Miyamasu-zaka exit of Shibuya station (JR Yamanote, Inokashira, and Tokyu Toyoko train lines, and Ginza and Hanzomon subway lines). An 8-minute walk from exit 4 of Meiji Jingu-mae station (Chiyoda subway line) or 10 minutes from Harajuku station (JR Yamanote line).

PARKING: free but space for only one car

COMMENTS: 5 and up, no English

Mom's Choice: Sunday in Aoyama

Aoyama Brunch • Nezu Institute of Fine Art and Gardens • National Children's Castle

Any day can be Mother's Day in upscale Aoyama. But we suggest a Sunday, when Aoyama is the place for brunch. Savor an elegant meal, then stroll past the boutiques of famous designers on your way to the Nezu Institute of Fine Art and its beautiful Japanese garden. Spend a serene afternoon far away from over-popular Yoyogi Park and Omotesando's throngs of window-shoppers tripping over each other. If a traditional garden doesn't suit your family, visit the Children's Castle instead. While parents may not find it as peaceful, they'll applaud the play equipment provided. Families with school-aged children may be able to see both Nezu and the castle, but most will opt for one or the other.

Start your day with a scrumptious meal you didn't have to cook yourself. There are many eateries in Aoyama, from fast food to four star. On Sundays, several outstanding restaurants suspend their regular lunch menus and offer special all-you-can-eat buffets. Here we offer Sunday brunch and weekday suggestions to fit any family, from French food in an elegant atmosphere to a casual health food buffet.

L'Orangerie de Paris, according to Tokyo's restaurant critics, is the city's best brunch and a relatively inexpensive way to sample the specialties of this delicious but high-priced French restaurant atop the Hanae Mori Building. Your table is set with fine French silver, and though there is no dress code this is an excellent excuse to get your little girl's finest dress out. Fashion designer Hanae Mori herself often comes for brunch.

The **Spiral Café** is just another upscale coffee shop on weekdays, but they put on a reasonably elegant Sunday brunch. They offer children's prices and welcome youngsters, although you will want to dress your kids in something better than play clothes.

Kids of all ages like the mini spiral art museum in the same building. Shoppers may also want to visit the Spiral Market upstairs for gifts and creative trinkets.

Brasserie Flo serves its regular menu on weekends but has a buffet lunch for those who might want to try this tour on a weekday. Their regular menu is also available during the buffet hours. At Flo's, modeled after the original in France, the food is not particularly outstanding, but the surroundings are worthy of Paris, the portions generous, and the prices reasonable. You'll be rubbing elbows with office workers and groups of lunching women.

Home on the basement level of the Crayon House bookstore serves a Japanese natural foods buffet seven days a week. The restaurant uses organic vegetables from the health food shop on the same level, has unique booster chairs that will even help babies sit so they can eat at the table, and was created for families so you don't have to worry about disrupting the atmosphere. The buffet is not vegetarian but there are enough vegetable dishes to satisfy those who want to avoid meat. Dress casually.

Bamboo doesn't serve a fancy brunch, but you can have a pleasant lunch of salad and sandwiches on the charming outdoor terrace.

Aoyama has dozens more delicious restaurants we don't have space to mention, but with these options we've tried to include the best Sunday brunches as well as suggestions for weekdays, whether you want to dress up or down. Your choice of clothing may also dictate where you go next: stroll in your Sunday finery to the Nezu Institute of Fine Art or race to the Children's Castle and subject your playclothes to a little more wear and tear.

The **Nezu Institute of Fine Art**'s small collection of Japanese, Chinese, and Korean pottery and art is a treat for aficionados. The museum contains seven works designated as National Treasures, seventy-nine Important Cultural Properties, and one hundred Important Art Works. For families, however, these delicate pieces take second place to the institute's impeccable garden, a rare and refreshing respite from the crowds and chaos of Tokyo. The garden is only open to museum patrons. So go in, pay your entrance fee, have a brief look at the antiquities and gift shop items, then head outside. Step into a leafy green retreat where pools and streams hush all sound except for the occasional splashing of bright-colored carp and the warbling of a songbird. Tall trees provide shade from the afternoon sun and block all sight of the city. Follow secret pathways through cool, velvety mosses and delicate ferns, discovering little bridges, steppingstones, teahouses, and stone lanterns. Relax and enjoy flowers and fragrance and fresh air.

Give yourself an hour for the museum and the garden, longer if you are with a toddler who will want to carefully inspect everything, including the odd bug. After you roam through the garden, have afternoon tea in the museum's Café Gazebo or, if there is still plenty of steam left in your engines, head for the next spot on the tour.

At the height of the bubble economy the Japanese government opened the **National Children's Castle**, a fabulous place to play, pretend, and learn. Children paint on the walls—17 meters of blank space—in the third-floor Fine Arts Studio. Next door, the Play Hall has great indoor climbing, sliding, and tunneling equipment, a computer playroom, and a corner for older kids with foos ball and pool tables. This place also has fantastic pretend play areas with all the trappings: a dreamy play kitchen, pretend shops, puppets and dolls, and legos of every variety to fashion your own castles, farmyards, and cities. There are shelves of books (including a few in English) and a special section with baby toys for the very wee ones to explore.

In the fourth-floor Music Lobby, kids can dance, sing, and even accompany a live band. Music Studios A and B are reserved for weekday classes, and on the weekends Music Studio B has concerts and movies. Check the daily schedule when you arrive. During Japa-

The castle can become more than just an occasional play spot for your family. They hold classes in Japanese on music, art, computers, and more. Occasionally you will even find instructors who speak English—we did for performing arts. If money is no object and you are looking for somewhere to hold a party, you can book an undecorated room on the eighth or ninth floor of the Children's Castle for about ¥20,000. Cake, drinks, and snacks can be ordered (at outrageous prices) from the castle's restaurant, and instead of preparing party games you can just let the kids loose in the Play Hall. You can also join the day care center. They take care of children at least two years old and have a variety of plans and schedules. If you want to register for a class or discuss the Japanese day care in English, ask if their English-speaking staff member is on duty. The receptionists speak some English too. They can also give you an English pamphlet about the Children's Castle.

nese school holidays, the castle's busy seasons, Music Studio A is open for infants and early walkers to pound on a plethora of music toys. On the same floor is an Audio/Visual Library where you can watch your requests in a booth. There is a large selection of videos in English. Parents and kids can take swimming lessons in the basement pool. The tenth floor has a personal computer room geared for older kids.

Don't forget to visit the roof. There are all sorts of bikes, trikes, and scooters you can ride on flat terrain or down slopes. There is outdoor swimming in the summer, and kids over age three can use the "play port," an enclosed jungle gym featuring slides, punching bags, tunnels, and the irresistible ball pool. The Aoyama Theater and the Aoyama Round Theater in the same complex sponsor musicals, ballets, concerts, and other performances your kids may be interested in.

Other Things to Do in the Area

Crayon House, brainchild of the feminist writer Keiko Ochiai, carries children's books in Japanese, English, and French, interesting toys including small musical instruments, stationery, and magazines, plus novels and an outstanding collection of English and Japanese books on women's issues. There is a large table with picture books and children's novels to sample. You can find Shel Silverstein, The Baby Sitters Club, Madeline books, Richard Scarry, Eric Carle, Beatrix Potter, Roald Dahl, Jan Pienkowski, and numerous recent publications, many in both English and Japanese. They stock books on cassette plus children's music tapes and videos. What you don't find on their shelves, they will order and ship to your house. You pay later by postal *furikae*, a transaction you can do at any post office. The store hosts storytelling hours in Japanese, a variety of contests, and book-signings.

Wise Mammy, two stores behind the Crayon House, carries European designer layettes and name-brand toddlers' clothing up to size 95 centimeters (U.S. 9 months).

On Sundays, Omotesando between Aoyama Dori and Harakuju station closes to traffic and fills to capacity with pedestrians. Most shops lining the street, dubbed Tokyo's "Champs Elysées," cater to the fashion elite, but a few focus on kids. **Kiddyland**, a high-priced toy and novelty store, carries American action figures and character merchandise, gag toys, stationery, and hair accessories for teens. You can always count on Kiddyland for Easter, Halloween, Valentine's Day, and Christmas decorations or birthday party paper goods and favors with Happy Birthday written on them in English, although both this store and **Dear Kids La Foret Part 2** are uncomfortably crowded on the weekends. The junior version of La Foret department store is on Meiji Dori, across from a large parking lot. Inside on the second and third floors are several little boutiques and restaurants catering to kids and their parents.

OTHER EATING OPTIONS

Restaurants If you're looking for a quick snack or meal, the Children's Castle has a restaurant on the ground floor level that caters to kids and families. Dear Kids Laforet Part 2 has a restaurant on the top floor with lots of kid-pleasing menu items. The Nezu garden's Café Gazebo sells Japanese and Western sweets and drinks.

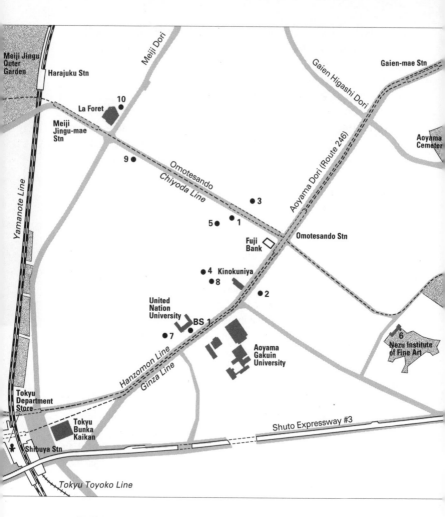

PLACES TO VISIT

1. L'Orangerie de Paris (Hanae Mori Building)
2. Spiral Café and Spiral Market
3. Brasserie Flo
4. Crayon House
5. Bamboo Sandwich Restaurant
6. Nezu Institute of Fine Art
7. National Children's Castle
8. Wise Mammy
9. Kiddyland
10. Dear Kids La Foret Part 2

BS 1. Aoyama Gakuin-mae Bus Stop

Picnic Possibilities At the Children's Castle, many people use the chairs or stairs outside the third-floor Play Hall to eat lunches, but there are also dining areas with tables and chairs on floors 2 and B1. When the cherries bloom, Aoyama Botchi (cemetery) actually becomes a popular picnic spot. It's just up the road from the Nezu museum. Bring a blanket and with luck you might find space to spread it out.

FOR INFANTS AND TODDLERS

If you absolutely need a highchair, head for Crayon House. It's the only restaurant mentioned that has special chairs for little ones. You will want your stroller to lug little ones around on this tour. However, if you go down Omotesando when it's crowded you might find you need to pick up the children for protection from the jostling shopping bags of passersby. The Nezu museum has no diaper-changing or nursing areas. The Children's Castle has a nursing room on the fourth floor, and diaper-changing facilities and baby beds on almost every floor. You can find hot water for bottles at the reception center on the fifth floor and even buy disposable diapers in the Atrium Shop. Crayon House has a baby bed on the third floor for diaper changing. Their first floor restroom is reserved for kids only because they often need to get to the facilities in a hurry. Kiddyland has a diaper-changing table in its fifth-floor ladies' room. Dear Kids Laforet Part 2 has a small nursing room on the second floor. Next door there is a toddler's toilet in the ladies' room.

WHERE & WHEN

L'Orangerie de Paris
オランジュリードパリ
Hanae Mori Building, 5F
3–6–1 Kita Aoyama, Minato-ku, Tokyo 107–0061
☎ (03) 3407–7461
東京都港区北青山3-6-1　ハナエモリビル5階　〒107-0061
OPEN: 11:30 A.M. to 2:30 P.M. and 5:30 P.M. to 10:30 P.M.; Sun brunch 11 A.M. to 2:30 P.M. Adults ¥4,000 for lunch, over ¥8,000 for dinner. Reservations strongly suggested.
DIRECTIONS: at the top of the Hanae Mori Building on Omotesando Dori just in front of exit A1 of Omotesando station (Hanzomon,

Ginza, or Chiyoda subway lines).
PARKING: no parking on Sun. Limited parking available on weekdays.

Spiral Café and Spiral Market
スパイラルカフェ、スパイラルマーケット
5–6–23 Minami Aoyama, Minato-ku, Tokyo 107–0062
☎ (03) 3498–5791 café; (03) 3498–5792 market (11 A.M. to 8 P.M.)
東京都港区南青山5-6-23　〒107-0062
OPEN: 11 A.M. to midnight weekdays; 11 A.M. to 8:30 P.M. weekends and hols; Sun brunch 11 A.M. to 2 P.M. Adults ¥3,000, children under 12

¥1,500. Reservations suggested. Brunch ¥1,000.
DIRECTIONS: take exit B2 from Omotesando station (Hanzomon, Ginza, or Chiyoda subway lines). By car, on Aoyama Dori just south of the intersection with Omotesando.
PARKING: hourly rate

Brasserie Flo

表参道ブラッセリーフロ

4–3–3 Jingu-mae, Shibuya-ku, Tokyo 150–0001

☎ (03) 5474–0611

東京都渋谷区神宮前4-3-3　〒150-0001

OPEN: 11:30 A.M. to 4 P.M. for lunch, 4 P.M. to 11:30 P.M. (last order 10:30) for dinner, buffet served from 11 A.M. to 3 P.M. on Sat (until 5 on Sun, hols) ¥1,600. No reservations required.
DIRECTIONS: a few minutes walk from exit A2 of Omotesando station (Hanzomon, Ginza, or Chiyoda subway lines).
PARKING: none

Home and Crayon House

クレヨンハウス

3–8–15 Kita Aoyama, Minato-ku, Tokyo 107–0061

☎ (03) 3406–6492 (books), (03) 3406–6409 (restaurant)

東京都港区北青山3-8-15　〒107-0061

OPEN: Crayon House, 11 A.M. to 7 P.M.; Home 11 A.M. to 10 P.M.; buffet 11 A.M. to 2 P.M.; adults ¥1,200, children 2–6 ¥600. No reservations required. Buffet served from 11 A.M. to 2 P.M.
DIRECTIONS: take exit A1 from Omotesando station (Hanzomon, Ginza, or Chiyoda subway lines) and turn left at the corner of the Hanae Mori Building. Crayon House will be on your left.
PARKING: none

Bamboo

バンブー

5–8–8 Jingu-mae, Shibuya-ku, Tokyo 150–0001

☎ (03) 3407–8427

東京都渋谷区神宮前5-8-8　〒150-0001

OPEN: 11 A.M. to 10 P.M daily
DIRECTIONS: a 7-minute walk from exit A1 of Omotesando station (Hanzomon, Ginza, or Chiyoda subway lines).
PARKING: none

Nezu Institute of Fine Art

根津美術館 (Nezu Bijutsu-kan)

6–5–1 Minami Aoyama, Minato-ku, Tokyo 107–0062

☎ (03) 3400–2536

東京都港区南青山6-5-1　〒107-0062

OPEN: 9:30 A.M. to 4:30 P.M. (enter by 4 P.M.)
FEES: adults ¥1,000, students ¥700, under 12 years free
CLOSED: Mon and New Year's hols
DIRECTIONS: an 8-minute walk from exit A5 of Omotesando station (Hanzomon, Ginza, or Chiyoda subway lines). By car, the institute is south of Route 246, just off Omotesando.
PARKING: free for patrons; lot holds six cars
COMMENTS: all ages, English pamphlet

National Children's Castle

子供の城 (Kodomo no Shiro)

5–53–1 Jingu-mae, Shibuya-ku, Tokyo 150–0001

☎ (03) 3797–5666

東京都渋谷区神宮前5-53-1　〒150-0001

OPEN: 12:30 A.M. to 5:30 P.M. weekdays; 10 A.M. to 5:30 P.M. weekends, school, and national hols
CLOSED: Mon (Tues if Mon is a school or national hol), Dec 29 to Jan 2
FEES: adults ¥500, children 3 to 17 ¥400
DIRECTIONS: 15-minute walk from the Miyamasuzaka exit of Shibuya station (JR Yamanote, Tokyu Toyoko, and Keio Inokashira train lines, or Shintamagawa, Ginza, and Hanzomon subway lines) or exit B2 of Omotesando station (Ginza, Hanzomon, or Chiyoda subway lines). 10 minutes by bus #81 or #88

from Shibuya station bound for Ochanomizu, Tokyo Tower, or Tokyo Yaesuguchi. Get out at Aoyama Gakuin-mae bus stop.

PARKING: 80-car lot, hourly rate

COMMENTS: all ages, adequate English, nursing room

Wise Mammy
ワイズマミー
3–8–12 Kita Aoyama, Minato-ku, Tokyo 107–0061
☎ (03) 3407–9007
東京都港区北青山3-8-12　〒107-0061
OPEN: 11 A.M. to 6 P.M.
CLOSED: irregularly
DIRECTIONS: see Crayon House. Wise Mammy is on the street behind Crayon House, two shops up toward Aoyama Dori.

Kiddyland
キディランド
6–1–9 Jingu-mae, Shibuya-ku, Tokyo 150–0001
☎ (03) 3409–3431
東京都渋谷区神宮前6-1-9　〒150-0001
OPEN: 10 A.M. to 8 P.M.

CLOSED: 3rd Tues of the month, also Jan 1

DIRECTIONS: on Omotesando Dori a few minutes walk from exit A1 of Omotesando station (Hanzomon, Ginza, or Chiyoda subway lines).

PARKING: none

Dear Kids La Foret Part 2
ディアキッド ラフォーレ パートⅡ
La Foret Part 2 Building, 2/3F
1–8–10 Jingu-mae, Shibuya-ku, Tokyo 150–0001
☎ (03) 3497–9631 (Control Room)
東京都渋谷区神宮前1-8-10　ラフォーレパートⅡ2/3階　〒150-0001
OPEN: 10 A.M. to 7 P.M.
DIRECTIONS: a 1-minute walk from Meiji Jingu-mae station exit 5 (Chiyoda subway line); a 7-minute walk from Harajuku station (JR Yamanote line); a 10-minute walk from Omotesando station exit A2 (Hanzomon, Ginza, or Chiyoda subway lines). By car, on Meiji Dori just north of intersection with Omotesando.
PARKING: none
COMMENTS: nursing room

Kichijoji Play Spots for Babies and Toddlers

0123 Kichijoji • Inokashira Park

If you lived nearby, you would take your baby or toddler to **0123 Kichijoji** every day. Here, Mom and Dad can relax while children ages 0 to 3 build motor skills and discover their own creativity in a place designed for action and games of let's pretend. There are no licensed character toys here. No videos, no computer screens. Beautifully constructed wooden climbing equipment, things to ride, and building blocks take their place. A few hours here is enough to make you listen to child educators who warn against too much television and expensive but uninspiring toys. New parents especially will find plenty of ideas for things to try at home.

Paid for by Musashino City, fundamentally 0123 Kichijoji is for use by city residents. However, although only Musashino residents can participate in classes, everyone is welcome to visit for a day of play. There is no entrance fee. Leave your stroller outside by the front door, put your shoes in the boxes at the entrance, store your excess gear in the coin lockers in the basement (your 10-yen coin will be returned), and request an English copy of the rules at the reception window. Read carefully; some rules may be unexpected. For example, you cannot throw away any garbage—including diapers. Be sure to come fed or bring something to eat if you want to have lunch here. The closest restaurant or place to buy takeout is back by the station at Sun Road Shopping Center, 15 minutes away on foot.

In the garden, log houses, benches, and baby swimming pools (in summer) sit under wisteria vines and plum trees. You'll find everything you need to build moats and castles in the sandbox. Inside, the main play space holds lots of wooden toys and play equipment, sponge blocks big enough to build a fort, a play kitchen, dress-up clothes, and a piano. Parents can play or read and drink coffee (¥30) or Japanese tea (free) in the adjacent lounge. Literature on child-rearing is available in Japanese. Bring extra clothes in the summer, since your kids will play in the water.

Upstairs, cuddle your child in your lap and enjoy one of the handful of English picture books in the library, or turn the pages of the many Japanese books. Take a break in the conversation area, where parents can chat and sip tea. You can eat lunch in the study on this floor from 11:45 A.M. to 1:30 P.M. A special room for babies has highchairs, a mini kitchen with everything you need to prepare formula, a tiny wooden slide, rattles, and other baby toys. There are no restrictions on infant feeding times in the babies' room.

You could easily make a day of it; 0123 Kichijoji closes at 4 P.M. But for a change of pace and some outdoor fun, follow the map to **Inokashira Park**. No description of Kichijoji would be complete without a mention of this large, two-part park. One of the best in Tokyo, it was designed to stimulate interest in natural science and it will—especially in your kids.

Rent rowboats or pedal boats and float lazily around the giant pond in the sub-park, home to many carp and ducks. It's a scenic spot in springtime, thick with cherry trees that encircle the pond and crowd against a small flowering plum grove. Food stands at the water's edge sell bags of food to feed the fish, and nearby is an old aquarium where you can learn about the inhabitants of Japanese rivers.

Cross Kichijoji Dori to get to Inokashira Shizen Bunka-en, which holds a small zoo with an animal petting corner, a tiny amusement park for toddlers, a tropical plant greenhouse, a sculpture garden and museum featuring the works of Seibo Kitamura, and a room used by poet Ujo Noguchi.

The park is a wonderful place to play, with plenty to keep you entertained. We have mixed feelings, however, about recommending the zoo. If you are looking for a place where a toddler can touch guinea pigs or rabbits, we suggest the petting zoos at Tama Zoo, Kodomo-no-Kuni, and Arakawa Amusement Park, where they do a much better job of protecting the animals from small children who don't

> Among Tokyo's zoos, Inokashira ranks third in the number of endangered species in residence. Ueno has sixteen, Tama fifteen, and Inokashira nine, a large number considering the size of the zoo. Many of these species are indigenous to Japan. The tiny Japanese squirrels are especially endearing.

know better than to hurt them. But if you have an interest in endangered species then you may want to visit.

Other Things to Do in the Area

If you want to get in some shopping—especially toy shopping—Kichijoji has a few noteworthy establishments.The entire fifth floor of **Isetan's** new Kichijoji annex is taken up by a fabulous toy department called Dr. Kids Town, which looks something like Disneyland's Main Street. Small, colorful boutiques sell lots of imported toys as well as the main Japanese brands. When ready for a break from shopping, the kids can climb into a big fire engine, dive into a pool of sponges, or play on the slide in the stuffed animal zoo. A tunnel-shaped rest area with tables connects the new annex to the older building. It's a good place to eat a packed lunch. Pass through the tunnel to get to the children's wear and maternity departments as well as the nursing and diaper-changing area.

Sleepers, near the end of the main drag in Sun Road, carries character pajamas and costumes for adults and children (sizes start at 100 centimeters). You'll find great possibilities for Halloween or dress-up here.

Nikki-Tikki sells great wooden toys from Northern Europe, puzzles, playhouse furniture, and more. You may have seen branches in Hiroo, Daikanyama, and Kobe, but the biggest and best is the Kichijoji main store. Look for the store's red and white sign on the right side of the street just after Cache, Cache. **Obaa-san no Tamatebako**, which translates as Grandmother's Treasure Box, carries children's books in Japanese and a nice selection of European toys. Tester models of the most popular toys entertain toddlers while parents select items to purchase. The store takes up the first two floors of the Yamazaki Building, a few minutes' walk beyond Nikki-Tikki.

If you've come to Kichijoji on a Thursday, don't miss the 11 A.M. English story time at **The Grab Bag**, a children's resale shop. The store carries next-to-new American and European brand clothing, toys, and English picture books. Owner, former New York elementary school teacher Ellen Motohashi, will sell your gently used items on consignment.

EATING OPTIONS

Restaurants There are plenty of restaurants and takeout places in Sun Road Shopping Center next to Kichijoji station, but none in the vicinity of 0123 Kichijoji. If you are bound for Inokashira Park you will find a cluster of noodle and snack shops in the sub-park and a snack shop in the main park.

Picnic Possibilities Bring your lunch to 0123 Kichijoji and eat it in the second-floor study. You can also eat a packed lunch in the tunnel rest area at Isetan. Inokashira Park has ample space for spreading a feast on a blanket or nibbling sandwiches on a bench.

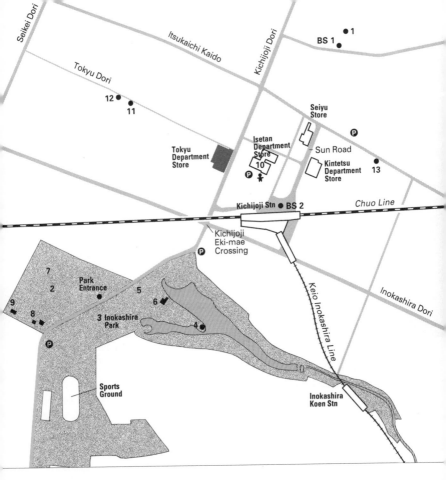

PLACES TO VISIT

1. 0123 Kichijoji
2. Inokashira Shizen Bunka-en
3. Inokashira Park
4. Boat Rental
5. Plum Grove
6. Aquarium
7. Zoo
8. Sculpture Garden
9. Seibo Kitamura Museum
10. Isetan Department Store
11. Nikki-Tikki
12. Obaa-san no Tamatebako
13. The Grab Bag

BS 1. Higashi Machi 1-chome Bus Stop
BS 2. Bus Terminal

FOR INFANTS AND TODDLERS

Of course 0123 Kichijoji has diaper-changing and bottle-feeding facilities. There are even tiny toilets for the newly potty-trained. Isetan has a baby room in its layette and maternity wear department, complete with diaper-changing tables, a nursing area, and hot water for bottles. There is a diaper-changing table in the aquarium in the Inokashira sub-park, but no other infant-care facilities in the park. The Grab Bag has a rocker for nursing in their Crawl Around Corner.

WHERE & WHEN

0123 Kichijoji

0123吉祥寺 (Zero, Ichi, Ni, San Kichijoji)
2–29–12 Kichijoji Higashi Machi, Musashino-shi, Tokyo 180–0002
☎ (0422) 20–3210
武蔵野市吉祥寺東町2-29-12　〒180-0002
OPEN: 9 A.M. to 4 P.M.
CLOSED: Sun, Mon, and all national hols except for Children's Day (May 5), as well as during the New Year's hols
FEES: none
DIRECTIONS: a 12-minute walk from the central exit of Kichijoji station (JR Chuo and Sobu or Keio Inokashira lines). From Kichijoji station, take Kanto bus #10 bound for Nishi Ogikubo, get off at Higashi Machi 2-chome and walk 2 minutes.
PARKING: no parking available, but there is a parking lot a block and a half south (fills up quickly on weekends)
COMMENTS: infants to preschoolers, English version of rules, nursing room

Inokashira Park

井の頭自然文化園 (Inokashira Shizen Bunka-en)
1–17–6 Goten Yama, Musashino-shi, Tokyo 180–0005
☎ (0422) 46–1100
東京都武蔵野市御殿山1-17-6　〒180-0005

OPEN: 9:30 A.M. to 4:30 P.M. (park admission until 4; squirrel and guinea pig areas close at 3)
CLOSED: Mon (Tues if Mon is a hol), Dec 29 to Jan 3
FEES: *Park Entrance*: adults ¥400, junior high school students ¥150, free for children of elementary school age or younger and adults over 65. *Rowboat Rental*: ¥600/hr, overtime at ¥300/half hour. *Cycle Boats*: ¥600/half hour, overtime at ¥600/half hour. *Aquarium*: adults over 16 ¥400, junior high school students ¥150, free for children under 12 and adults over 60.
DIRECTIONS: a 10-minute walk from Kichijoji station (JR Chuo and Sobu lines). Or, take the Keio Inokashira line to Inokashira Koen station. The station's exit is at the far end of the park. It will take you about 10 minutes to get to the heart of the park, more if your kids get distracted on the way. By car, take Inokashira Dori to Kichijoji station crossing, turn south onto Kichijoji Dori. You will see the garden and zoo portion of the park on your right; the parking lot will be on the left.
PARKING: limited parking is available at an hourly rate in a 60-car lot on Kichijoji Dori across from the main park. You are asked to come by public transportation if possible.
COMMENTS: all ages, English pamphlet

Sun Road Shopping Center
サンロードショッピングセンター

• Isetan Department Store
伊勢丹

1–11–5 Kichijoji Honmachi, Musashino-shi, Tokyo 180–0004

☎ (0422) 21–1111

東京都武蔵野市吉祥寺本町1-11-5

〒180-0004

OPEN: 10 A.M. to 7:30 P.M.; restaurants on 8th floor open 11 A.M. to 9 P.M.

CLOSED: on some Wed

DIRECTIONS: short walk from Kichijoji station central exit (JR Chuo and Sobu or Keio Inokashira lines). By car, take Itsukaichi Kaido toward Mitaka, turn left at Kichijoji Odori, then right at the signal in front of Kintetsu Department Store, which you will see on your left. The entrance to the parking lot is about 100 meters down on your left.

PARKING: free for 1 hour with a stamped receipt for ¥2,000 in purchases, for 2 hours with ¥5,000 in purchases. Or, pay an hourly rate at the F&F parking lot at Kichijoji Parking Plaza.

COMMENTS: all ages, some English, nursing room

• The Grab Bag
グラップバーグ

1–34–11 Honcho, 2F, Kichijoji, Musashino-shi, 180–0004

☎ (0422) 21–7057

東京都武蔵野市吉祥寺本町1-34-11　〒180-0004

OPEN: 10 A.M. to 5 P.M.

CLOSED: Tues, national hols, Dec 31–Jan 5

DIRECTIONS: a 7-minute walk from Kichijoji station on JR Chuo and Sobu or Keio Inokashira lines. By car, drive to Musashino-shi on Inokashira Dori, turn right at the stop light in front of the Tokyu Inn, drive to the end of the street and turn right onto Itsukaichi Kaido. The Grab Bag is on the second floor of a gray-tiled three-story building on the right side of the street; look for a green awning.

PARKING: 3 spaces, call ahead for directions to lot

COMMENTS: rocker for nursing, owner speaks English

• Nikki-Tikki
ニキティキ

2–28–3 Kichijoji Honmachi, Musashino-shi, Tokyo 180–0004

☎ (0422) 21–3137

東京都武蔵野市吉祥寺本町2-28-3　〒180-0004

OPEN: 10 A.M. to 7 P.M.

CLOSED: Thurs

DIRECTIONS: a 10-minute walk from the north exit of Kichijoji station

• Obaa-chan no Tamatebako
おばちゃんの玉手箱

Yamazaki Building floors 1/2F

2–31–1 Kichijoji Honmachi, Musashino-shi, Tokyo 180–0004

☎ (0422) 21–0921

東京都武蔵野市吉祥寺本町2-31-1　山崎ビル1/2階　〒180-0004

OPEN: 10 A.M. to 7 P.M.

CLOSED: Dec 29 to Jan 3

DIRECTIONS: a 12-minute walk from the north exit of Kichijoji station

Things That Go!

Rev your engines for some exciting outings that center around wheels, wings, tracks, and motors.

*With lots of shiny red engines to admire, entertaining displays, and a rescue helicopter to pilot, the **Yotsuya Fire Museum** is such a favorite with our younger kids that we take them there as a reward for good behavior. Watercraft and seashore fun are the focus of the **maritime museum** tour, where you take a boat to a large, informative museum that includes two retired ocean-going vessels.*

*For a slow-paced, old-fashioned excursion, climb aboard the city's only remaining **streetcar** and pick from a variety of activities, from nature parks and secret gardens to a toddler-size amusement park or, for older kids, a museum with informative displays that teach about paper-making and paper crafts.*

*Aviation enthusiasts can listen in and watch as real air traffic controllers guide flights in and out of **Narita** airport from a fascinating museum located just off one of the runways. Kids will enjoy learning about the principles of flight, pretending to pilot aircraft, and examining the museum's extensive collection of models.*

Fight Fires in Yotsuya

Yotsuya Fire Museum • Shinjuku Gyoen

Free, filled with fire engines, and directly connected to the subway station, the **Yotsuya Fire Museum** is the perfect place to visit when the weather is bad or you just don't feel like walking. Using interactive displays and games, the museum introduces the history of firefighting in Japan.

The country's first firemen were samurai, and instead of squirting water on a blaze they tore down the surrounding wooden buildings to stop the fire from spreading, then let it burn out. Their demolition tactics are illustrated by a diorama on the fifth floor of the museum, which also has some artifacts and a collection of the banners these fiercely competitive brigades carried as they rushed off to a fire. Outside on the terrace, you can climb into a retired fire helicopter perched near the edge to give pretend pilots a terrific view of the streets below and even Mount Fuji on clear days.

On the fourth floor, a collection of photos, uniforms, and equipment illustrates how firefighting has evolved

Avid firebugs won't want to miss the annual Shobo Dezome Fire Engine Festival, highlighted by a parade of over a hundred fire engines and firefighters in Edo-period attire who compete in an acrobatics contest atop bamboo ladders. Tokyo firefighters hold their festival every January 6. In 1998 the festival moved from Harumi to Ariake with plans to hold it there every year. Yokohama's parade is the second Sunday in January at the Minato Mirai 21 Heliport east of Rinkoh Seaside Park (see Tour 28 for more information on Minato Mirai).

over the years. The third floor is devoted to firefighting today. Small children and adults alike will be entranced as toy fire engines with sirens wailing race to put out a fire and save a cartoon character in one display. Those who are old enough will want to try the computer games, including one that lets you fight your way out of a burning building. People with good Japanese reading skills can test how much they've learned on computer terminals. Throughout the museum, many tidbits of information are written only in Japanese, but there is enough English to make it enjoyable.

Vintage fire trucks, a helicopter, and other firefighting equipment fill the first floor and the basement, where a small museum shop is located. Unfortunately, you are not allowed to climb on the equipment, but there are plenty of intriguing exhibits, like a horse-drawn fire wagon and a steam pump used in the late 1800s. If you happen to be near the first-floor entrance closest to the information desk when the hour changes, step outside the door and listen to a serenade by a figurine clock with a tiny marching band.

If you are exceptionally interested in firefighting, you may want to check on the special exhibitions held twice a year, or make reservations to watch some of the many Japanese and English films on the sixth floor. There is also a library with materials on firefighting on the seventh floor, open only on Wednesday, Friday, and Sunday afternoons. The receptionists at the information desk should be able to help you.

All floors are accessible by elevator. Wandering through the museum should take about an hour, longer if you stop to play.

If the weather is nice, take a short ride on bus #70 from just outside the building to Shinjuku 1-chome stop, or walk 15 minutes along Shinjuku Dori to **Shinjuku Gyoen**. Wide open spaces and formal flower beds await you. The park has Japanese, English, and French gardens, along with plenty of soft grass to sprawl on—a relatively rare commodity in Tokyo. With about ten thousand cherry trees, Shinjuku Gyoen is breathtaking when the blossoms are out and gorgeous any other time. The prime minister himself traditionally makes an official visit to the park to view the cherry blossoms; the park's front gate is opened only for his annual pilgrimage or for rare visits from other dignitaries. November 1 to 15 is another good time to visit Shinjuku Gyoen. That's when the park holds its famous Chrysanthemum Festival. During the Chrysanthemum Festival and cherry blossom season, regular holidays are canceled and Shinjuku Gyoen remains open every day.

Whenever you visit, you're sure to enjoy yourself. The entrance fee, small as it is, tends to discourage people, so you generally don't have to worry about rowdy crowds (except when the blossoms are out). Restaurant facilities on the grounds mean there's no reason to leave if you get hungry. Spend a lazy afternoon playing on the grassy lawns, feeding the fish, or watching artists at work. While you may see people with balls, badminton sets, or frisbees, Japanese announcements throughout the park request visitors not to play with them in the park. Instead you may want to wander the winding garden paths, trying to identify the plants. If your children read Japanese, they can follow the Green Adventure Course, which challenges you to guess the names of trees, flowers, and shrubs as you walk through the park. Pick up your score-card at the Shinjuku Gyoen Information Center just outside the Shinjuku gate. At the center you'll also find the souvenir shop, botany exhibits, and a gallery with shows that usually have a nature theme. Some of them can be quite fun, even if you don't read Japanese.

Other Things to Do in the Area

Shinjuku's development from the Paleolithic period to the end of World War II is illustrated in the **Shinjuku Historical Museum** just 7 minutes on foot from Yotsuya 3-chome station. Although it takes only 20 or 30 minutes to look around, visitors will be entertained by a life-sized trolley car, a typical dwelling, and personal effects from the early twentieth century. Step into the hallway of an old-time salaried worker's home, and inspect the braised potatoes, *kinpira* (sauteed root vegetables), miso soup, and rice set out for dinner while listening to music from the period. The museum ends with a huge black-and-white photo of the rubble that Shinjuku was reduced to by American firebombs, and another of the skyscrapers that were built on the ashes. If you'd like to stop and take a break on the way, **San-ei Park**, located between the museum and the station, has lots of good things to climb on.

When bad weather rules out a trip to Shinjuku Gyoen, you may want to hop on the Marunouchi line for a 15-minute ride to Awajicho station and the **Transportation Museum**, 5-minutes' walk away. One of Tokyo's old favorites, this large museum covers every mode of transportation from palanquins and rickshaws to spacecraft, but as you might expect in Japan, trains are the highlight. Models of every train line in Tokyo, including whichever one your child takes most often, run on a large model track set in the museum's famous train panorama. Beyond the train show, there are two old-fashioned locomotives to climb on, a model of the newest *shinkansen* bullet train, and many other rail-related exhibits. You can even drive a *shinkansen* with the help of a video simulator. The second floor houses ship exhibits for aspiring seafarers as well as displays on buses, model cars, motorcycles, and bikes. Floor three is mainly dedicated to airplanes, with a JAL plane you can board, a model helicopter cockpit, several old-style planes, and exhibits on rockets. The museum shop near the first-floor entrance sells realistic models of all the trains and buses in the Tokyo area.

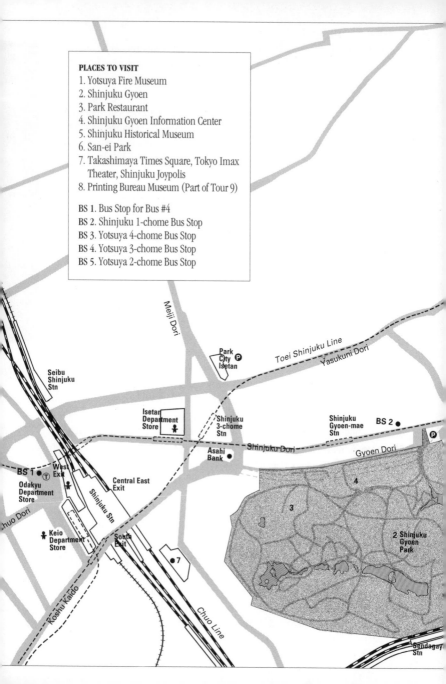

PLACES TO VISIT
1. Yotsuya Fire Museum
2. Shinjuku Gyoen
3. Park Restaurant
4. Shinjuku Gyoen Information Center
5. Shinjuku Historical Museum
6. San-ei Park
7. Takashimaya Times Square, Tokyo Imax
   Theater, Shinjuku Joypolis
8. Printing Bureau Museum (Part of Tour 9)

BS 1. Bus Stop for Bus #4
BS 2. Shinjuku 1-chome Bus Stop
BS 3. Yotsuya 4-chome Bus Stop
BS 4. Yotsuya 3-chome Bus Stop
BS 5. Yotsuya 2-chome Bus Stop

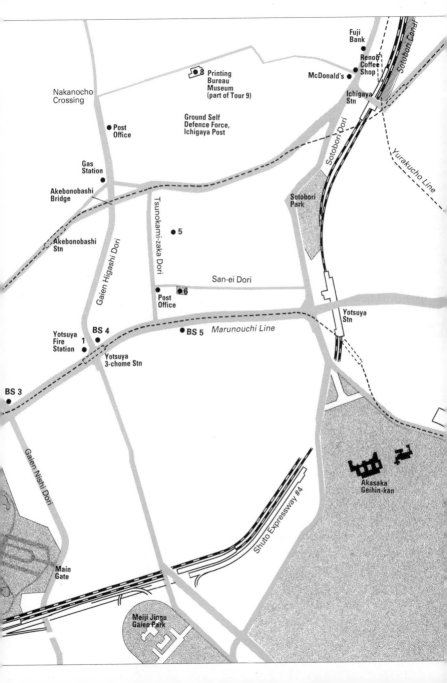

Fuji
Bank

Renoir
Coffee
Shop

McDonald's ●

Ichigaya
Stn

Nakanocho
Crossing

🏛8 Printing
Bureau
Museum
(part of Tour 9)

Ground Self
Defence Force,
Ichigaya Post

● Post
Office

Sotobori Dori

Yurakucho Line

Gas
Station ●

Akebonobashi
Bridge

Sotobori
Park

Tsunokami-zaka Dori

● 5

Akebonobashi
Stn

Gaien Higashi Dori

San-ei Dori

Post
Office ● ●6

Yotsuya
Stn

BS 4

Yotsuya
Fire
Station
1 ●

● BS 5   *Marunouchi Line*

Yotsuya
3-chome Stn

BS 3

Gaien Nishi Dori

Akasaka
Geihin-kan

Shuto Expressway #4

Main
Gate

Meiji Jingu
Gaien Park

Experience a movie as if you were actually in it at Tokyo **Imax Theater** in Takashimaya's Times Square building. All-new 3D movies with general audience ratings play on the 18-by-25-meter screen ten times a day. To hear the film in English, tune the speaker on the 3D headgear to channel one. The theater's lobby has a commanding view of Shinjuku Gyoen and Tokyo Tower.

Sega's **Shinjuku Joypolis** game center/theme park, in the same building, is a quick way for a kid to blow his entire allowance. The favorite attractions are Ghost Hunter, a roller coaster shooting game combination, and the Power Sled, a bobsled race simulator. The Shinjuku location is the smallest Joypolis; there are bigger versions in Odaiba (see Tour 18) and Yokohama. All are extremely popular and often uncomfortably crowded. A strong command of Japanese is essential for many of the attractions.

EATING OPTIONS

Restaurants Kentucky Fried Chicken and a few other fast-food restaurants are located in the neighborhood of the Fire Museum. Several nearby coffee shops serve Western and Japanese food. Restaurant facilities in Shinjuku Gyoen offer a short menu of light meals. The Transportation Museum has a restaurant car on the fourth floor that serves curry and spaghetti for ¥700. And there are many restaurants to choose from on the twelfth, thirteenth, and fourteenth floors of the Takashimaya Times Square Building.

Picnic Possibilities The lunchroom on the tenth floor of the Fire Museum is clean and airy, with a nice view. Bring something to eat; whole milk, fruit juice, and other drinks are available. Picnics are a pleasure at both Shinjuku Gyoen and Sanei Park. At the Transportation Museum, you can take your lunch up to the benches on the museum's roof if the weather is fine. There is also a large room with tables and drink machines on the second floor, where you can eat a homemade lunch or, when available, purchase an *eki bento*. These boxed lunches featuring local delicacies are sold at nearly every train station (*eki*) in Japan, and some stations are so famous for having delicious food that trains make longer stops to give the passengers time to shop. Several of the very best "station lunches" are shipped in on Sundays and national holidays for museum visitors to try, but be warned that they go fast.

FOR INFANTS AND TODDLERS

While there is no diaper-changing spot, we were told the Fire Museum's many benches could be used. The museum's Western and Japanese toilets are clean and new; the tenth floor has a smaller toilet for tots in training. The Transportation Museum has a diaper-changing table in the ladies' bathroom on the first floor. There is no elevator in the four-story building, so you may not want to bring your stroller.

WHERE & WHEN

Yotsuya Fire Museum
消防博物館 (Shobo Hakubutsu-kan)
3–10 Yotsuya, Shinjuku-ku, Tokyo 160–0004
☎ (03) 3353–9119
東京都新宿区四ツ谷3-10　〒160-0004
OPEN: 9:30 A.M. to 5 P.M. (entry until 4:30)
CLOSED: Mon (Tues if Mon is a hol), Dec 28 to Jan 4
FEES: none
DIRECTIONS: Yotsuya 3-chome station (Marunouchi line) exit 2. Toei bus #3 bound for Harumi Futo from bus stop #4 near the west exit of Shinjuku station, bus #97 bound for Yotsuya station from Shinagawa (west exit) and Hiroo stations, bus #70 bound for Shinjuku station from Tamachi and Roppongi stations, and bus #81 bound for Waseda University from bus stop #7 near the west exit of Shibuya station all stop at Yotsuya 3-chome. By car take Shinjuku Dori to the Gaien-Higashi Dori crossing.
PARKING: none
COMMENTS: all ages, some English

Shinjuku Gyoen
新宿御苑
11 Naito-cho, Shinjuku-ku, Tokyo 160–0014
☎ (03) 3350–0151
東京都新宿区内藤町11　〒160-0014
OPEN: 9 A.M. to 4:30 P.M. (entry until 4)
CLOSED: Mon (Tues if Mon is a hol), Dec 29 to Jan 3. No hols from March 25 to April 24 and

Nov 1–15.
FEES: adults ¥200, junior/senior high students ¥50
DIRECTIONS: a 5-minute walk from Shinjuku Gyoen-mae station (Marunouchi line) or Sendagaya station (JR Sobu line). Toei bus #3 or #70 to Shinjuku 1-chome or bus #81 to Yotsuya 4-chome (for more bus details see Yotsuya Fire Museum).
PARKING: just off Shinjuku Dori, at the northeast corner of the park, hourly rate
COMMENTS: all ages, English pamphlet

Shinjuku Historical Museum
新宿歴史博物館 (Shinjuku Rekishi Haku-butsu-kan)
22 Sanei-cho, Shinjuku-ku, Tokyo 160–0008
☎ (03) 3359–2131
東京都新宿区三栄町22　〒160-0008
OPEN: 9 A.M. to 5 P.M. (entry until 4:30)
CLOSED: Mon (Tues if Mon is a hol), Dec 29 to Jan 3
FEES: adults ¥200, elementary/junior high students ¥100
DIRECTIONS: 8 minutes from Yotsuya 3-chome station (Marunouchi line), 10 minutes from Yotsuya station (JR Chuo and Sobu lines), 8 minutes from Akebonobashi station (Toei Shinjuku subway line). Toei buses #3 and #97 stop at Yotsuya 2-chome on Shinjuku Dori a few minutes' walk from the museum (see bus information under Yotsuya Fire

Museum for details). By car take Shinjuku Dori and turn north one street east of Tsunokamizaka Dori.

PARKING: limited parking available

COMMENTS: 5 and up, English pamphlet

San-ei Park

三栄公園 (San-ei Koen)

24 San-ei-cho, Shinjuku-ku, Tokyo 160–0008

東京都新宿区佐三栄町24　〒160-0008

OPEN: 24 hours

FEES: none

DIRECTIONS: see Shinjuku Historical Museum. The park is located on Sanei Dori near the museum.

PARKING: none

COMMENTS: younger children, no English

Transportation Museum

交通博物館 (Kotsu Hakubutsu-kan)

1–25 Kanda-Sudacho, Chiyoda-ku, Tokyo 101–0041

☎ (03) 3251–8481

東京都千代田区神田須田町1-25　〒101-0041

OPEN: 9:30 A.M. to 5 P.M. (entry until 4:30)

CLOSED: Mon and Dec 29 to Jan 3

FEES: adults ¥310, children 4 to 15 years old ¥150, preschoolers under 4 free

DIRECTIONS: a 5-minute walk from exit A3 of Awajicho station (Marunouchi line) and Ogawamachi station (Shinjuku line), 5 minutes from the exit for Electric Goods Town of JR Akihabara station (JR Yamanote, Keihin Tohoku, Sobu lines), 5 minutes from the exit for Showa Dori in Akihabara station (Hibiya line), a 10-minute walk from exit 6 of Kanda station (Ginza line). By car, on Chuo Dori near Manseibashi bridge.

PARKING: 30-car lot, daily rate; spots are frequently available on weekdays, but on weekends parking is next to impossible

COMMENTS: all ages, sketchy English

Tokyo Imax Theater

東京アイマックスシアター

Takashimaya Times Square, 12F

5–24–2 Sendagaya, Shibuya-ku, Tokyo 151–0051

☎ (03) 5361–3030

東京都渋谷区千駄ヶ谷5-24-2　高島屋タイムズスクエア12階　〒151-0051

OPEN: 9 times a day between 10 A.M. to 10 P.M. Sun to Thurs and 10 A.M. to 11:30 P.M. Fri, Sat, and national hols.

CLOSED: Times Square Building's three annual hols are scheduled differently every year.

FEES: adults ¥1,300, ages 13 to 18 and over 60 ¥1,000, under 12 ¥800

DIRECTIONS: visible from the new south exit of Shinjuku station (JR Yamanote, JR Chuo, Odakyu, and Keio lines; Shinjuku and Marunouchi subway lines)

PARKING: space for 900 cars in the Times Square lot. Customers spending at least ¥3,000 on entrance tickets may receive a discount worth 60 minutes of parking. Inquire at the ticket counter.

COMMENTS: 8 and up, adequate English

Shinjuku Joypolis

新宿ジョイポリス

Takashimaya Times Square, 10F/11F

5–24–2 Sendagaya, Shibuya-ku, Tokyo 151–0051

☎ (03) 5361–3040

東京都渋谷区千駄ヶ谷5-24-2　高島屋タイムズスクエア10/11階　〒151-0051

OPEN: 10 A.M. to midnight

FEES: entrance under high school ¥100, over high school ¥300. Attractions are ¥500 to ¥700 each.

DIRECTIONS: see Tokyo Imax Theater

COMMENTS: 8 and up, no English

A Streetcar Adventure

Arakawa Streetcar Line • Asukayama Park • Shibusawa Memorial Museum • Kita Ward Historical Museum • Paper Museum • Otonashi Shinsui Park • Nanushinotaki Garden • Arakawa Amusement Park • Arakawa Nature Park

Clang! Clang! goes the bell. There's a slight jolt, and you are coursing the roads on Tokyo's only remaining streetcar. The **Arakawa Streetcar Line** has a nostalgic appeal for both kids and adults, and along the route are lots of great places for families. Get off at a few of our favorite stops to soak up some local flavor and let the kids romp through the playgrounds that dot the route. We've highlighted more than enough to fill a day, so you can pick and choose whatever is right for your family.

Catching the streetcar is easy. The line intersects with other train and subway lines at Higashi Ikebukuro station (Yurakucho subway line), Otsuka station (JR Yamanote line), Oji station (JR Keihin Tohoku line and Nanboku subway line), Machiya station (Keisei

Originally built in 1911 as Oji Electric Railways, the line became part of the Tokyo Metropolitan Streetcar Lines (Toden) in 1943. Toden was once a major public transportation system carrying passengers and cargo on nearly 40 lines, but poor management and the growing popularity of the automobile were generating large losses as early as the mid-1950s. When the Tokyo government decided to cut costs by terminating the streetcar lines, residents pleaded to keep passenger lines 27 and 32. The two lines were reorganized into one and renamed the Arakawa Streetcar Line.

line and Chiyoda subway line), and Minowa station (Hibiya subway line). Find seats near the driver for the best view as you travel the city streets and avenues.

Our first stop: Asukayama station, where there are several spots of interest for school-age kids. **Asukayama Park** has more than 70,000 square meters of space to stretch your legs in, with pavilions, fountains, cascades, and spectacular cherry trees. The park also has one of the widest ranges of playground equipment we have come across, including several types of jungle gyms, an old steam locomotive that you can climb in, an old street-car that you can't, a concrete boat, a concrete castle with hide-outs, slides, and interesting walls to climb, playhouses, swings, and more. The park will also soon have three museums: the Shibusawa Memorial Museum is open now, while the Kita Ward Historical Museum and the Paper Museum are both slated to relocate to the park by 1998.

The **Paper Museum**, now located on the other side of Oji station, holds the most promise for entertaining and enlightening young minds. Learn about the history of paper, its manufacture, and its many practical and artistic uses. The current museum has an English pamphlet, English explanations on many of the exhibits, and outstanding displays; the new museum promises to be even better. *Kouzo*, *mitsumata*, and *ganpi* trees, the raw materials for making Japanese *washi* paper, grow outside on the museum's lawn at both locations. Examples of pre-paper writing materials—papyrus, parchment made of goat and sheep skin, calfskin vellum, and palm leaves—give visitors an understanding of the importance of paper in human development. A look at early paper-making machines, the history of pioneers in this industry, and the process of making paper by hand gives visitors a whole new appreciation for the value of a single sheet. There are also exhibits on the technologies used to make disposable diapers, cardboard, tissues, toilet paper, labels, postage stamps, milk and egg cartons, writing paper, newspapers, and other products.

The section highlighting paper crafts has lots of fun examples, like an origami peacock, paper flowers arranged *ikebana* style, miniature books and Bibles you need a magnifying glass to read, papier mâché animals of the Chinese zodiac, and large paper castles. You can compare grades of handmade *washi* with machine-made paper. Watch an English video on paper-making (inquire at the reception desk) or participate in a class that shows you how to make new postcards by recycling milk cartons and newspaper. Postcard classes at the old museum were held on Sundays. Call in Japanese to confirm times for this or one of the dozens of paper craft classes offered when the new museum opens its doors.

Eichi Shibusawa's mansion was destroyed in bomb raids on Tokyo, but his elegant library and stained-glass windows, guest house, and gardens remain as a memorial to the founder of Dai-Ichi Kangyo Bank, a man widely regarded as Japan's

Andrew Carnegie. For foreigners, a letter from Thomas Edison to Viscount Shibusawa is perhaps the most memorable exhibit in the **Shibusawa Memorial Museum**. Not much else here will appeal to the foreign visitor. There are no English explanations, but this might change when the other two museums open.

At this time, we have little information on the **Kita Ward Historical Museum**, which will soon move from a dilapidated facility to a new modern structure in the park, the largest of the three museums. The museum's collection includes antiques and pottery excavated from the soil of Kita Ward.

All aboard for the next stop, Oji station. Here you can take off your shoes, roll up your pants, and go wading at **Otonashi Shinsui Park**, a short walk from the station. Chosen as one of Tokyo's top one hundred parks, this one is small but wonderfully landscaped. The whole park is just a short, shallow section of the Shakujii river and its banks, but bridges made from curious pieces of driftwood and artfully positioned rocks, a water wheel, Meiji-period street lanterns, and stone staircases create a special ambiance. In spring, the north bank is lined with pink cherry blossoms, and a large weeping willow at the end of the park sports lovely pale green leaves.

You can continue down the riverbank for some bird watching or follow the map to **Nanushinotaki Garden**, an old Japanese garden with a teahouse, creeks, waterfalls, and ponds inhabited by ducks and bright-colored carp. Artistic bridges and Japanese-style gazebos are scattered among waterways and dense groves of trees. The main entrance to the park with its old-style wooden signboard looks almost like a temple gate. The garden, originally built in the late Edo period, underwent several changes and improvements in the Meiji period, including the planting of over a hundred maple trees. Maps posted near the gates and throughout the park come in handy in finding the waterfalls, as tall trees sometimes block your view of the landscape. This is a great place to seek some relief on a scorching summer day or to view the autumn colors in an oasis of calm. Just don't forget your bug spray.

Preschoolers or young elementary school students in your group? Get off the streetcar at Arakawa Yuenchi-mae station for the ward-owned **Arakawa Amusement Park**, priced to please parents experiencing yen shock. And it only feels cheap to your pocket book. A merry-go-round, a Ferris wheel, and a train have no age limitations for passengers. You must be four to ride the Sky Cycle and the Coffee Cups and at least in elementary school to ride the roller coaster. All rides cost ¥100 each for kids, ¥200 for adults—and if you buy tickets in sheets of seven or fourteen you get a discount. There are a number of coin-operated rides, plus a fishing hole with poles and bait, a crafts center (craft instructions in Japanese only), playground equipment, a pond with swans, and a water play area that opens in the summer.

The park's top-notch petting zoo wins kudos from parents for the way the attendants teach kids to respect the animals, which include guinea pigs, rabbits, sheep, goats, monkeys, meerkats, raccoons, kangaroos, cows, ponies, and birds of all sorts. Bring along carrot sticks and cabbage leaves, or *komatsuna*, a leafy vegetable resembling spinach, so you can feed the guinea pigs. (Bring only these vegetables as the attendants won't let you feed anything else to the furry creatures.) The guinea pig and rabbit cages are available for 20 minutes at a time with a 10-minute rest interval for the animals between sessions. Kids from ages four to ten can ride the ponies for free all year round; just ask for a pony ride ticket at the front gate. Only thirty children can ride at each of the three sessions: 10:30 to 11 A.M., 1:30 to 2 P.M., and 3 to 3:30 P.M. Tickets are available on a first-come, first-served basis starting 1 hour before the session and closing 10 minutes before it starts.

Arakawa Yuenchi can take all day, especially if you want to fish or try out the crafts center. They have a long list of crafts projects for every age from toddlers (play dough, painting) up to fourth graders and beyond (making tops, kites, various levels of origami, etc.). But the amusement park is just one of the attractions in this area. In fact, you might have a little trouble getting your kids to it. On the way you pass colorful playground equipment, the Sports House's heated indoor pool and training room, and an outdoor roller-skating rink that becomes a pool in July and August. All of these are adjacent to each other on one street with Arakawa Amusement Park at the end, and all are open to the public.

Beyond the amusement park is a water bus pier. **Tokyo Mizube Cruising Lines** operates water buses from the pier on Fridays, Saturdays, Sundays, and national holidays. There are two routes: the Daimawari Course takes you up the Sumidagawa and down the Arakawa to Kasai Seaside Park (see Tour 23), and the Sumidagawa river Course takes you past Sakurabashi to Ryogoku (Tour 2). Schedules change seasonally.

Ride the streetcar six more stops as it curves south beyond the end of our map. Step down at Arakawa 2-chome station and look for the entrance to **Arakawa Nature Park** on the east side of the tracks. This three-part park appeals to kids from toddlers through grade school. The park's "Athletic Ground" includes wall scaling, a rope-and-pulley coaster to sail your body across the little field, a pyramid of nets to climb, and an assortment of wooden jungle gyms. A playground for toddlers and preschoolers has the regular assortment of small swings, slides, and see-saws. In the bug observatory, you can see specimens of Japan's famous *kabuto* (helmet) beetles. A pond with swans, ducks, and carp creates a pleasant atmosphere. One edge of the pond has beds of native grasses, like *shobu,* which Japanese put in their baths on Children's Day, May 5. The park also has a large variety of blooming trees, shrubs, and flowers, carefully chosen to ensure that visitors can enjoy flowers throughout the year.

The far end of the nature park has a fabulous place to ride bikes. Well land-scaped, this traffic park, like others in the city, has small streets and stoplights to teach kids about traffic safety. The park lends out a wide variety of things to ride: little pedal cars, tricycles, go-carts, bikes in sizes 14 to 24 inches, and two sizes of unicycles, 16 and 20 inches. To borrow a bike, pick one out, fill out a registration form (it's in Japanese but the people there will kindly walk you through it), and receive a plastic card and vehicle, free of charge. Then you're off. Fountains and benches are refresh-ing for parents who wait while the kids wear themselves out. One warning: certain square areas of the park are reserved for either tricycles and pedal cars, go-carts, or unicycles. If your school-aged child takes his big go-cart to the tricycle section where the little ones ride, he'll hear a pretty vociferous *"dame"* (that's forbidden!) from the otherwise avuncular senior citizens who run the traffic park. So be sure to look at what types of cycles are in the square before your child enters, although any cycle can be ridden on the "streets" that surround the squares.

We're nearing the end of the streetcar line now, but even though we skipped some expensive and well-known spots like Ikebukuro's overpriced Sunshine City, we've described far more places than you can visit in one trip. Spend a day at the Arakawa Amusement Park, then return to see Asukayama and Oji, or combine one of the latter two with Arakawa Nature Park. Any way you do it, you are sure to have a memorable streetcar adventure.

EATING OPTIONS

Restaurants There are a few restaurants in the Asukayama area but nothing worth mentioning—if you want to eat there, we suggest you bring your lunch. There are many Japanese restaurants between Otonashi Shinsui Park and Nanushinotaki Garden. Arakawa Amusement Park has no restaurants but near the station are a Mos Burger with picture books to keep kids occupied, a sushi restaurant, and a couple of coffee shops. Keep your ticket stub and you can reenter the amusement park. Arakawa Nature Park also has no restaurants and there are few in the neighborhood.

Picnic Possibilities Asukayama Park has lots of places to sit down but few tables and no vending machines for drinks. The same goes for Otonashi Shinsui Park and Nanushinotaki Garden. Still, you'll find lots of picnickers in all of these places. Arakawa Yuenchi has tables and benches outdoors. You can buy snacks and drinks on the first floor of the rest house and eat at the indoor tables on the second floor; the rest

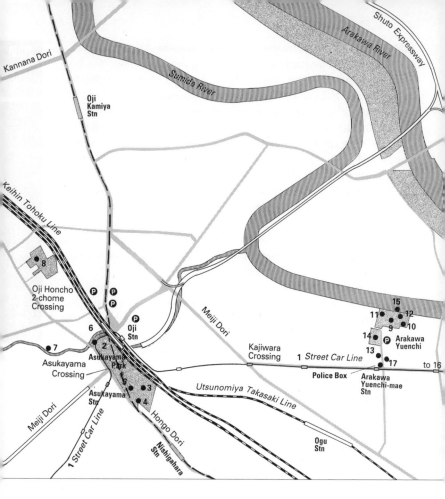

PLACES TO VISIT

1. Street Car Line
2. Asukayama Park
3. Shibusawa Memorial Museum
4. Paper Museum
5. Kita Ward Historical Museum
6. Otonashi Shinsui Park
7. Shakujiigawa River
8. Nanushinotaki Garden
9. Arakawa Amusement Park
10. Fishing
11. Water Play Area
12. Petting Zoo
13. Sports House
14. Roller Skating
15. Water Bus Stop
16. Arakawa Nature Park
17. Mos Burger

house is located close to the back of the section with the rides. Arakawa Nature Park has vending machines in several areas as well as benches and tables. Near the pond is the most scenic spot to eat your lunch.

FOR INFANTS AND TODDLERS

Asukayama Park has no diapering or nursing facilities at the time of this writing, although when the Kita Ward Historical Museum and the Paper Museum reopen there, they may have facilities. The park does have a lot of toddler-friendly play equipment and large low-lying flat rocks where you can make a quick change if necessary. Arakawa Amusement Park has scores of tame coin-operated rides as well as a merry-go-round and a train that toddlers can ride. You'll find a diaper-changing table in the restroom for the handicapped near the fishing hole, but no private place to nurse. Free stroller rental is available at the front gate. Arakawa Nature Park has no nursing facilities but there is a diaper-changing table in the ladies' restroom near the traffic park.

WHERE & WHEN

Asukayama Park
飛鳥山公園 (Asukayama Koen)
1–1–3 Oji, Kita-ku, Tokyo 114–0002
☎ (03) 3910–8882 (9 A.M. to 5 P.M.)
東京都北区王子1-1-3　〒114-0002
OPEN: 24 hours
DIRECTIONS: a 5-minute walk from Oji station (Arakawa streetcar line) or a 1-minute walk from the south exit of Oji station (JR Keihin Tohoku line). By car, at Asukayama intersection of Meiji Dori and Hongo Dori.
PARKING: none
COMMENTS: all ages, no English

Paper Museum
紙の博物館 (Kami no Hakubutsu-kan)
1–1–3 Oji, Kita-ku, Tokyo 114–0002
☎ (03) 3911–3545
東京都北区王子1-1-3　〒114-0002
(no other information available at the time of this writing)

COMMENTS: 5 and up, English pamphlet

Shibusawa Memorial Museum
渋沢栄一資料館 (Shibusawa Eiichi Shiryo-kan)
2–16–1 Nishigahara, Kita-ku, Tokyo 114–0024
☎ (03) 3910–0005
東京都北区西ヶ原2-16-1　〒114-0024
OPEN: 10 A.M. to 4 P.M.
CLOSED: Sun and national hols, also Dec 20 to Jan 10
FEES: adults ¥300, students ¥150
DIRECTIONS: see Asukayama Park
COMMENTS: 5 and up, no English

Kita Ward Historical Museum
北区立郷土博物館 (Kita Kuritsu Kyodo Hakubutsu-kan)
1–1–3 Oji, Kita-ku, Tokyo 114–0002
☎ (03) 3914–4820

東京都北区王子1-1-3　〒114-0002
(no other information available at the time
of this writing)

COMMENTS: 5 and up, no English

Otonashi Shinsui Park

音無親水公園 (Otonashi Shinsui Koen)
1–1 Saki Oji Honcho, Kita-ku, Tokyo 114–0022
☎ (03) 3908–1111 (Kita Ward Office Parks
Division)
東京都北区王子本町1-1先　〒114-0022

OPEN: 24 hours

DIRECTIONS: short walk from the north exit of
Oji station (Arakawa and JR Keihin Tohoku
lines, and Nanboku subway line). By car,
turn left at Asukayama intersection of Meiji
Dori and Hongo Dori.

PARKING: none

COMMENTS: all ages, no English

Nanushinotaki Garden

名主の滝公園 (Nanushinotaki Koen)
1–15–25 Kishi Machi, Kita-ku, Tokyo 114–
0021
☎ (03) 3908–1111 (Kita Ward Office Parks
Division)
東京都北区岸町1-15-25　〒114-0021

OPEN: 9 A.M. to 5 P.M., until 6 from July 15 to
Sept 15. Admission until 30 minutes before
closing.

CLOSED: Dec 29 to Jan 3

FEES: none

DIRECTIONS: a 10-minute walk from the north
exit of Oji station (Arakawa and JR Keihin
Tohoku lines, and Nanboku subway line). By
car, take Meiji Dori to Asukayama intersection and turn left. Turn right at the 1st traffic
light past Oji Honcho 2 crossing, and the
park will be on the right.

PARKING: none

COMMENTS: all ages, no English

Arakawa Amusement Park, Roller-Skating Rink/Pool, Sports House

荒川遊園地 (Arakawa Yuenchi)
6–35–11 Nishi Ogu, Arakawa-ku, Tokyo 116–
0011
☎ (03) 3893–6003 (amusement park and skating rink/pool), (03) 3800–7333 (Sports House)
東京都荒川区西尾久6-35-11　〒116-0011

OPEN: 9 A.M. to 6 P.M.

CLOSED: Mon (Tues if Mon is a hol), Dec 29 to
Jan 3

FEES: admission is ¥130 for those over 15,
younger children and senior citizens over 65
enter free. Rides are ¥200 for adults and ¥100
for kids. Fishing costs include poles and nets;
bait is ¥60 and hooks are ¥10.

Fishing Cost	Children	Adults
all day	¥400	¥1,300
4 hours	¥250	¥800
1 hour	¥100	¥350
overtime	¥100	¥350

Sports House	Time	Children	Adults
Pools	2 hours	¥250	¥500
Training Room	3 hours		¥300
Arena	3 hours	¥200	¥400

Roller-skating, available from Oct through
May, costs ¥100 for adults and ¥50 for children per hour. Skate rental is ¥60 for adults
and ¥50 for children. Sizes to 28 centimeters.

The outdoor pool, available in July and
Aug, costs ¥350 for adults and ¥150 for children for 2 hours.

DIRECTIONS: a 3-minute walk from Arakawa
Yuenchi-mae streetcar stop. On Sat, a mini city
bus takes twenty passengers at a time from the
park to Minami Senju station (Hibiya subway
line, JR Joban line) at 12 P.M., 2 P.M., and 4
P.M., and to Nippori station (JR Yamanote,
Keihin Tohoku, and Keisei lines) at 1 P.M.

and 3 P.M. By car, take Meiji Dori at Kajiwara crossing; turn left and drive along the streetcar tracks. Arakawa Amusement Park will appear on your left. At the police box turn left into the small shopping street. Parking is on your left in front of the Sports House.

PARKING: available for cars less than 2.1 meters high from 8:30 A.M. to 8 P.M., at an hourly rate. Lot holds 114 cars.

COMMENTS: toddlers to younger elementary school students, no English; remember to bring carrots or cabbage so your kids can feed the rabbits

Tokyo Mizube Cruising Lines
東京都公園協会水辺ライン

☎ (03) 5608–8922

OPEN: stops at Arakawa Amusement Park pier on Fri, Sat, Sun, and national hols. Schedules change with the season.

FEES: *Sumida River Course*: ¥500 to ¥1,500 for adults, ¥250 to ¥750 for children. *Grand Trip Course*: ¥500 to ¥2,000 for adults, ¥250 to ¥1,000 for children.

DIRECTIONS: see Arakawa Amusement Park
COMMENTS: all ages, no English pamphlet

Arakawa Nature Park
荒川自然公園 (Arakawa Shizen Koen)
8–25–3 Arakawa, Arakawa-ku, Tokyo 116–0002
☎ (03) 3803–4042
東京都荒川区荒川8-25-3　〒116-0002

OPEN: 9 A.M. to 5 P.M. Oct to April; 7 A.M. to 7 P.M. May to Sept

CLOSED: Mon (Tues if Mon is a hol)

FEES: none

DIRECTIONS: less than 1 minute from the east side of Arakawa 2-chome station (Arakawa line). By car, take Meiji Dori to Sun Pearl Arakawa-mae crossing, turn left past Sun Pearl Arakawa and Arakawa Park. At Sun Pearl Arakawa Kita crossing turn left and continue straight until you see the nature park on your right.

PARKING: none

COMMENTS: toddler to younger elementary school students, no English

18

Sail Away to the Museum of Maritime Science

**Water Bus • Museum of Maritime Science • Seaside
Pools • Shiokaze Park • Yurikamome Monorail**

Six floors jam-packed with ways to learn about ships await you at the Museum
of Maritime Science. We suggest you arrive by boat and, after exploring the
museum, head for Shiokaze Park to soak up some rays, stroll the shoreline, or
romp in the playground.

The Tokyo harbor is one of the busiest in the world; ships glide in and out carrying
everything from bananas to oil to cars. You'll get an excellent view of this easy-to-miss
side of the city as you take the **water bus from Hinode Pier** in Hamamatsucho
to the **Museum of Maritime Science**. Your 40-minute ride on the ferry offers a
scenic harbor view of the new architectural developments in the area. Before you
reach your destination, Ome Pier, the boat stops at Harumi and Odaiba Seaside Park.
Boats run every 45 minutes starting at 10 A.M. You can also buy discount tickets at the
pier that include the ferry and entrance to the Museum of Maritime Science. See Tour
18 for a map of the water bus routes.

When you dock, you'll see the museum—a huge white building in the shape of
a 60,000-ton passenger liner. Head inside to learn all about oceangoing vessels. The
glass and marble entrance hall resembles the lobby of a deluxe cruise ship, and the
displays throughout are modern and attractive. The museum has English titles on all
display cases that will satisfy the questions of most preschool kids, and the contents of
many exhibits speak for themselves. Older visitors with a strong interest in seafaring
may want to bring along a friend who can translate.

The exhibits tell the history of ships from ancient boats to modern tankers, container vessels, and nuclear-powered ships. You will see models of some of the most

famous vessels to sail the seas. An exhibit called "Ships Carrying Culture and Civilization" houses a model of a Viking ship and Christopher Columbus's *Santa Maria*. In the next glass case you'll see a ship belonging to Holland's East India Company, and Captain Nelson's *Victory*. The case labeled "The First Revolution of Materials and Propulsion" holds two famous clippers: the *Sea Witch* and the *Cutty Sark*. Ships from Japan's Meiji and Showa periods take up several cases, and a whole section on future concepts in shipbuilding introduces techno-superliners with no engines or screw propellers. In keeping with the ship design of the structure, there's a giant engine room on the first floor to teach visitors about propulsion.

Marine development is, appropriately, the theme of the basement floor, where cleverly constructed panoramas illustrate prospective ways to use the sea floor. You'll see ideas on how to extract minerals and oil, survey marine life, and use the sea as an energy source as well as for living and leisure space.

On the second floor, you'll learn about marine transportation and the ports and harbors that ships sail between, as well as maritime safety rules and fishing regulations. Exhibits teach lighthouse codes and tell of dramatic water rescues. Compare model ships designed for various uses and see how those for transporting raw materials or cars differ from oil tankers, ferries, conventional passenger liners, or high-speed passenger ships with jet foils. The submarine corner is one of the highlights of the naval defense section, also located on the second floor. Check for unfriendly vessels in the Periscope Room.

On the third floor, models and real wooden canoes represent "Ships of the World." Notable exhibits include a model of an ancient Thai ship used to transport the king, and the floating wooden buckets used by *ama*, the famous female pearl divers of Japan who dive without oxygen tanks. There is also a room dedicated to the late Ryoichi Sasagawa, founder of the ship museum, who made his fortune in boat racing and was once a prominent figure in Japan. Follow the corridor to your right, where you can steer a radio-controlled model ship around an island and through the waters of an artificial sea for ¥100.

The fourth floor is occupied by a Chinese restaurant—decorated to look like the dining room of a luxury passenger ship—offering diners an excellent view of the surrounding harbor, while the fifth floor is mainly used for private parties. As you explore the ship, don't miss the "bridge" on the sixth floor. Take a turn at the tiller of a simulator and navigate a 28,000-ton ship through Tokyo harbor, then examine the wide array of instrumentation used to navigate a ship this size across the ocean. You'll also want to visit the observatory high above the upper deck, since it has a fantastic view of Tokyo as well as of the harbor and its boats.

Outside the museum are a number of related attractions. Near the parking lot is a "flying boat," a Kawanishi H8K2 seaplane used by the Japanese navy in WWII. The Anorizaki lighthouse, built in 1873, is Japan's oldest wooden lighthouse. The *Soya*, a former Japanese research vessel, made six trips to Antarctica before permanently docking next to the museum. Climb aboard the bright orange ship and explore her narrow passageways and tiny cabins. Then head for the *Yotei Maru*, the large ferry resting at anchor just beyond the *Soya*. The *Yotei Maru* carried steam locomotives and later electric trains plus their passengers from Aomori, the northern tip of Honshu, to Hakodate in Hokkaido. Now it is a floating playland. Look at what life is like under the sea, listen to sounds of the ocean, take a virtual reality ride on the back of a dolphin, or go zooming through fish habitats on an underwater scooter simulator.

Downstairs you can watch a film about the adventures of a dolphin and a little boy, and relive a bit of human drama from Aomori in 1955. Mechanical mannequins, sound effects, stage sets, and period props create an early-morning atmosphere. In the market, the fishmonger fusses with his wife in a northern dialect; hawkers sell apples and *yaki-imo* (hot sweet potatoes). At the station, an overburdened mother asks the station manager about departure schedules. Passengers and porters deal with baggage as the people and the train itself are moved aboard the ferry. Exit near the old-style kiosk and head upstairs for the gift shop, the video game center, and the view from the ship's deck.

From mid-July to the end of August, you can cool off in the waters of the Museum of Maritime Science's **Seaside Pools**, although we thought the prices were quite steep. Swim in the rectangular jumbo pool, pretend to river-raft in the 200-meter circular current pool, or try the thrills of a curving waterslide. On Sundays and holidays during the pool's off-season you can hop into pedal boats in the jumbo pool for a reasonable price. There is also a kiddie pool for those over three.

Beyond the museum's parking lot is **Shiokaze Park**, a large, two-part seaside park that makes an excellent place to enjoy harbor action. Watch giant freighters plow through the waves as gulls wheel overhead. Green lawns, Washington palm trees, fountains, sunbathing areas, and a play area featuring a wooden ship with a roller slide on its stern make the south part of the park a great spot to dry off after a dip in the pool. To go home you can take the new **Yurikamome Monorail** from either Fune-no-Kagakukan station near the Museum of Maritime Science or Daiba station near Odaiba Seaside Park (see Other Things to Do in the Area) behind the Nikko Tokyo Hotel. The new unmanned monorail, running from Shinbashi to Ariake, takes you across the Rainbow bridge and makes a good choice for families who want a full day out. The last water bus leaves for Hinode Pier at 4:30 P.M., half an hour before the Museum of Maritime Science closes.

Other Things to Do in the Area

Follow one of Shiokaze Park's walking courses and look at the sights. The longest course, 1.7 kilometers one way, leads you across a small bridge, through the north part of Shiokaze, and on to **Odaiba Seaside Park**. (You can also get to Odaiba from the Museum of Maritime Science by water bus.) Halfway through the park, a rocky shoreline turns into a thin strip of sandy beach where the kids can fish, swim, or build sandcastles. This area is also the local windsurfers' haven and has a board-storage facility. You can have an after-swim shower in the Marine House.

Behind Odaiba Seaside Park lies **Decks**, six floors of restaurants and shopping. Many of the stores are American camping and sporting goods chains, but the prices are Japanese.

At Odaiba, walk round the curving beach to the furthest tip of land, **Daisan Daiba**, to relive a page in Japan's history. This land was reclaimed in 1853 to use in defending Tokyo Bay from the return of Commodore Perry's black ships. Destroyed in the Great Kanto Earthquake of 1923, the few remains of the fortress and its cannonry tell wordlessly of Tokugawa Japan's fear of the outside world. The tiny rectangular islands further out in the water were created as a battery at the same time.

Next door, **Sega's Tokyo Joypolis** is another good way to spend money and have little to show for it. But if you've said no to snowboards or hotdogging on rollerblades or skateboards, this place has a safe alternative for kids over 130 centimeters (about 4'3"). The Halfpipe Canyon swings 7 meters high at 36 kilometers an hour. Among the ten other large attractions are an indoor roller coaster with a shooting game and a freefall ride. There are also rooms full of Sega coin-operated games. Many of the games and attractions require substantial Japanese for full participation.

EATING OPTIONS

Restaurants   Kaio, a Chinese restaurant on the fourth floor of the Museum of Maritime Science, offers good food, a pleasant atmosphere, and a great view of the harbor. For about half the price you can have snacks or a small meal of spaghetti or hot dogs at Cabin, a fast-food café located outside the "stern" of the museum building

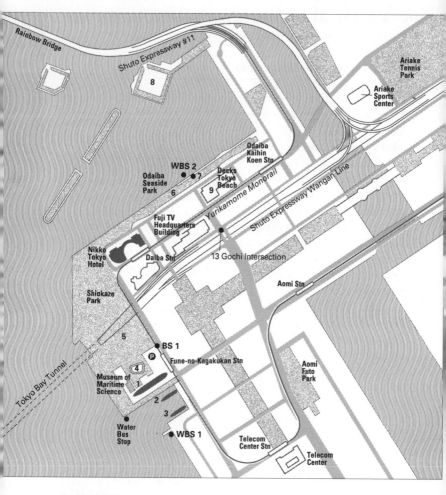

PLACES TO VISIT

1. Museum of Maritime Science, Cabin Restaurant
2. The *Soya*
3. The *Yotei Maru*
4. Seaside Pools
5. Shiokaze Park
6. Odaiba Seaside Park

7. Marine House
8. Daisan Daiba
9. Decks Tokyo Beach, Tokyo Joypolis

BS 1. Kaijo Koen-mae Bus Stop
WBS 1. Water Bus for Ship Museum
WBS 2. Water Bus for Odaiba Seaside Park

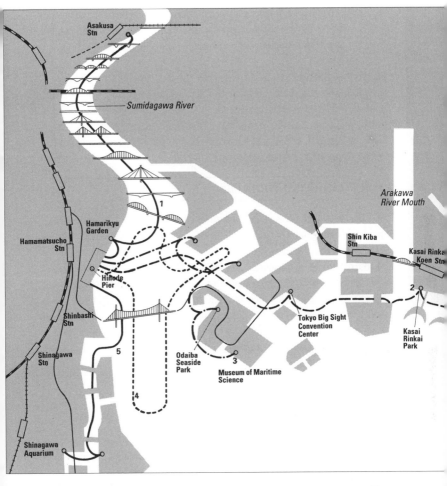

1. **Sumida River Line**——(Asakusa to Hinode, 40 minutes). Go under the river's 12 different brigades through *Shitamachi*, old downtown Tokyo (see Tour 1).

2. **Kasai Sealife Park Line**——(Hinode to Kasai Rinkai Park, 55 minutes). See the newly developed area over the Rainbow Bridge with stops at Wakasu Kaihin Park and Kasai (Tours 27 and 23).

3. **Museum of Maritime Science Line**——(Hinode to Museum of Maritime Science, 35 minutes). Use this line for Tour 18.

4. **Harbor Cruise Line**——(Roundtrip from Hinode Pier, 45 minutes). Good for summer nights or when you don't particularly want to get anywhere.

5. **Canal Cruise Line**————(Hinode to Shinagawa Aquarium via Oi Kaihin Park, 35 minutes). A fun way to take young children to the Shinagawa Aquarium (see Tour 23).

opposite the parking lot. Neither place caters especially to children, but Cabin does have a terrace, so you can enjoy an open-air feast if you choose. There are a handful of restaurants in Odaiba Seaside Park, and over two floors of restaurants at Decks.

Picnic Possibilities There are picnic tables in front of the Museum of Maritime Science, and Shiozake Park is just next door. If you'd like something to round out the lunch you've brought, drinks and ice cream are available from vending machines in the corridor on the right side of the museum entrance, and there is a shop in Shiokaze Park that sells snacks for picnickers. You can also spread a blanket at Odaiba Seaside Park or Daisan Daiba.

FOR INFANTS AND TODDLERS

All of the ladies' bathrooms in the museum building have cribs for diaper-changing. You should be able to get hot water from the café or the restaurant. Bringing a stroller is probably a good idea as the museum is so large, but make it a lightweight one because not all parts of the ship can be reached by elevator. Also, you'll have to park it at the entrance when you explore the *Soya* or the *Yotei Maru*—they have lots of staircases, making a stroller more of a burden than an aid. You can easily take a stroller from Shiokaze Park to Odaiba. Watch your toddlers carefully on Daisan Daiba, where it would be easy for them to plunge into the sea. Decks has a nursing room and diaper-changing area on the fourth floor.

WHERE & WHEN

Hinode Pier Water Bus
観光汽船水上バス

2–7–104 Kaigan, Minato-ku, Tokyo 105– 0022
☎ (03) 3457–7830
東京都港区海岸2-7-104　〒105-0022
SCHEDULE: boats leave for the Ship Museum at 10, 10:45, 11:30, 12:15, 1, 1:45, 2:30, 3:15, 4, and 4:45. In the summer months, schedules may vary, with more departures.
CLOSED: Dec 29–31
FEES: adults ¥520, children ¥260. Discount ticket for a one-way trip to Ship Museum and entrance to Ship Museum, *Soya,* and *Yotei Maru* costs ¥1,270 for adults, ¥870 for junior

high students, and ¥640 for younger children.

DIRECTIONS: see Sumida River Ferry in Tour 1.
PARKING: none, but there are garages in buildings in the area

Museum of Maritime Science
船の科学館 (Fune-no-Kagaku-kan)

3–1 Higashi Yashio, Shinagawa-ku, Tokyo 135–0092
☎ (03) 5500–1111
東京都品川区東八潮3-1　〒135-0092
OPEN: 10 A.M. to 5 P.M. weekdays, (6 P.M. Sat, Sun, and hols)

CLOSED: Dec 28 to Dec 31

FEES: Pool fees are ¥2,800 for adults and ¥1,400 for children. The pedal boats are ¥300.

	Hon Kan and Soya Ticket	Soya and Yotei Maru Ticket	Kyotsu Ticket
Adult	¥700	¥600	¥1,000
Child	¥400	¥350	¥600

Note: *Hon Kan* Ticket includes entrance to museum and *Soya Yotei Maru* Ticket includes entrance to *Yotei Maru* and *Soya*. *Kyotsu* Ticket includes entrance to museum, *Soya*, and *Yotei Maru* Child's fee is for children aged five through junior high school.

DIRECTIONS: see Hinode Pier Water Bus above for directions by water bus. By rail, the museum is a 1-minute walk from Fune-no-Kagakukan station on the Yurikamome Monorail. Or, take bus #01 bound for Monzen-Nakacho station from bus stop #12 on the east side (Konan exit) of Shinagawa station. Get off at Kaijo Koen-mae. From exit 3 of Monzen-Nakacho station (Tozai subway line) turn left on Eitai Dori and board bus #01 bound for Shinagawa. Get off at Kaijo Koen-mae. By car, take expressway #11 and exit at Daiba. You can also take the Bayshore line expressway (Kosoku Wangansen) and exit at 13 Gochi if you are coming from the southwest or the Ariake ramp if you are coming from the northeast.

PARKING: large outdoor lot, hourly rate

COMMENTS: 5 and up, sketchy English

Shiokaze Park

潮風公園 (Shiokaze Koen)

1–2 Higashi Yashio, Shinagawa-ku, Tokyo 135–0092

☎ (03) 5500–2455

東京都品川区東八潮1-2　〒135-0092

OPEN: 24 hours

DIRECTIONS: see Museum of Maritime Science. The park is northwest and adjacent to the museum grounds.

PARKING: Shiokaze has two parking lots. The south lot holds 70 cars and the north lot holds 120. Hourly rate up to 7 hours, after which a daily rate applies.

COMMENTS: all ages, good English map on sign boards

Odaiba Seaside Park

お台場海浜公園 (Odaiba Kaihin Koen)

1–4–1 Daiba 1-chome, Minato-ku, Tokyo 135–0091

東京都港区台場1-4-1　〒135-0091

OPEN: 24 hours

DIRECTIONS: a few minutes' walk from Daiba station on the Yurikamome Monorail line, behind the Nikko Tokyo Hotel. By car, from the Rainbow bridge use the Daiba interchange or the Ariake interchange from the Bayshore line expressway (Kosoku Wangansen). The park is adjacent to Shiokaze Park.

PARKING: 100-car lot, hourly rate

COMMENTS: all ages, English pamphlet of park

Decks Tokyo Beach

デックス トーキョウ ビーチ

1–6–1 Daiba, Minato-ku, Tokyo 135–0091

☎ (03) 5500–5050

東京都港区台場1-6-1　〒135-0091

OPEN: daily 11 A.M. to 9 P.M. (boutique), or 11 P.M. (restaurant)

DIRECTIONS: see Odaiba Seaside Park

PARKING: 400-car lot, hourly rate

COMMENTS: nursing room

Take Off and Land at Narita's Aviation Museum

Narita Museum of Aeronautical Sciences • Narita Airport Course

Noses aimed skyward, sleek 747s speed down the Narita runway and thrust themselves into flight just a stone's throw away from the **Narita Museum of Aeronautical Sciences**. While Narita is about 70 minutes from Tokyo, most people find reasons to visit Japan's main international airport fairly regularly. Though the airport has observation decks on both of its terminals, the view, blocked by buildings, cannot compare to the museum's. A field full of aircraft and five floors of hands-on fun will take the sting out of seeing off relatives, prepare children for plane trips, and entertain any would-be pilot or airplane aficionado. The English at the museum is limited, but the displays are excellent so we've provided some explanations.

Climb into the cockpit of a small Mitsubishi plane and pretend to pilot it to an exotic destination, or race a friend taking a turn at the controls of a nearby Puma helicopter. You are allowed to board and explore five of the aircraft that decorate the museum lawn, including an American-made Aero Commander. A radar antenna and beacon lights make it all seem real.

Inside the museum are more planes and explanations on how they work. Buttons start propellers, switch on lights, engage engines, and even let you hear the roar of a jet. On the first floor you'll find information on important principles behind the miracle of flight. Although heavier than air, planes fly because their engines are powerful enough to provide swift forward motion. Air flowing over the curved top of the wing travels faster than air moving under the wing's flat bottom, resulting in a difference in air pressure. The air below the wings is heavier and provides more resistance than the air above, creating lift and keeping the plane in the air. In one large exhibit, actual wings are sliced up like a cucumber to show in cross sections how different parts of a wing's airfoil shape vary in thickness.

Wings are slightly slanted so that the plane pushes down on the surrounding air, which pushes back up against it. This also moves the plane aloft, as you'll learn by pulling the levers on one exhibit. These let you vary the angle of the wing and hence the wing lift. Helicopters use the same principles, except that their "wings" are rotating blades. One display illustrates how pilots maneuver helicopters by altering the propeller pitch, or angle.

Test your understanding of these concepts in one of the cockpits or simulators in the museum. The most exciting, the DC-8 simulator in Playroom 2, takes you over Tokyo Bay. (Check the time schedule for this soon after entering the museum.) You can also experience the early days of flight on a man-powered aircraft simulator that estimates your flying speed and distance. Japanese-language films, books, and other materials explaining aviation can be found in the event hall and library, both on the first floor.

The second floor has more hands-on exhibits illustrating various airplane functions, plus a detailed model of Narita Airport complete with buttons that light up runways and point out interesting parts of the facility. Several hundred models donated by hobbyists show how aircraft engineering has developed through the years, from the first small, light planes to supersonic jets and helicopters.

The museum's location at the end of Narita runway #1 makes the upper floors one of the best places in the world to view airport action. Bring binoculars for an even better view of airplanes taking off and landing, or pulling into the hangars nearby. The third floor is an outdoor observation deck, while floors four and five are built in the shape of a control tower. Divide your party into pairs if you decide to visit the museum's small restaurant on the fourth floor, the best spot around to sit and watch jets while sipping drinks or spooning down ice cream. The small tables by the window seat only two people. Order before you are seated by purchasing tickets for the food you want at a machine just inside the entrance.

Listen to actual radio conversations between Narita's traffic controllers and the pilots of incoming and outgoing flights in the fifth-floor control room exhibit. While English speakers will have no trouble following these exchanges, volunteers are sometimes present to translate them into Japanese for local visitors. The museum director suggests 40 minutes to 2 hours to see everything. We suggest 2 hours minimum. Even on weekends, the museum is usually not crowded—unless you have the bad luck to come at the same time as a tour group.

If you still have several hours of daylight left before 5 P.M., head to **Narita Airport Course** for some energy-burning outdoor fun. Scale, slide, climb, and jump. You will use muscles you never even realized were part of your body on the forty-point nature obstacle course. Crawl like a crab, swing like Tarzan, traverse swaying rope bridges like Indiana Jones, and race across sinking steps like a character in a video game. The Champion Course takes an estimated 80 minutes to complete. There is also a tamer course for preschoolers. Dress for dirt unless it has rained the day before—then dress for mud.

The park has shower facilities, coin lockers, uniform and shoe rental (to sizes L and 27 centimeters, respectively), and a first aid station. For a little extra money, you can ride on all sorts of crazy-shaped cycles, do a crafts project, try your hand at miniature golf, or find your way through the Family Maze. This is much trickier than it looks from the outside; you are supposed to collect five stamps while you work your way through. The attendant will take your ticket, clock you in, and give you a card to put the stamps on. At the fishing hole, bamboo poles and bait are provided for you. Catch all you like but you can only keep two (depending on the size), and the staff will bag them. This is actually generous, as most fishing holes we have researched charge more for fishing, then either prohibit you from taking the catch or charge you per fish.

You can plant peanuts and potatoes in the spring or come later for the autumn harvest. Those with Japanese language skills may also participate in a 5-kilometer orienteering course and several types of nature quizzes. No one speaks English here and everything is written in Japanese only, but the people are warm-hearted and gestures (plus the glossary in this book) will go a long way.

Other Things to Do in the Area

Children enjoy the calming environment, beautiful blossoms, and spacious grounds of **Chiba Prefectural Botanical Garden**. Over 41,000 plants belonging to 264 species and 66 families fill the garden. Not all are named on the English pamphlet, but this is one of the best places here to teach your kids what plants and flowers are called in English-speaking countries. Get a copy at the main office; it also contains a map. The garden has a traditional Japanese section featuring ponds with little stone bridges and winding paths, rock gardens, and thick groves of trees, including a little orchard of Japanese apricots. Small woods of conifers, deciduous trees, and evergreens help youngsters learn the difference between tree families. If you aren't up to the Narita Airport Course, Chiba Prefectural Botanical Garden makes a good option. It's lovely and it's free.

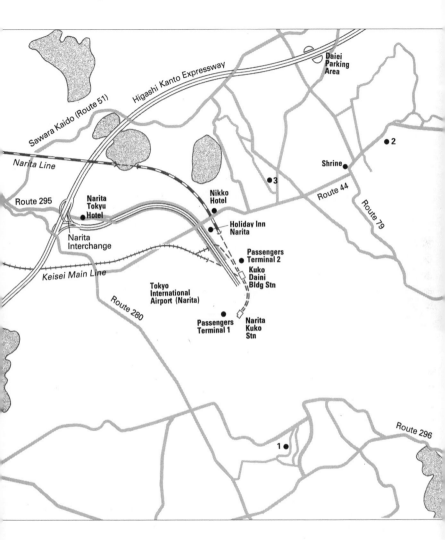

PLACES TO VISIT

1. Narita Museum of Aeronautical Science
2. Narita Airport Course
3. Chiba Prefectural Botanical Garden

EATING OPTIONS

Restaurants Balloon, located on the fourth floor of the Museum of Aeronautical Sciences, serves light Western dishes, noodles, and a child's lunch that comes on a plate shaped like a jet. We suggest, however, that you stick to ice cream and drinks. There's a better variety of food at Narita Airport itself, where there are quite a few restaurants. Ikoi-no-Mori, located west of the entrance to Narita Airport Course and beyond the parking lot, serves home-style Japanese food. A little restaurant inside the park behind the windmill sells *soba* and *udon* noodles and corn dogs.

Picnic Possibilities You can eat a packed lunch in the lounge on the fifth floor of the museum, which also has a view of the runway. Vending machines inside the museum sell drinks. Narita Airport Course has picnic tables for homemade lunches, or call in Japanese to reserve a cookout. Request Day Camp service and bring your own food or have them provide all the ingredients for a Japanese-style barbecue. They supply all the cooking equipment either way. Spread a blanket on the large lawn at Chiba Prefectural Botanical Garden for a homemade feast.

FOR INFANTS AND TODDLERS

The Museum of Aeronautical Sciences has a diaper-changing table near the restrooms on the first floor. There is no nursing room here or at Narita Airport Course, although there is a diaper-changing table in the women's restroom near the reception area and store. The shower rooms have coin lockers but unfortunately no benches for nursing privacy. Chiba Prefectural Botanical Garden has no toddler facilities, but you can spread a towel on the lawn for a quick change.

WHERE & WHEN

Narita Museum of Aeronautical Sciences
航空科学博物館
(Koku Kagaku Hakubutsu-kan)
Iwayama, Shibayama-machi, Sanbu-gun, Chiba-ken 289–1608
☎ (0479) 78–0557
千葉県山武郡芝山町岩山　〒289-1608
OPEN: 10 A.M. to 5 P.M. (entry until 4:30)

CLOSED: Mon (Tues if Mon is a hol), Dec 30, 31
FEES: adults ¥500, junior/senior high school students ¥300, children ¥200
DIRECTIONS: 15 minutes by bus from stop #11, outside Narita Passenger Terminal 1. There are free shuttles from Terminal 2 to Terminal 1. (No shuttles from noon to 1.) Reserve seats on the Narita Express at any of the Kanto area's major stations for the quickest ride to

Narita airport, or take a slower, less expensive train from Ueno on the Keisei line. You can also take an airport limousine from major hotels or Tokyo City Air Terminal (TCAT) directly above Suitengu-mae station (Hanzomon subway line). By car, take Tokyo Bay expressway (Wangan Doro) to Higashi Kanto expressway and get off at the Narita interchange. (Upon request the toll booth farthest to the left can provide you with a map to the museum.) Head toward the airport. At the Narita Airport signal go straight in the direction of Shibayama. The museum will appear on the right about 10 minutes down the road.

PARKING: free and plentiful

COMMENTS: all ages, some English

Narita Airport Course
成田エアポートコース

817 Maebayashi, Taiei-machi, Katori-gun, Chiba-ken 287–0222

☎ (0478) 73–5121

千葉県香取群大栄町前林817　〒287-0222

OPEN: 9 A.M. to 5 P.M. (entry until 4)

CLOSED: rainy days and Dec 30 to Jan 1

FEES: adults ¥800, junior/senior high school students ¥700, elementary school students ¥600, children over 4 ¥500. Price includes nature obstacle course and special events. Discount tickets for other attractions are sold at the reception desk or you can pay regular price at the attraction gate.

DIRECTIONS: take the bus bound for Wada-kagaku from Keisei Higashi Narita station and get off at Narita Airport Course-mae bus stop. Or, call the park and ask them to send a shuttle to pick you up at Keisei Higashi Narita station. The bus will return you to Kuuko Dai 2 Biru station (airport building #2). Shuttle

fees are ¥400 for adults and ¥200 for students. By car, take the Bayshore line expressway (Kosoku Wangansen) to Higashi Kanto expressway and get off at the Narita interchange. Turn right onto Route 295 and drive to the signal in front of Holiday Inn Tobu Hotel. Turn left and drive 3 or 4 km to a T intersection. Turn left, drive about 1 km and you will see the park on your right. If you are coming from the Museum of Aeronautical Sciences, drive back toward the Narita interchange going between the two airport terminals. About 500 meters from the airport check spot Tokyo bridge will appear. Cross it and you will see Holiday Inn Tobu on your left. Follow directions above to the park.

PARKING: lots hold up to 500 cars. Parking fees are only charged during Golden Week.

COMMENTS: all ages, no English

Chiba Prefectural Botanical Garden
千葉花植木センター

(Chiba Hana Ueki Center)

80–1 Dojo, Tenjinmine, Narita-shi, Chiba-ken 286–0102

☎ (0476) 32–0237

千葉県成田市天神峰字道場80-1　〒286-0102

OPEN: 9 A.M. to 4:30 P.M.

CLOSED: Mon (Tues if Mon is a hol)

FEES: none

DIRECTIONS: by car, take Bayshore line expressway (Kosoku Wangansen) to Higashi Kanto expressway and get off at the Narita interchange. Turn right onto Route 295 and drive to the signal in front of Holiday Inn Tobu Hotel. Turn left and follow the English signs to the garden.

PARKING: free for 100 cars

COMMENTS: all ages, English pamphlet

Fins, Fur, and Things with Wings

Tokyo has scores of zoos and aquariums, with a wide range of locations, sizes, and prices. We picked out the very best, beautiful, relaxing places where the animals are well treated and families can truly enjoy visiting them.

*At the top of the list: **Tama Zoo**. It takes a while to get there, but spacious pens that recreate the animals' natural habitats make this zoo the most pleasant. Special features like a lion safari ride and a tropical butterfly garden draw visitors from hours away. **Kodomo-no-Kuni** is the closest place that provides a real farmyard experience, with sheep, a working dairy, pony rides, and all kinds of farm fowl—as well as swimming, ice skating, and some fantastic play equipment.*

***Kasai Rinkai Park** and **Tokyo Sea Life Park** offer nice beaches and lots of space for active kids of all ages to play in. This is the place to see penguins and puffins, and the aquarium also has the largest touching pool in town, with plenty of starfish, shellfish, and other hardy sea creatures. The publicly funded aquarium is outstanding and inexpensive in comparison with others around town.*

*Black Beauty fans will enjoy Negishi's **Equine Museum** and **Memorial Racetrack Park**. See the differences between Shetland ponies, quarter horses, thoroughbreds, and other breeds by watching the horses in the Pony Center—the living exhibits of the museum. Located on the former racetrack in Yokohama's foreign settlement, this quiet park and excellent museum make a perfect half-day outing for horse fans.*

While we couldn't include it here, Yokohama will be opening its new Tsuzuki Zoo sometime in the next few years. Early plans show a facility that will probably be the best in Japan. Be on the lookout for it.

Negishi: Horse Lover's Paradise

Negishi Memorial Racetrack Park • Equine Museum of Japan • Pony Center • Negishi Forest Park

Yokohama's first foreign residents brought their love of fast horses with them. By 1866 they had tried racing at several sites before getting permission to use the green hills of Negishi, where they built the track that popularized Western-style horse racing in Japan. No horses gallop around the course at **Negishi Memorial Racetrack Park** today, but the old track and stands, a stable where you can compare different breeds of horses, and an outstanding equine museum will please the horse lover in your family.

The **Equine Museum of Japan** traces the evolution of the horse, and explains man's history with horses, describing the folklore that surrounds them. Here you can learn about horses around the world and study tack both ancient and modern. Inspect embellished saddles from Japan's Edo period, China, Burma, and Russia. Japanese lacquer saddles, stagecoaches, stirrups inlaid with silver, bits from ancient Persia, Italy, and eighteenth-century India, and bridles from eras long gone stand as evidence to man's close relationship with the horse. A life-size model of an Edo-era *magariya,* a building where farmers and horses lived under the same roof, is the largest exhibit. Inside you'll hear the sounds of country life from long ago, and see stables, straw saddles, farm implements, and living quarters. The museum also has a collection of art and crafts featuring horse motifs, from recent watercolor paintings to antique *netsuke,* exquisitely carved ivory figures once used as accessories with traditional Japanese attire. There are several video booths with films featuring styles of horsemanship from acrobatics to sleigh-pulling, Japanese horse-related festivals, different species of domestic horses, and famous horse races. A video in English outlines the history of horse racing in Japan.

Negishi's **Pony Center**, a few minutes' walk from the museum building, provides an exhibit of living horses. Want to know the differences between a Shetland pony, an American quarter horse, and a thoroughbred? Several types of horses and ponies live in the center, so visitors can compare their size and features, learn to distinguish different breeds, and find out about their daily life. Signs in Japanese behind each horse describe how much they eat, what they weigh, and other data. Residents of the Pony Center adhere to a fixed daily schedule. Breakfast starts at 9 A.M. in their stalls. At 9:30 they go to the paddock for free play until it's time to prepare for their 1:30 riding exercise. At 3 the horses are groomed, then returned to their stalls for dinner and sleep. Several of the horses and ponies are made available to visitors for a short mosey around the paddock every third Sunday starting at 1:30 P.M. If you want to participate, arrive early and get in line by at least 1 to get a numbered badge. Only the first 150 elementary and middle school students get to ride. During the winter, when fewer kids come to the park, adults sometimes get a chance to ride too. You can also feed carrots to the horses on Saturdays from 1:30 to 1:45 P.M.

When you're ready, take a stroll through the lovely forest on the hill behind the museum and Pony Center. A smooth sidewalk in **Negishi Forest Park** takes you past the pond, through the trees, and under the crumbling remains of Negishi Racetrack's once-glorious stands. The sidewalk was once the track itself. In the stands above, curious Japanese aristocrats mingled with the elite—and lowlife—of Yokohama society, all dressed in their finest clothes. Horses raced this track from 1866 until 1942, when the wartime government closed the track because of its strategic view of the harbor. After the war the grounds were used by the U.S. military, and naval facilities still border the park. The original stands were destroyed in the Great Kanto Earthquake of 1923. What remains today was built in 1929. You cannot enter the building, but if you want a closer look, walk past the Yokohama Detachment of the U.S. Yokosuka Base and you'll see it on the right. Behind the stands, a playground with a roller slide, a pulley ride, a sandbox, and play equipment that combines playhouses, jungle gyms, and slides will delight young children.

You could see everything here in half a day. But we suggest coming with a lazy picnic in mind on a day when the horses are available to ride, and spending a slow-footed day at this once-upon-a-time racetrack.

Other Things to Do in the Area

If you've got serious train fanatics in your group, make time for the **Yokohama Streetcar Museum**, a 17-minute bus ride from Negishi Forest Park. Located next to a bus parking area on the first floor of an apartment building, this place has all the ambiance of a musty old garage, but it boasts one of the best collections of model trains in the country. Climb aboard six retired streetcars that made their way along Yokohama's avenues in different decades. A 160-square-meter panorama has 348 meters of O-gauge track laid in six lines and 114 meters of HO-gauge track laid in two lines. Shows at the large panorama feature all kinds of trains, from early steam models to the latest *shinkansen*. Visitors can participate in the show by operating the streetcars, and between shows guests can operate the two train lines in the switch yard for ¥100.

Bring your own handmade model trains to run on the N-gauge tracks of a smaller panorama or use one of the museum's (toy trains are not allowed). Also in the museum is a high-tech simulator of the Yokohama subway that runs three times a day (10–11 A.M., 12–1 P.M., and 2–3 P.M.), and a collection of over seven hundred model trains donated to the museum by a single hobbyist who made them all. Train buffs will need an hour or two to get their fill. If your interest in trains is only passing, you might just pass on this one.

More Pony Rides

Tokyo's Setagaya Ward also has a horse park, built for the equestrian events of the 1964 Olympics. Visit when **Baji Park** holds its *Uma no Shitamu Hi* (day for getting to know horses), one Sunday every month (usually the third weekend but that changes occasionally). Young girls perform balancing acts on horseback and trained horses do tricks in the horse show that starts around 1:30 P.M. Around 2, children ages four to ten can have a quick ride on a horse or pony. Next to the horse rides, smaller kids can ride in an old-fashioned, Clydesdale-drawn cart that goes round a flower garden. Pick up free tickets for rides at the reception desk on the left as you enter the park. If you're lucky there may also be a jumping competition to watch in the adjacent ring. The park holds an annual horse show during Golden Week, with jumping competitions and trained horse acts. On September 23 there is a festival with horses and riders dressed in traditional Japanese garb. Horse competitions are held frequently on weekends throughout the year. Surprisingly, the park is hardly ever crowded, even when the horse rides are available. The horse motif is everywhere—on sculptures, water fountains, landscaping, even the play equipment.

The down side to the horses in Negishi and Baji parks is that you have to wait for the once-a-month opportunity to ride them. For more frequent access to horses, visit Kodomo-no-Kuni (see Tour 21), Arakawa Amusement Park (see Tour 17), or one of

Edogawa Ward's Ponylands. **Shinozaki Ponyland** on the banks of the Edogawa river is the larger of the two, offering free pony rides to kids in sixth grade or younger and horse cart rides to everyone. While the **Nagisa Ponyland** is smaller and doesn't offer horse cart rides, there is more to do in the area. Nagisa Park is connected by shuttle to a string of parks with flower gardens, camping, and recreational facilities. At either Ponyland, a park attendant will lead the pony around a track as your child sits in the saddle. You can ride as many times as you want on slow days, but on busy days you can only ride once. While there is an upper age limit (sixth grade), there seems to be no lower one. We've seen parents holding babies round their waists so they can stay on the pony as they amble down the track. The Ponylands also offer riding lessons to women who live, work, or attend school in Edogawa Ward.

EATING OPTIONS

Restaurants Dolphin Restaurant, across the street from the southeast side of Negishi Park, has a terrace with a view of the harbor and serves Western cuisine. This famous restaurant has appeared in movies and on TV, and is even mentioned in a popular song. Dinner starts at around ¥5,000, but there is a lunch special for ¥1,500 on weekdays. Spaghetti and other à la carte choices are even cheaper and always available at lunchtime. There are no restaurants near the Streetcar Museum. There is a Royal Host in front of the main gate of Baji Park, plus several other restaurants in the vicinity. You'll have trouble finding a place to eat at either Ponyland.

Picnic Possibilities Spread a blanket on one of the wide lawns or find a bench for a picnic in Negishi. The rest house at the southeast entrance sells snacks and drinks. Benches near the drink machines opposite the restrooms in the Streetcar Museum come in handy when you've got a hungry toddler who can't wait for a place with atmosphere. Baji Park has a Japanese-style garden that makes a lovely picnic spot. A shop round the corner to the left after you pass through the main gate sells drinks and snacks. Bring a picnic blanket and a basket of goodies for either Ponyland location.

FOR INFANTS AND TODDLERS

Negishi has no designated nursing or diapering facilities, but the bench in the ladies' room on the ground floor under the rest house is a good possibility when you have to make do. The locker room in the rest house also offers privacy and there are showers

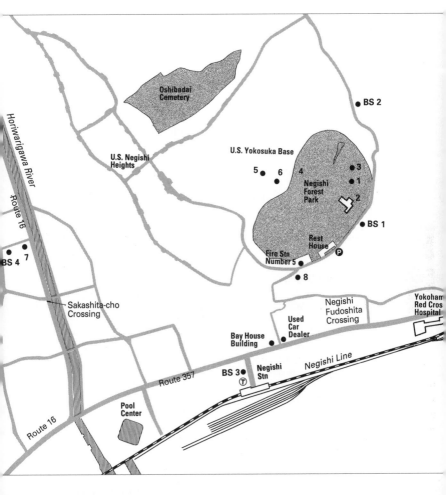

PLACES TO VISIT

1. Negishi Memorial Race Track Park
2. Equine Museum of Japan
3. Pony Center
4. Negishi Forest Park
5. Playground
6. Old Race Track Stands
7. Yokohama Street Car Museum

8. Dolphin Restaurant

BS 1. Taki-no-Ue Bus Stop
BS 2. Yamamoto-cho 4-chome Bus Stop
BS 3. Bus Stop
BS 4. Shiden Hozon-kan-mae Bus Stop

that might come in handy if you have kids like some of ours. Parents with strollers using mass transit should definitely ride the bus from Negishi station instead of climbing all the stairs to the park. The Equine Museum has one flight of stairs and no elevators. The Streetcar Museum provides nothing in the way of diaper-changing or nursing spots, but you may be able to use a bench to change a diaper or an empty streetcar exhibit for feeding. There is a diaper-changing table in the women's restroom inside the shop at Baji Park. Parents of infants may want to bring a stroller. At Shinozaki Ponyland, keep an eye on toddlers so they don't toddle into the river.

WHERE & WHEN

Negishi Memorial Racetrack Park
根岸競馬記念公園
(Negishi Keiba Kinen Koen)
1–3 Negishi-dai, Naka-ku, Yokohama-shi, Kanagawa-ken 231–0853
☎ (045) 662–7581
神奈川県横浜市中区根岸台1-3　〒231-0853
OPEN: 9:30 A.M. to 5 P.M.
CLOSED: Mon, April 1, Dec 29 to Jan 4
FEES: none
DIRECTIONS: a 20-minute uphill walk from Negishi station (JR Keihin Tohoku and Negishi lines), or take city bus #21 from stop #2 bound for Sakuragicho station and get off at Taki-no-Ue bus stop. By car, take route 357; at Negishi Fudoshita intersection drive uphill and you will soon see the park on the left.
PARKING: hourly, open 24 hours
COMMENTS: all ages but children must be at least 4 to ride, no English

Equine Museum of Japan and Pony Center
馬の博物館 (Uma no Hakubutsu-kan)
1–3 Negishi-dai, Naka-ku, Yokohama-shi, Kanagawa-ken 231–0853
☎ (045) 662–7581
神奈川県横浜市中区根岸台1-3　〒231-0853
OPEN: 10 A.M. to 4 P.M. for museum, 9:30 A.M. to 4:30 P.M. for Pony Center
CLOSED: Mon except national hols, April 1 (the

park's anniversary), and Dec 28 to Jan 4
FEES: adults ¥100, school-age children ¥30 for museum entrance. Fees may change during special exhibits. The Pony Center is free of charge.
DIRECTIONS: see Negishi Memorial Racetrack Park
COMMENTS: 5 and up, adequate English

Negishi Forest Park
根岸森林公園 (Negishi Shinrin Koen)
Negishi-dai, Naka-ku, Yokohama-shi, Kanagawa-ken 231–0853
☎ (045) 641–9185
神奈川県横浜市中区根岸台
OPEN: 24 hours
CLOSED: no hols
FEES: none
DIRECTIONS: see Negishi Memorial Racetrack Park
COMMENTS: all ages, no English

Yokohama Streetcar Museum
横浜市市電保存会
(Yokohama-shi Shiden Hozon-kai)
3–1–53 Takigashira, Isogo-ku, Yokohama-shi, Kanagawa-ken 235–0012
☎ (045) 754–8505
神奈川県横浜市磯子区滝頭3-1-53　〒235-0012
OPEN: 9:30 A.M. to 4:30 P.M.
CLOSED: Mon (Tues if Mon is a hol). Closed

for New Year's hol and occasionally in winter to set up new exhibits.

FEES: adults ¥200, elementary school students and younger ¥100

DIRECTIONS: from Negishi Forest Park take bus #21 to Shiden Hozon-kan-mae bus stop—it's about a 17-minute ride. From bus stop #4 at Negishi station (JR Keihin Tohoku and Negishi lines) it's a 10-minute ride on bus #21.

PARKING: none

COMMENTS: 5 and up, no English

Baji Park
馬事公苑 (Baji Koen)

2–1–1 Kami Yoga, Setagaya-ku, Tokyo 158–0098

☎ (03) 3429–5101

東京都世田谷区上用賀2-1-1　〒158-0098

OPEN: daily 9 A.M. to 5 P.M. (until 4 in winter)

FEES: none

DIRECTIONS: from the south exit of Shibuya station (JR Yamanote, Tokyu Toyoko, Tokyu Shintamagawa, and Inokashira train lines, Hanzomon and Ginza subway lines) take bus #24 or bus #26 and get off at Nodai-mae stop; the park is a 3-minute walk. You can also get to Nodai-mae bus stop via bus #12 or bus #1 from the north exit of Yoga station (Shintamagawa line) or bus #23, #1, or #11 from Chitosefunabashi station (Odakyu line). It's a 15-minute walk from Sakurashinmachi station (Shintamagawa line), or a 20-minute walk from either Kyodo station (Odakyu line) or Kamimachi station (Tokyu Setagaya line). By car, several blocks northeast of the intersection of Setagaya Dori and Kanpachi Dori.

PARKING: none

COMMENTS: all ages, no English

Shinozaki Ponyland
篠崎ポニーランド

3–12–17 Shinozaki, Edogawa-ku, Tokyo 133–0061

☎ (03) 3678–7520

東京都江戸川区篠崎3-12-17　〒133-0061

OPEN: 10 to 11:30 A.M., 1:30 to 3 P.M. (from July 21 to Aug 31 open 9 to 11:30 A.M. only)

CLOSED: Mon (Tues if Mon is a hol) and Dec 29 to Jan 1; also closed for rain or strong winds

FEES: none

DIRECTIONS: take bus #72 from bus stop #2 bound for Ichinoe station at the south exit of Koiwa station (JR Sobu line) or bus #73 bound for Edogawa Sports Land and get off at Shinozaki Toshokan/Ponyland-mae. By car, take Keiyo Doro or expressway #7 and exit at Keiyo Deiriguchi.

PARKING: none

COMMENTS: must be 10 or younger to ride, no English

Nagisa Ponyland
なぎさポニーランド

Nagisa Park

7–3 Minami Kasai, Edogawa-ku, Tokyo 134–0085

☎ (03) 5658–5720

東京都江戸川区南葛西7-3　〒134-0085

OPEN: 10 to 11:30 A.M., 1:30 to 3 P.M.; from July 21 to Aug 31 open 9 to 11:30 A.M. only

CLOSED: Mon (Tues if Mon is a hol) and Dec 29 to Jan 1; also closed for rain or strong winds

FEES: none

DIRECTIONS: take bus #24 from Kasai station (Tozai line) or bus #20 from Nishikasai station (Tozai line). By car, take the Express Bayshore line to Kasai and travel north on Kannana Dori until you reach Sogo Recreation Park. Turn right, continue to Nagisa Park.

PARKING: free; two 20-car lots

COMMENTS: must be 10 or younger to ride, no English

21

Farmyard Feeling and Country Lanes

Kodomo-no-Kuni

P onies nicker and whinny for their young riders while sheep graze peacefully on the hillside at **Kodomo-no-Kuni**. Ducks and waterfowl of all kinds splash and preen in a nearby pond, a sight you can enjoy while savoring rich, creamy homemade ice cream with the special taste that only comes when you use milk straight from the cow. Country life has many pleasures, especially for children, but in the Tokyo area these things can be hard to find. Kodomo-no-Kuni brings a farmyard experience together with fantastic playground equipment, a maze, pools, ice skating, cycling, beautiful gardens, and more.

Kodomo-no-Kuni, or Children's Land, is 45 minutes and a world away from downtown Tokyo. Green rolling hills block out any signs of urban life, and secluded paths through thick woods make you feel as if you are wandering through a quiet corner of the Japanese countryside—until you hit one of the park's many attractions. You won't find any thrills-and-chills rides here; instead of jet coasters, there's bicycling through a cherry grove, a complex maze to challenge directional skills, and a working dairy. Although there is an additional charge for some of the more exciting activities, none of them

O riginally peaceful, rolling farmland, the site that became Kodomo-no-Kuni was used by the Imperial Japanese forces and later the U.S. military as a storage depot. You can still see the remains of ammunition storehouses on the inner ring road. With the goal of helping to develop children with sound minds and bodies, the park opened in 1965 to commemorate the marriage of Emperor Akihito and Empress Michiko six years earlier.

will break your pocketbook. Plan to spend an extra ¥500 to ¥2,000 per person for activities (see prices in the Where & When section), depending on the age and interests of your group. It's not much for the kind of fun you'll find at Kodomo-no-Kuni. Come early and spend the whole day in this huge park, which occupies just shy of one million square meters. Ask for an English map when you purchase your tickets, but consider it just a general directional guide, since it doesn't include all the paths. Get a Japanese map too, and match the characters with those on the more accurate signposts throughout the park if you can't read them on your own.

Fresh air, open spaces, and lots of opportunities to exercise your muscles make this a great place for energetic people to play. Just past the entrance on the left, older children can experience the thrills of an action adventure film, hanging onto an overhead pulley and swooping swiftly downhill as it slides along a cable. Follow the paths along the park's spacious lawns, where you'll encounter plenty more free fun spots: a roller slide, a maze, a fort, and two exotic indoor botanical gardens with the warmth of a tropical jungle, to name just a few.

No matter what time of year you come, there's something special to do. During Japanese school holidays from mid-July to the end of August, visitors can cool off in nine outdoor pools. There are five waterslides, including two spiral tubes and three open slides that aim you straight at the water and take you over plenty of bumps. The longest slide is 91 meters. From mid-December to the end of February a large tent-covered area amid the pools is used for ice-skating. In other months, you can stroll along paths lined with colorful autumn leaves, sit under blossoming trees, or take a peek at animal babies.

The campground is near quiet, tree-lined Swan Lake, where you can rent pedal boats and rowboats or borrow a free raft, and learn about animals habits at the nearby Visitor Center. From here it is a long, pleasant walk—past tunnels, play equipment, a splashing spot, and a plum grove—to the zoo and farmyard area.

More farm animals than any other spot within easy reach of Tokyo are reason enough to visit Kodomo-no-Kuni. Screeching turkeys, colorful roosters, and other farm fowl peck and scratch in large pens inside the park's small zoo, a real bargain among the attractions. Deer, goats, and donkeys greet curious young guests, and of course there are guinea pigs and bunnies to cuddle. Brightly colored birds play with visitors who enter their net-covered dome; the blue and green parakeets in particular seem to enjoy swooping and diving just centimeters above your head. There are about three hundred birds (fourteen varieties) including an albino peacock and a splendidly decorated Chinese pheasant. Benches and vending machines are plentiful in this area, making it a good spot for a well-earned rest when you've seen the animals.

The sound of cattle munching and mooing is a sure sign that you're near the park's working dairy. You can walk right up to the cows, and watch as the workers feed and milk them at 3 every afternoon. The ice cream stand at one end of the milk plant sells drinks and snacks, and ice cream made from the dairy's milk. The ice cream is soft, sold by the cone, and comes in only one flavor: vanilla. The cones are generously filled and even those who never order plain vanilla will feel like they've had a special treat. One side of the milk plant has large windows so visitors can peer in and watch as milk cartons are mechanically filled, closed, and sent down the conveyor belt. The milk sold at Kodomo-no-Kuni also comes from the dairy cows, so it is very fresh.

The grazing sheep in the nearby meadow are equally approachable. They'll nose their way to the fence and bleat out a greeting for friendly children. By the barn are more sheep, and you can purchase feed to give them for a small price. Short pony rides are available just up the hill, near a pond where all kinds of ducks and geese gather for the winter.

The soccer field, Memorial Hall, and various outdoor grounds can be rented cheaply for games, events, school field trips, and the like, but generally you must make reservations one year to six months in advance. Tennis courts require a one-month advance booking. With a little planning, you can also camp out or have a barbecue. Camping is mostly for large groups of around thirty people, and is only available to families during summer school holidays. Apply by postcard six months ahead of time. If you want to have a cookout, call ahead in Japanese to reserve one of several *teppanyaki* (grilled food) "courses" and Kodomo-no-Kuni will provide the food, or you can rent the grill and bring all your own ingredients and matches. Special events and activities are held each month. Call in Japanese to find out about them.

EATING OPTIONS

Restaurants   Noodle dishes and other inexpensive Japanese cafeteria foods are available at a large restaurant about 3 minutes from the entrance. You can also buy light meals like pilaf and fried rice balls at a little kiosk near the ponies. Vending machines in other locations sell items like drinks and ice cream.

Picnic Possibilities   With plenty of woods, picnic tables, and secluded benches, Kodomo-no-Kuni is a great place for outdoor eating. Bring along food from home or stop and pick up a *bento* boxed lunch in Shibuya or one of the other large stations on your way. You can round out your meal with homemade ice cream and other snacks sold in the park.

FOR INFANTS AND TODDLERS

Diaper-changing facilities are plentiful and easy to spot, but since they are in the park's unheated bathrooms, winter visitors may want to select children's clothing carefully so they can remain mostly dressed during changes. The General Information Office just to the right of the front gate as you enter the park will accommodate nursing mothers. It is also the lost child center, first aid station, and lost and found. There are also diapering and nursing facilities in the Visitor Center.

A stroller can make the long walk around this spacious park much more enjoyable. Some of the paths are gravel or rough tracks, but you should be able to get almost everywhere on the large paved roads. For families who want to ditch their stroller for awhile so they can use the pool or hike through the camellia woods, the park has a designated stroller parking lot near the pools. You can also rent strollers near the main entrance.

WHERE & WHEN

Kodomo-no-Kuni
こどもの国

700 Naramachi, Aoba-ku, Yokohama-shi, Kanagawa-ken
☎ (045) 961–2111 to 3
神奈川県横浜市青葉区奈良町700
OPEN: 9:30 A.M. to 4:30 P.M. (entry until 3:30)
CLOSED: Mon (when Mon is a hol, the following day), Dec 31 and Jan 1
FEES: *Entrance only*: adults and high school students ¥600, middle and elementary school students ¥200, preschoolers over 3 ¥100.

Entrance and 2 hours in the pool: adults ¥1,000, students ¥450, preschoolers ¥350. *Entrance, 2 hours of skating and skate rental* adults ¥1,300, students ¥700, preschoolers ¥600. *Ponies*: ¥350/ride (3-year-olds to sixth graders); hours from 10 A.M. to noon, 1 to 2:30 P.M., and 3 to 4 P.M. *Boats*: ¥400/half hour (up to 3 passengers). *Cycle boats*: ¥600/half hour (up to 2 passengers).
Zoo: ¥150. *Bicycle Rental*: ¥150 for adults and

¥100 for children. *Stroller Rental*: ¥200
Cart for bags and coats: ¥300. *Teppanyaki*: ¥1,300 to ¥1,800/person plus ¥400/person cooking fees. *Cookouts*: ¥400 for adults, ¥250 for children plus ¥1,300 for grill rental (coal and firewood sold separately). For *Teppanyaki* and *Cookouts*, call in advance in Japanese for reservations and list of what to bring.

DIRECTIONS: take the Hanzomon/Shintamagawa/Den'entoshi line or JR Yokohama line to Nagatsuda and change; Kodomo-no-Kuni is one stop on a special line that leaves from platform 7, which is only accessible by stairs from platforms 3, 4, 5, and 6 of the Den'entoshi line. If you've come on the Yokohama line, buy your ticket for Kodomo-no-Kuni near the Den'entoshi wicket, then pass through the wicket and follow the signs to platform 7. There are also buses from Tsurukawa station (Odakyu Odawara line). Turn right as you exit the station and take any bus from stop #3. By car, the park is 5 minutes south of Setagaya Dori. Exit at Tsurukawa station, and follow Route 139; the park will be on your left. It takes 20 minutes from the Yokohama interchange on the Tomei expressway; follow Route 16 to Route 246, exit at Tama station, and turn left at the 7th traffic light and right onto Route 139. The park will be on your right.

PARKING: Daily rate. The lot fills up on Sun.

COMMENTS: all ages, English map/pamphlet, nursing area in General Information Office

On Safari at Tokyo's Best Zoo

Tama Zoo

Ten meters away, a lion crouches in the shade of a tree. The bus draws closer. Suddenly, the animal lunges at the vehicle. Its jaws open wide to reveal a set of razor-sharp teeth and a tongue aimed at the tiny chunks of meat attached to the outside of the window. Providing many of the thrills of a real African safari, the zebra-striped Lion Bus is just one of the many special features that make **Tama Zoo** the best in the greater Tokyo area.

Situated in the rolling foothills of the Tama area a few stops from Mount Takao, the zoo is spacious, modern, and clean. Japan's first natural habitat zoo, it covers 52.3 hectares (129 acres). With ramps and elevators thoughtfully located near its few stairs, Tama Zoo is designed for strollers and wheelchairs, although the hills make walking strenuous at times. Instead of pacing up and down drab pens crowded into a small area, many of the animals roam large, open spaces designed to resemble their native habitats, interacting with other species from the same part of the world. Although this means much more walking for visitors, the paths between attractions take you through beautiful woods that provide plenty of shade in summer.

Climbing the steep hill that leads to the **Insectarium** is a good way to start. As you toil up the incline, remind yourself that the walking will be mostly downhill from here. Inside the facility is a host of wonders, starting with the biggest bug collection in town. The best part: many of the creepy-crawlies are still alive and wiggling, munching, and walking as they would in nature. Ants and beetles, bees and bugs thrill amateur entomologists and send gentle chills up the spines of the squeamish. Glow-worms, fireflies, and other luminous insects light up one section without much help from electric lamps.

Hundreds of exotic flowers and a lovely waterfall add to the beauty of the zoo's tropical butterfly garden in the central section of the Insectarium. Colorful specimens flutter from flower to flower, winging past the hummingbirds that share their home. Inside this beautiful dome, zoo volunteers lend magnifying glasses to interested visitors, explaining about the garden's tinier inhabitants. Though more comfortable using Japanese, some of these guides do speak English, and throughout the zoo the English explanations are fairly good. You will definitely want one of the English maps available at the ticket gate. Use it to find the outer loop of the **Africa Garden**, a very short walk from the Insectarium.

Cheetahs, chimpanzees, and elephants will return your stare as you stroll down Safari Road; you'll also have a chance to see the zoo's pride of lions from afar and decide whether you want to pay ¥350 (¥100 for children age three through middle school and senior citizens over sixty-five) to ride the Lion Bus. The lines can be long when the zoo is crowded, but the close-up view is unforgettable. If your kids are tall enough to see over the seats, you may want to stand so that you can see the lions from the windows on both sides of the bus. The mini-safari lasts less than 10 minutes, so you shouldn't get too tired. Plain, inexpensive Japanese food can be found at the zoo's only cafeteria, located near the Lion Bus exit. Across the street, giraffes munch on their lunch, while oryx and zebras race across a large stretch of red earth that simulates the African savannah they came from. Colorful wading birds pick their way gracefully around the edges. When you, too, have skirted this wide enclosure, turn left or backtrack to just before the cafeteria to reach the **Asia Garden**.

Snorting Mongolian horses, chattering Japanese monkeys, playful bears, and placid water buffalo are just a few of the animals that live on the forested hillside of the zoo's largest section. Waterfowl of all kinds splash and preen in a charming pond near the petting zoo, a favorite spot for small children. On weekends and national holidays, guinea pigs and rabbits can be cuddled in the mornings from 11 A.M. to 12 P.M. and in the afternoons from 1 P.M. to 2 P.M. Rhinos, reindeer, snow leopards, tigers, elephants, and others will entertain you on your way to the last section of the zoo, the **Australia Garden**.

Here, cuddly koalas cling to trees in an environment that closely resembles their arid homeland. The zoo takes special care of the heat-loving koalas and their compatriots the wallabies, wombats, and emus. Spring and fall they play in a large outdoor space, winter and summer they take refuge from the elements in the Koala House, a special building that has desert plants and even realistic sunsets. Visitors will enjoy the informative displays on some of the more unusual features of Australian animals.

Near the edge of the Australia Garden senior citizens and disabled visitors can board a shuttle bus back to the entrance. If you have time to spare, you'll want to stop in the **Watching Center** near the exit. The center's entertaining displays, which challenge visitors to do things like match fur patterns or tails with the right animals, make this a great place to recap the highlights of your visit to the zoo. It's also a good way to save the day if you get caught in a sudden shower. The zoo shop next door sells a wide variety of animal goods, but they're a little on the expensive side.

Exploring Tama Zoo will take a minimum of 2 hours, longer if you want to experience all the attractions. The animals, hills, and wide open spaces make this zoo an all-day adventure you won't soon forget.

Other Things to Do in the Area

Wheels and engines are the focus of **Tama Tech**, an excellent amusement park located on the same road 1.5 kilometers left from Tama Dobutsu Koen train station. Adults and kids will have a great time racing go-carts, mini dune buggies, and robot walkers; roller coasters, water rides, and miniature golf add to the thrills. You can even barbecue in one area. This Honda-affiliated theme park is among Tokyo's best, with attractions that will keep you entertained for at least 2 or 3 hours. Because both the zoo and the amusement park are large and exciting, most people will want to visit them on separate days.

EATING OPTIONS

Eating Out   Located in the African section near the Lion Bus, the zoo's cafeteria offers typical Japanese-style dishes at very reasonable prices. Soft ice cream, drinks, corn dogs, *yakisoba*, and the like are also available for as little as ¥300. There are also snack bars down the hill from the Koala House and inside the Watching Center. Tama Tech has a curry restaurant and a *ramen* shop.

Picnic Possibilities   Benches throughout the zoo provide plenty of opportunities to munch on homemade goodies while watching your favorite animals. Tama Tech has open grassy areas and several picnic tables too.

FOR INFANTS AND TODDLERS

There are two diaper-changing tables, one in the rest area in the cafeteria and one in the rest area of the snack bar near the Koala House. If you need hot water for bottles, ask at the cafeteria or one of the snack bars. Nursing moms can find privacy in the

First Aid Center at the Watching Center. There is no designated nursing space, but just ask and the nurses there will let you use a bed to feed your baby. The Lost Child Center is also in the Watching Center.

Tama Tech has diaper-changing in three places: the restroom in the curry restaurant, the restroom next to the Wild River Adventure ride, and the First Aid station. You can also nurse your child in the First Aid station.

WHERE & WHEN

Tama Zoological Park
多摩動物公園 (Tama Dobutsu Koen)
7–1–1 Hodokubo, Hino-shi, Tokyo 191– 0042
☎ (0425) 91–1611
東京都日野市帆土窪7-1-1　〒191-0042
OPEN: 9:30 A.M. to 5 P.M. (ticket booth and Lion Bus until 4)
CLOSED: Mon (Tues if Mon is a hol), Dec 29 to Jan 3
FEES: adults ¥500, junior high students ¥200, younger children and those 65 and over free; no fees charged on April 29, May 5, and Oct 1
DIRECTIONS: 2 minutes from Tama Dobutsu Koen station (Keio Dobutsuen line: take Keio line from Shinjuku and change at Takahata Fudo station). 15 minutes by bus #14 from Keio Tama Center station (Keio Sagamihara line); get off at Tama Dobutsuen Eki bus stop. In the future accessible by Tama Toshi monorail, which is under construction at the time of this writing. By car, take the Chuo highway to the Hachioji #1 interchange, then travel south on the Hachioji Bypass (toll road) to Utchikoshi. Turn left on to Kitano Kaido, turn right at Hirayama 5-chome intersection, and take the right side of the next fork. Tama Tech will appear on your left and the zoo will be about 1.5 kilometers down the road on your right.

PARKING: the zoo has no parking, but there are several lots in the area
COMMENTS: all ages, English pamphlet

Tama Tech Amusement Park
タマテック
5–22–1 Hodokubo, Hino-shi, Tokyo 191– 0042
☎ (0425) 91–0820
東京都日野市程久保5-22-1　〒191-0042
OPEN: 9:30 A.M. to 5 P.M.
FEES: adults ¥1,600, children 3 to 12 ¥800, for entrance only or buy a passport ticket at ¥3,300 for people over 13 and ¥2,700 for children 3 to 12.
DIRECTIONS: 10 minutes by bus from Takahata Fudo station (Keio line). Buses leave from stop #1. 5 minutes by bus #12 or #22 from Tama Dobutsu Koen station (Keio Dobutsuen line). 12 minutes by bus from bus stop #4 at Toyoda station (JR Chuo line). 15 minutes by bus #33 from Keio Tama Center station (Keio Sagamihara line). Buses leave from bus stop #13. For directions by car, see Tama Zoological Park.
PARKING: space for 1,000 cars, daily rate
COMMENTS: all ages, English map, nursery

Kasai's Sea Life: An All-Day Ocean Experience

Kasai Rinkai Park and Bird Park • Tokyo Sea Life Park • Kasai Marine and Beach Park

A humble fishing village where clam boats once chugged along the shore, Kasai resisted modernization for a surprisingly long time. The delicious seaweed raised there—Asakusa *nori*—was once the only kind of *nori* our Japanese mothers-in-law gave as gifts. For the locals the sea was a living, a pastime, a lifestyle. But in the middle of the Showa emperor's reign (1926–89), a flood embankment separated the peaceful village from the ocean, and pollution from Japan's industrial development worsened, crippling the local fishing industry. In the early 1970s, a project team set about reclaiming the area. Today, the birds and fish are gradually returning to their homes, and the people have part of their beach back, but with a modern twist.

A cluster of three connected seaside parks now protects area wildlife, teaches visitors about sea life and birds, and provides plenty of play space. Easily accessible by rail, bus, car, and even ferry, Kasai makes for an outing as hassle-free as it is wholesome, fun, and educational. Bring along binoculars and, if you are coming by car, shovels and pails, bicycles, and kites.

When it's operating, the park train will give you an overall view of the area. Then, head east to **Kasai Rinkai Park's Bird Park**, a breeding ground for egrets, herons, ducks, snipes, and other waterfowl. New reed growth in the area is also luring land birds. Follow the main path to the circular Watching Center, where you can pick up a map of the bird park and check out the Japanese displays in the second-floor exhibition room. Then steal along the more intimate trails to the blinds for a closer look at the magpies, martins, warblers, thrushes, and shrikes flitting through the bush or bathing in the ponds. Stay quiet so as not to disturb the birds. Watching Center personnel can field questions in Japanese about the park and its residents for individual visitors and groups. There are no telescopes for visitors to use, so don't forget your own viewing lenses. Spend about an hour bird-watching, then double back to the main promenade for a look at creatures that live under the water.

Tokyo Sea Life Park houses the city's best aquarium. No dolphins or seals jump through hoops here, but the aquarium has one of the best presentations of sea life you'll find without donning scuba gear. When you stop at the gate to purchase your ticket, ask for a brochure; they have English, Russian, Chinese, and Korean versions. Guide in hand, head for the big glass bubble roof of the aquarium.

Inside you'll find malicious-looking hammerhead sharks, giant bluefin tuna, colorful exotic fish, a forest of kelp, and organisms so small you must view them with a microscope—creatures from all the world's oceans and the Caribbean Sea. You can explore the underwater world at the 3-D Theater in Japanese, or watch the library's four English videos on fish, each 14 to thirty 30 minutes long. The aquarium puts on grand-scale special exhibits which change about once a year. Staff do scheduled Spot Guides, explaining about marine life in front of the tanks, and publish a monthly newsletter, both in Japanese only.

Kasai is the place to come to watch penguins. Several varieties of these formal but fun-loving sea birds splash and play in a large pool just outside the aquarium building. You can compare these southern avians, fast swimmers who can't fly, with their cousins from the icy north. The aquarium's puffins walk like Charlie Chaplin, fly well, and swim duck fashion. The reconstructed tidal basin has small but real waves and tides, as well as coastal life. A Touch Corner at one end of the basin is filled with starfish and sea urchins. Touch as much as you like, but don't take the creatures out of the water.

As you exit the building, you'll pass through the aquarium's family-oriented cafeteria. Tables inside and out and an elegant Tent Deck built over a salt pond make this a relaxing spot for a break before venturing on to the outdoor exhibits that enliven the well-manicured grounds. In another corner of the park, you can study the inhabitants of a small freshwater lake and stream from above and below the surface.

The tanks and exhibits at the Sea Life Park take about 2 hours, longer if you want to watch videos or listen to the Spot Guides. Spend the rest of your day flying kites, fishing from the rocky shore, sprawling on a grassy lawn, wheeling down the cycling course, or just checking out the scenery from Crystal View, the large white-and-glass building in the center of the park. Bucket and pail in hand, cross the Kasai Beach bridge (Nagisa Bashi) to **Kasai Marine and Beach Park** and build sandcastles or hunt for seashells. Serious birders set up high-tech scopes here and study the birds perched on distant reeds. Only the west beach of the park is open to the public and you cannot swim or fish here, but this is a fine place to watch the waves roll in or stare out at the wide open sea. A billboard advises visitors to beware of red stingrays and high tide. Stake out a spot in the soft wet sand; as your castles get higher and higher the sun will slip down in an orange sky and disappear into the ocean.

Other Things to Do in the Area

Just because you can't swim in Kasai doesn't mean you can't ride the waves. Forgo land travel and take the ferry from Hinode Pier (see Tour 1 for directions to pier and Tour 18 for map of water bus routes).

The **Subway Museum**, a 15-minute bus ride away, combines well with the aquarium on days too cold for Kasai's outdoor parks to be appealing. High-tech simulators and hands-on exhibits make it a great half-day outing all on its own. The museum has an easy-to-drive streetcar, and youngsters love playing with the automatic doors and pretending to be passengers. Three video simulators make the ride through Tokyo's subway system seem incredibly real. Drivers each have their own set of simulator controls, and strategically located "engineers" (mostly retired subway workers) show you the ropes. Metro Panorama shows of the miniature subway trains start at 11 A.M. and 1, 2, and 3:30 P.M. While waiting, learn how subways are constructed and maintained from viewer-activated displays. Or take a nostalgic look at the subways of Japan's past, inspecting the antique appointments and all-wood interiors of old subway cars. A movie/lecture hall shows films about Japanese subways.

Ward-owned **Hotel Seaside Edogawa**, located in Kasai Rinkai Park, makes a cozy haven for a family in search of a reasonably priced seaside vacation. Room rates include breakfast and dinner, with discounts for kids.

More Fish and Fowl

Spending time in **Tokyo Port Wild Bird Park** will teach your children not only about birds, but also about the fragile nature of an ecosystem and the responsibility we must all take for nature conservation. The volunteers who started the park and now run it with the guidance of Japan's Wild Bird Society provide an excellent example of how citizens can band together to do something valuable. We've seen even kids permanently attached to a computer utter soft gasps of amazement as they become engrossin the daily activities of wild birds in their natural habitat.

Visitors range from serious birders to first-timers. If you fall into the latter category, English-speaking rangers are sometimes on hand in the Nature Center and can answer questions. Stop by the center to pick up an English pamphlet with color photos of the birds that frequent the nature preserve. If your family really enjoys bird watching, you may want to study more about it with *A Field Guide to the Birds of Japan*, written by the Wild Bird Society of Japan and published by Kodansha International. Japanese speakers may enjoy a park-sponsored bird-watching session for beginners, held on Sundays and national holidays from 11 to noon in the Nature Center. The Nature Center also has exhibits, films, and lectures on birds and other topics of interest to naturalists. Telescopes are provided in the Nature Center and in the blinds, but if you have binoculars at home bring them along. Shorter children will find them easier to use than the telescopes—and after all, a close-up view is what bird-watching is all about.

Shinagawa Aquarium is Tokyo's second-best aquarium—unless you are a toddler; then it's number one. It's just the right size, boasts the city's only dolphin show, and is fairly easy to maneuver with a stroller. Feeding times (posted on the tanks) mesmerize small children. The dolphin and sea lion shows are in the small first-floor stadium. Be sure to double-check the schedule as soon as you arrive, and plan to stake out your seats at least half an hour in advance on weekends. Monday to Saturday, the dolphin shows start at 11:30 A.M., 2 P.M., and 3:30, and the sea lion show at 1 P.M. On Sundays and holidays, the dolphins perform at 11 A.M., 1:30 P.M., and 4, and the sea lions at noon and 2:45. When choosing a spot, be forewarned: when the dolphins leap, they can splash out enough water to soak people halfway to the top of the stands.

The best part of the aquarium is on the lower level; take the stairs or elevator, designed to make you feel as if you are descending below the waves. You'll find yourself at the edge of a gigantic tank filled with a wide variety of sea creatures. Right through the middle of it is a glass tunnel that gives you the sensation of an undersea adventure, without getting wet.

Stepping out of the aquarium, you enter **Shinagawa Kumin Park**, nicely landscaped with a large, stone-rimmed pond. Children will want to walk northward through the park, passing under a motorway, until they come to the playground. A clean sandbox, swings, and a slide will entertain little ones. In July and August, you can take a dip in the outdoor pool. The north part of the park also has tennis courts and cookout spaces. To barbecue, call the park in Japanese for reservations. You must bring your own food and cooking equipment. Active families can easily see the Tokyo Wild Bird Park and the Shinagawa Aquarium in one day. Go by car; the poorly timed train and bus connections can waste more than an hour.

A **ferry from Hinode Pier** will take families who want to skip the bird park straight to the Shinagawa Aquarium. The trip takes 40 minutes. Call Tokyo Cruise Ship Company in Japanese at ☎ (03) 3457–7830 for schedules and ticket prices. Boat schedules are also posted at the dock at the aquarium and outside next to the aquarium entrance. See Tour 18 for map of water bus routes.

EATING OPTIONS

Restaurants   Tokyo Sea Life Park's large cafeteria outshines most of the eating options we have seen at parks and zoos, with a large range of nutritious choices at reasonable prices. Crystal View has a smaller-scale cafeteria downstairs. The hotel has several restaurants, and just outside the Sea Life Park is another cafeteria-style restaurant. Near Kasai Rinkai Koen station are three more eateries. Restaurants are scarce around the Subway Museum. Dolphin, a small restaurant with an excellent pond view and a variety of fish on its menu, is located near the entrance to the Shinagawa Aquarium. Lunch is about ¥1,500. There are no restaurants at or near Tokyo Port Wild Bird Park.

Picnic Possibilities   Beautiful ocean views make Kasai Rinkai Park a great place to spread your picnic blanket. Bring food from home or buy snacks at the stalls near the entrance to the aquarium. The Subway Museum also has a place where you can eat your lunch, located in the back next to the theater. Vending machines sell hamburgers in addition to beverages. While you munch, you can leaf through a small collection of books on trains. Tokyo Port Wild Bird Park and Kumin Park have picnic tables and drink machines. You can also reserve barbecue facilities at Kumin Park.

FOR INFANTS AND TODDLERS

There is a nursing room in the souvenir shop just after you enter the first gate of Kasai Rinkai Park. You can also change diapers on beds in the ladies' rooms in the aquarium and the handicapped restroom in Crystal View. No strollers are allowed inside the Tokyo Sea Life Park aquarium on weekends or national holidays; you must park them opposite the ticket vending machines. For lost children or lost articles inquire at the aquarium's second-floor information desk. The Subway Museum has a diaper-changing table in the ladies' room. On the ground floor of the Shinagawa Aquarium near the entrance, there is a diaper-changing table in the handicapped restroom. Tokyo Port Wild Bird Park has no special facilities for diapering or nursing, but if you are looking for a place to make do we suggest trying the Nature Center.

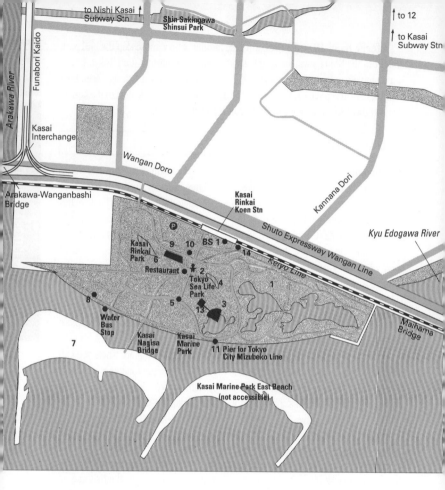

PLACES TO VISIT

1. Kasai Rinkai Bird Park
2. Tokyo Sea Life Park
3. Aquarium
4. Fresh Water Exhibits
5. Crystal View
6. Kasai Rinkai Park
7. Kasai Marine and Park
8. Fishing Spot

9. Hotel Seaside Edogawa
10. Park Train
11. Pier for Tokyo City Mizubeko Line
12. Subway Museum
13. Restaurants
14. Parking Lot Entrance

BS 1. Kasai Rinkai Koen Bus Stop

WHERE & WHEN

Kasai Rinkai Park and Bird Park

葛西臨海公園 (Kasai Rinkai Koen)

6–2–1 Rinkai-cho, Edogawa-ku, Tokyo 134–0086

☎ (03) 5696–1331

東京都江戸川区臨海町6-2-1 〒134-0086

OPEN: park 24 hours, bird-watching center 9:30 A.M. to 4:30 P.M., park train 9:30 A.M. to 3 P.M. (only Sat and Sun, call to check at 03–3877–0725)

FEES: no entry fee; park train ¥300 for junior high and older, ¥150 for primary school students

DIRECTIONS: a 5-minute walk from Kasai Rinkai Koen station (JR Keiyo line). The Musashino line also stops at Kasai Rinkai Koen station, but only on Sun and hols. Red double-decker buses from Koiwa station (JR Sobu line), Ichinoe station (Shinjuku subway line), or Kasai station (Tozai subway line) will take you to Kasai Rinkai Koen station. Or, take Toei bus #20 bound for Kasai Rinkai Koen Eki from bus stop #2 at Nishi Kasai station (Tozai line). There are two #20 buses that go different routes, so Toei advises you to check with the driver before boarding. If you are coming from the Subway Museum, take bus #28 bound for Kasai Rinkai Koen from stop #8 or a red double-decker bus from stop #7; Kasai Rinkai Koen is the last stop. Kasai Rinkai Koen Pier is accessible by Tokyo-to-Kankokisen ferry from Hinode Pier (see Tour 1 Sumida River Ferry for directions). By car, take the Bayshore line expressway (Kosoku Wangansen), exit at Kasai interchange, and turn right at the first light.

PARKING: two large lots, daily rate

COMMENTS: all ages, no English, nursing room

Tokyo Sea Life Park

葛西臨海水族園 (Kasai Rinkai Suizo Koen)

6–2–3 Rinkai-cho, Edogawa-ku, Tokyo 134–0086

☎ (03) 3869–5152

東京都江戸川区臨海町6-2-3 〒134-0086

OPEN: 9:30 A.M. to 5 P.M. (admission until 4)

CLOSED: Mon (Tues if Mon is a hol), Dec 29 to Jan 3

FEES: adults ¥800, middle school students ¥300, free for preschoolers, elementary school students, and adults over 65

DIRECTIONS: see Kasai Rinkai Park

PARKING: park at Kasai Rinkai Park

COMMENTS: all ages, English pamphlet

Kasai Marine and Beach Park

葛西海浜公園 (Kasai Kaihin Koen)

6–2–4 Rinkai-cho, Edogawa-ku, Tokyo 134–0086

☎ (03) 5696–4741

東京都江戸川区臨海町6-2-4 〒134-0086

OPEN: 9 A.M. to around 5 P.M. (until sunset in winter)

FEES: none

DIRECTIONS: see Kasai Rinkai Park

PARKING: park at Kasai Rinkai Park

COMMENTS: all ages, no English

Subway Museum

地下鉄博物館 (Chikatetsu Hakubutsu-kan)

6–3–1 Higashi Kasai, Edogawa-ku, Tokyo 134–0084

☎ (03) 3878–5011

東京都江戸川区東葛西6-3-1 〒134-0084

OPEN: 10 A.M. to 5:30 P.M. (admission until 5)

CLOSED: Mon (Tues if Mon is a hol), Dec 28 to Jan 4

FEES: adults ¥210 adults, elementary and middle school students ¥100

DIRECTIONS: across the street from Kasai station (Tozai subway line). If you are coming from Kasai Rinkai Park, board a red double-decker bus or bus #28 on the east side of the square in front of Kasai Rinkai station and get off at Kasai Eki bus stop. By car, exit the Bayshore line expressway (Kosoku Wangansen) at the Kasai interchange and take Kannana Dori; the museum is on the east side of the street across from Kasai subway station.

PARKING: free parking for 20 cars is available a few blocks to the east. Use the entrance on the other side of the Subway Museum.

COMMENTS: all ages, English pamphlet

Hotel Seaside Edogawa
ホテルシーサイド江戸川

6–2–2 Rinkai-cho, Edogawa-ku, Tokyo 134–0086

☎ (03) 3804–1180

東京都江戸川区臨海町6-2-2　〒134-0086

FEES: adults ¥11,000 to ¥13,500, children over 7 ¥8,400 to ¥10,900, children ages 2–7 ¥6,900 to ¥9,400. Rates include breakfast and dinner and vary according to the room and number of guests per room.

DIRECTIONS: see Kasai Rinkai Park above. The hotel is inside the park.

Tokyo Port Wild Bird Park
東京港野鳥公園 (Tokyo-ko Yacho Koen)

3–1 Tokai, Ota-ku, Tokyo 143–0001

☎ (03) 3799–5031

東京都大田区東海3-1　〒143-0001

OPEN: 9 A.M. to 5 P.M. except for Nov through Jan, when the park closes at 4:30. Admission until 30 minutes before closing.

CLOSED: Mon (Tues if Mon is a national or Tokyo city hol), Dec 29 to Jan 3

FEES: adults ¥300, junior/senior high students ¥150, small children and visitors over age 65 free

DIRECTIONS: a 15-minute walk from Ryutsu Center station (monorail from Hamamatsu-cho). Or take the central exit of JR Omori station (JR Keihin Tohoku line) and use the stairs next to Primo to get to the stops for

Keikyu bus #24, 25, 32, 36, 39, or 43 bound for Heiwajima, Keihinjima, or Jonanjima Junkan, which also stop at Omori Kaigan station (Keihin Kyuko line) before reaching Yacho Koen bus stop. From there the bird park is a 5-minute walk. From the east exit of Oimachi station (Oimachi and JR Keihin Tohoku lines) take Toei bus #98 bound for Shinagawa Eki Higashi Guchi to Tokyo Yacho Koen Iriguchi stop and walk 1 minute. By car, the park is on Kannana Dori west of the Bayshore line expressway (Kosoku Wangansen) overpass.

PARKING: free for about 55 cars

COMMENTS: all ages, good English pamphlets

Shinagawa Aquarium
品川水族館 (Shinagawa Suizoku-kan)

3–2–1 Katsushima, Shinagawa-ku, Tokyo 140–0012

☎ (03) 3762–3431

東京都品川区勝島3-2-1　〒140-0012

OPEN: 10 A.M. to 5 P.M. (admission until 4:30)

CLOSED: Tues, the day after national hols, Dec 29 to Jan 1

FEES: adults ¥900, elementary and middle school students ¥500, preschoolers age 4 and up ¥300

DIRECTIONS: the aquarium is a 5-minute walk from Omori Kaigan station (Keihin Kyuko line) and a 15-minute walk from the central exit (use the stairs next to Primo) of JR Omori station (JR Keihin Tohoku line). Shuttle buses from Oimachi station (JR Keihin Tohoku or Tokyu Oimachi lines) to the aquarium run about every hour on an irregular schedule. The bus leaves from stop #6 opposite Marui Department Store. Or come by ferry from Hinode Pier (directions in Tour 18). By car, the aquarium is located along Daiichi Keihin near the Suzugamori ramp of expressway #1.

If you are coming from the Wild Bird Park and are traveling by bus, take Keikyu bus #24, 25, 32, 36, 39, or 43 bound for Omori station and get off at Omori Kaigan Eki (station).

PARKING: available at the Shinagawa Kumin

Koen Minami parking area for an hourly rate. To reach the lot from the main entrance of the aquarium, travel south to the 4th traffic signal. Turn left, stay in the far left lane, and do not go up the elevated street. Turn left at the 1st corner and go over a bridge. The lot will be on your left at the foot of the bridge.

COMMENTS: all ages, sketchy bilingual pamphlet

Shinagawa Kumin Park

品川区民公園 (Shinagawa Kumin Koen)
3-chome Katsushima, Shinagawa-ku, Tokyo 140–0012
☎ (03) 3762–0655

東京都品川区克島3丁目   〒140-0012

OPEN: *Park*: 6 A.M.–6:30 P.M. (Dec–March), 6 A.M.–8:30 P.M. (April–Nov). *Outdoor pool*: 9 A.M. to 8 P.M., open to individuals from April–Nov. Morning session 9:30 to 12:30; afternoon session 1:15 to 5:15; and night session, held three times a week, Sat, Sun, Wed 5 to 8.

FEES: none for park; *pool* is ¥400 for adults, ¥200 for junior high school students, ¥100 for elementary school students

DIRECTIONS: see Shinagawa Aquarium

COMMENTS: all ages, no English

Nature in the City

You don't have to leave Tokyo to rejuvenate your family with fresh air and exercise in a natural environment. Following a narrow stream through tree-filled **Todoroki Ravine**, *it's easy to forget you're in one of the world's largest cities, and the park that fills the banks of the nearby Tama river offers plenty of spots for picnicking and soaking up sunshine.*

The best obstacle course in town challenges athletes of all ages at **Heiwa-no-Mori Park**, *where you can run, jump, and swing through a forest. After working out, wash up in a fashionable urban hot spring resort with heated pools and a wide variety of tubs.*

Have all the fun of camping out at the shore just a 20-minute drive from the center of Tokyo in **Wakasu Kaihin Park**. *Fish and watch the waves, or bike around a golf course to work up an appetite for a cookout. Be sure to save some time for a visit to the rain forest inside* **Yumenoshima's Tropical Greenhouse Dome**, *where waterfalls splash, bananas ripen, and bright-colored flowers bloom.*

Lots of things in Japan are small, but not **Showa Kinen Park**. *Children will love wandering through a forest where around each bend is a creative new kind of play equipment. Jump in giant, billowing clouds, slide down the back of larger-than-life dragons sleeping in a massive sandbox, splash in one of nine swimming pools. Wake up early and plan to stay late—the fun never stops here and there's more than you could possibly do in one day.*

Sweat and Soak in Heiwajima

Obstacle Course at Heiwa-no-Mori Park • Heiwajima Kurhaus Hot Spring

N othing ensures a good night's sleep better than fresh air, exercise, and a long, relaxing soak in a hot spring. Kids and adults will enjoy working up a sweat on a woodland athletics course, then splashing and soaking in an *onsen*, or hot spring, with heated swimming pools. **Heiwa-no-Mori Park** in southeast Tokyo is the place to come when you want to get your children worn out, fed, and bathed, and then home to sleep at, or even before, bedtime. There will be no complaints about taking a bath and no hemming and hawing about lights out, so you won't feel guilty when your charges are in dreamland and you have time to yourself.

Heiwajima's Heiwa-no-Mori Park has a pond for fishing, open fields for picnics and play, archery targets, tennis courts, obstacle courses, and a gateball (similar to croquet) field. And while all of these are enjoyable, the obstacle courses are the best. Layers of tall pines, willows, and flowering trees shield you from the clutter and noise of the city, and songbirds serenade you as you race across the forest floor. Go in the spring, the fall, on a clear winter day or a cool summer morning. You will feel your blood oxygenating, your stress dissipating, and your whole body relaxing as you start the course. When you're done, you'll have that good tired feeling that comes from physical exercise and a sense of accomplishment. So will your kids.

Two well-built courses serve any shape or size of family: a little seven-point course for the under-six crowd and a more extensive course for everyone else. The larger course has six color-coded levels of difficulty. The hardest level includes forty-five activities, the easiest twenty-eight. Age recommendations and activities for each level are posted in Japanese near the starting place. Choose the level you want, record your starting time, and you're off. Signs show which color levels should complete each item. The course crosses water in three places, and you have to pole a barrel around an obstacle in the pond. You'll be climbing, crawling, leaping, pulling, balancing, hanging, and having a good time. Give yourself two points if you did an item perfectly, one point if you did it but not so perfectly, and no points if you looked at it and ran away. Or, make up your own scoring system. Here's a rough translation of the course levels.

Levels for Obstacle Course

Color	Number of Items	Handicap	Age for Men	Age for Women
Red	28	34	7–10	7–10
Yellow	42	6	11–14	11–14
Blue	45	0	15–24	15–24
Green	43	4	25–35	15–24
Orange	37	16	36–45	25–35
Pink	30	30	above 46	above 36

An elevated section of Kannana Dori cuts the park in two. The park office, obstacle courses, and tennis courts are on the south side. You can get a map of the park's facilities at the office. You can also buy tickets for the larger obstacle course at a vending machine nearby. Go down the hall past the office and you will see the course entrance on the left. The seven-point course for preschoolers is free. Walk past the entrance for the large course to the street and turn left. In a few seconds you will come to a fork; take the right side and in a minute or so you will see the little course on the left.

If you want to make reservations for tennis or archery, call the park in Japanese. You must bring your own equipment for those sports, as well as for fishing. Anything you catch has to be thrown back—you are not allowed to take the fish home.

There are no showers in the locker rooms at the obstacle course, so bring a few hand towels to wash up with and a change of clothes to wear to the next spot: **Heiwajima Kurhaus**, part of the Heiwajima Leisure Land complex. If you are walking from the obstacle course, go under Kannana Dori and head for the opposite end of the park. There you will see steps leading to a statue of a mother and child. Follow the walkway behind the statue across the overpass, where you will come to cascading water. Go down the staircase on the right and walk straight to the corner. Cross the street and go left. Heiwajima Kurhaus is on the second floor of the large white building with blue stripes and pink window shutters.

Heiwajima Kurhaus is a plush, modern *onsen* with a round current pool, a heated kiddie pool, a gym, and loads of other amenities. The *onsen*'s water comes from a natural hot spring 2,000 meters underground, and the urban resort is set up so you can drop in without any preparation and enjoy all of the facilities. Your entrance fee includes saunas, a dozen different baths for each of the two sexes, pools, workout machines, water aerobics classes, studio aerobics classes, and movies on video (some in English). Pay more and you can get a sports massage, time in the aromatherapy room, or the use of body sonic therapy equipment. They provide towels and comfortable lounge wear (from one-size-fits-all for small kids to Japanese adult sizes S–LL). Soap, shampoo, razors, toothbrushes, and hairbrushes are available at no charge in the locker rooms. You can rent swimwear and workout shoes. They have a list of prices and an explanation of their facilities in English.

Take off your shoes as you enter the building and put them in shoe lockers in the room on your right. Bring the keys from your shoe lockers to the front desk. They will hold the shoe locker keys, charge you for entrance, and give you keys for the locker room. Pick up kits with towels and loungewear at the next counter. If you speak Japanese, you can also have *onsen* personnel evaluate your physical condition and give a recommendation on which baths you should enter and how long you should soak in each one. Put on a swimsuit and go to the pool, get into your loungewear and go to the restaurant or a relaxation zone, or stay in your birthday suit and hit the baths. You'll need coins for drinks from machines or for the game center, if the kids play there. For restaurant and massage charges, the clerk or waiter will scan the bar code on your locker key band and put the charges on your account.

When you enter the bath area, splash yourself with Kaburi-yu (hot water for dousing) from one of the tubs near the entrance. Digital temperature displays on each tub let you choose the one you like. Then enter the scrubbing area to soap up and rinse off. Now you are ready for the baths. Some are hot, some are warm, and one is tepid so even a young child will find it comfortable. One bath has a stream of hot water that falls from the ceiling. Put an aching part of your body under it for a water massage. Another has a chair that shoots water up from underneath. Plus there are all sorts of bubbling and soaking baths, saunas, and a wooden rest area. Little kids up to age seven or so can choose whether they want to bathe with mom or dad.

Between dips in the pools and baths, you can have a meal at the restaurant (just wear the loungewear and go barefoot), a drink at the pool-side juice bar, or a rest in one of the recliners in the large lounge. There is a separate smoking room so the main lounge stays smoke-free. You can even take your forty winks here, or let small children take a nap while parents read and take turns going to the gym.

Parents adore this place and kids have a great time as well. The different baths and the swimming pool are a fun, easy way to get the children cleaned up. When everyone has that rosy, relaxed, post-bathing glow, return the kit of used towels and loungewear, pay restaurant and massage bills at the front counter, pick up the keys to your shoe lockers and head home.

Other Things to Do in the Area

The round pool at Kurhaus isn't good for lap swimming and the entrance fee, though cheap compared to a mountainside *onsen* resort, can be a bit of a shock to newcomers who have not adjusted to Tokyo prices. If you are looking for a vigorous swim or just lots of splashing fun in a kiddie pool, try the inexpensive ward-funded pools at **Heiwajima Park**. From September 14 to June 30, the park has two heated indoor pools: a 25-meter pool for adults and school-aged children and a kiddie pool for those over three. From July 10 to August 31, the dome is opened and the two indoor pools become outdoor pools, plus two more pools are put into use. One is a 50-meter pool, the other a circular pool with slides. Also, children under age three are allowed to swim in the summer. Sorry, but no diving.

The pool has locker rooms with showers. The facilities are fairly new, clean, and in good repair. Bring your towels and swimwear, including bathing caps—required even for the guys. Be sure to check the pool holidays listed in the When & Where section. If you come with a child too young to swim, you can find a baby bed and a table with chairs in the lounge area on the second floor of the building. One parent can swim with the bigger kids while the other supervises the little one. The second-floor lounge looks out over the action in the pool.

In addition to Kurhaus, Heiwajima Leisure Land has boat races and a bowling alley. The bowling alley is on the fourth floor of the same building Kurhaus is in; the boat races are across the street. Oi Keibajo, a racetrack, is a short drive up the Shuto expressway.

EATING OPTIONS

Restaurants There is a restaurant inside Kurhaus and two others in the same building. If you want Italian food, try the restaurant in the Leisure Land complex.

Picnic Possibilities Both Heiwa-no-Mori Park and Heiwajima Park have grassy areas and tables for picnics. Machines selling cold drinks are located near the office

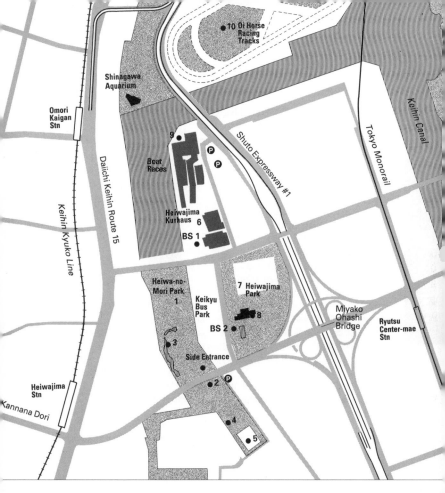

PLACES TO VISIT

1. Heiwa-no-Mori Park
2. Obstacle Course
3. Fishing Pond
4. Archery
5. Tennis Courts
6. Heiwajima Kurhaus and Bowling Alley
7. Heiwajima Park

8. Pools
9. Boat Races
10. Oi Horse Racing Track

BS 1. Heiwajima Leisure Land Bus Stop
BS 2. Omori Egyosho-mae Bus Stop

in Heiwa-no-Mori Park. You can also reserve space for a cookout at Heiwajima Park. Bring your own food, fire, grill, and cookware. Contact the park office in Japanese for reservations.

FOR INFANTS AND TODDLERS

There are no designated facilities for diapering or nursing in Heiwa-no-Mori Park, but you should find many spots that will do. Kurhaus has a baby bed and stools that you can use for nursing in the women's locker room. At Heiwajima Park, use the locker room. There is also a baby bed on the second floor.

WHERE & WHEN

Heiwa-no-Mori Park
平和の森公園 (Heiwa-no-Mori Koen)
2–1 Heiwa-no-Mori Koen, Ota-ku, Tokyo 143–0005
☎ (03) 3766–1607
東京都大田区平和の森公園2-1　〒143-0005
OPEN: obstacle course 9:30 A.M. to 4:30 P.M. (admission until 3)
CLOSED: Mon (Tues if Mon is a hol), Dec 29 to Jan 3
FEES: adults ¥330, elementary/junior high students ¥100. The seven-point course for preschoolers is free.
DIRECTIONS: a 5-minute walk from Heiwajima station on the Keihin Kyuko line or a 5-minute bus ride from the central exit (east side) at JR Omori station (JR Keihin Tohoku line). Use the Heiwajima Junkan (loop) bus at stop #9 and get off at Leisure Land bus stop. By car, travel east on Kannana Dori past Daiichi Keihin Dori and take the left off-ramp as you go over Miyako Ohashi bridge. Travel expressway #1 and take the 1st left, then turn left again heading back toward Miyako Ohashi bridge. Parking will be on your right underneath the bridge.
PARKING: Hourly rates. Parking from 8:30 A.M. until 9:30 P.M. No entrance to lot after 8:30 P.M.
COMMENTS: all ages, no English

Heiwajima Kurhaus
平和島クアハウス
1–1–1 Heiwajima, Ota-ku, Tokyo 143–0006
☎ (03) 3768–9121
東京都大田区平和島1-1-1　〒143-0006
OPEN: 10 A.M. to 10 P.M.
CLOSED: New Year's hols and a two-day hol in Oct vary each year
FEES: adults ¥2,550, children under 11 ¥1,225
DIRECTIONS: a 10-minute walk from Heiwajima station (Keihin Kyuko line) or a 5-minute bus ride from the central exit (east side) of JR Omori station. Board the Keikyu Heiwajima Junkan (loop) bus at stop #9 and get off at Leisure Land bus stop. By car, travel east on Kannana Dori past Daiichi Keihin Dori and take the left off-ramp as you go over Miyako Ohashi bridge. Drive along expressway #1 and take the 1st left and then the second right. Kurhaus is in the second building on the right.
PARKING: free
COMMENTS: all ages, English pamphlets, locker rooms can be used for nursing

Heiwajima Park
平和島公園
2–2–4 Heiwajima, Ota-ku, Tokyo 143–0006
☎ (03) 3764–8424 (Pool), (03) 3764–1414 (Park Office)

OPEN: Sept 14 to June 30 from 9:30 A.M. to 5:30 P.M. and 6 P.M. to 9 P.M. From July 10 to Aug 31, there are 3-hour morning and afternoon swimming sessions every day and a 3-hour evening session every day except Mon and Thurs. Only the 50-meter pool is open in the evenings. Summer sessions are 9:30 A.M. to 12:30 P.M., 1:15 to 4:15, and 5 to 8.

CLOSED: Mon. The pools are reserved for groups on Wed all day and Fri until 5:30. No individual swimmers allowed on those days. The pool is closed for a two-week summer hol that changes every year.

FEES: adults and high school students ¥440/2 hours, plus ¥100 for every additional half hour; children ¥200, plus ¥50 for every 30 minutes overtime

DIRECTIONS: S 15-minute walk from Heiwajima station (Keihin Kyuko line). From JR Omori station's east exit take the Heiwajima Junkan (loop) bus at stop #9 and get off at Leisure Land bus stop. By car, travel east on Kannana Dori past Daiichi Keihin Dori and take the left off-ramp as you go over Miyako Ohashi bridge. Travel expressway #1 and take the 1st left and turn left again. The parking lot will be on your left.

PARKING: hourly rate, open from 8:30 A.M. to 9:30 P.M. No entrance to lot after 8:30 P.M.

COMMENTS: all ages (note that kids under 3 cannot swim in winter), no English, no nursing room but locker rooms can be used for nursing

SIX

SWEAT AND SOAK

Tour 24

The Granddaddy of Tokyo's Family Parks

Showa Kinen Park

The sun is shining, the sky is blue, the temperature is just right, and you can't wait to get outside. When the weather is perfect, head for the perfect park. **Showa Kinen Park** is a whopping 120 hectares and still growing, with more than enough to entertain even the most active of children. We call it the granddaddy of local parks because here you'll find fun on a giant scale. Enjoy genteel sports like bird watching and lawn bowling or play rough-and-tumble in a forest turned into the most creative playground we have ever seen.

A former U.S. Air Force base, Showa Kinen Park commemorates the fiftieth anniversary of the Showa emperor's reign. Once finished, it will be the largest park of its kind in Japan. The park is in Tachikawa-shi, just over 20 minutes from Shinjuku by express train or 40 minutes by expressway. It is so big that you'll probably want to rent bicycles to get around, and maps are absolutely essential. As you enter the gate, ask for an English map of the entire park. Kodomo-no-Mori (Children's Woodland) is the first place to go. It has its own map, which is only in Japanese, but the pictures will help you get around. Hours can pass as you wander through the enchanted forest. Thick woods hide the dozen or so enormous play places so well that it seems to children as if you chance upon one wondrous thing after another.

The forest's spectacular sandbox is guarded by giant mosaic dragons with stomachs you can walk through, scales you can climb on, and tongues you can slide down. At the Kumo-no-Umi, billowy white tarps stretch across the hillside, creating a "sea of clouds" you can jump on. Kids—and adults—love bouncing high on the springy material beneath the fabric. Huge, bright-colored hammocks, a roller slide, and a mist-filled maze are some of the other play elements you'll encounter. Climb to the top of the Taiyo-no-Pyramid (Sun Pyramid) to admire the view or play king of the mountain.

In the heart of the forest, a rest house called Mori-no-Ie (Woodland House) holds free classes in Japanese on reed pipe–making the first Sunday of each month from 1 to 2 P.M., and classes on varying topics on the second Saturday of each month from 10 A.M. to 3:30 P.M. There is also a woodworking house for crafts open from 10 A.M. till 1 hour before the park closes. Individuals may use the facilities on Sundays, national holidays, and Japanese school holidays free of charge by applying at Mori-no-Ie. On weekdays and Saturdays, individuals may use the room if no group has reserved it. Tools and supplies can be borrowed at Mori-no-Ie.

Showa Kinen Park has its own train with six or seven stops. Use it to get from Kodomo-no-Mori back to the main gate, or to take a look at the whole park before deciding where to go next. In other parts of the park you can try your hand at croquet, petanque, frisbee golf, horseshoes, lawn bowling, and mini golf. Rent the equipment you need from Yurt Sports Equipment Rental, easy to find with the English map. If these games are new to you, lessons are held in Japanese on the fourth Sunday of every month from 10 A.M. to noon at the appropriate locations for each.

If cycling is your sport, there are 11 kilometers of road to pedal on one wheel or two. Bring your own bike or use one of the park's. Conventional bikes are rented out at the Tachikawa Gate and the South Gate. Unicycles are rented out only at the Tachikawa Gate. Boaters can choose from pedal boats, rowboats, and canoes, then maneuver around the fish in the large pond.

When you've worked up a sweat, cool off in the water-play area. In spring and autumn, five free outdoor pools tempt visitors to dip their toes. In summer (mid-July to September), four more pools open, admission is charged, and the Rainbow Pool area goes into full swing. One of the pools has four waterslides; the longer ones send you curving and swerving down 100 meters. You must be at least ten years old and 110 centimeters (3' 7") to use this pool. There is a big current pool to raft in a rubber boat or inner tube and a 180-meter wave pool with a Caribbean atmosphere. Jumbo-size nets you can climb stretch across the center of another pool. Adventurous swimmers clamber up and over to a wide slide that whooshes you back down into the water. A large clover-shaped pool in the center has roped-off lanes for lap swims and races. The nearby waterfall pool has five pleasant waterfalls to splash underneath, the largest 5 meters high. Smaller children will play happily in the kiddie pool and another shallow pool with a colorful monument. In winter, part of the pool area becomes an outdoor skating rink.

If you're in the mood to commune with nature, sprawl out on one of the spacious lawns or pick your way along the 700-meter mountain stream that flows through the center of the park. It ends in a dragonfly marsh where you can see eighteen different varieties of this well-loved summertime bug. There are both flower and herb gardens in various parts of the park and a large variety of trees. Japanese readers can get free maps for orienteering and green adventure courses near the Tachikawa Gate. If you'd like to get to know the park's inhabitants a little better, borrow binoculars from the Kabokuen Exhibition Center, bring them to the bird sanctuary blind, and take a peek at waterfowl like kingfishers and herons. Free bird watching meetings are held on the fourth Sunday of each month from 10 A.M. to noon. Meet in the morning at the south gate for a bird-watchers' tour of the park.

Don't try to race from attraction to attraction: there's far more than you can possibly do in a single outing at Showa Kinen Park, and it's growing every day. At the time of this writing, a Japanese garden is being built next to Kodomo-no-Mori. Other expansions are also planned, including a section to be called the Northern Forest. With all the variety and seasonal activities, there are plenty of reasons to come back again and again—like spring blossoms, summer fireworks, and the Tachikawa marathon.

EATING OPTIONS

Restaurants   The park has three restaurants that sell light meals. To eat indoors, buy tickets for the drinks and food you want and give them to the counter person. Pick up the food when your number is called. If you want to eat on the terrace at one of the restaurants, order from the Japanese menu at the window outside.

Picnic Possibilities   There is an eleven-hectare lawn just for picnics and sports, and many other lawns and picnic tables throughout the park. Snack shops and vending machines located near restrooms, restaurants, and rest areas lighten the load you must bring in your picnic basket. Call for barbecue reservations. You can use space for free and bring your own cooking gear and food, or rent equipment and buy ingredients for *yakisoba* (fried noodles) and *teppanyaki* (grilled meat and vegetables) at the park. You can even rent a tarp if the weather turns sour or the sun is too strong.

FOR INFANTS AND TODDLERS

Smooth paths make it easy for parents pushing strollers, either your own or a park rental. The park train makes it even easier. They put your stroller in a storage section in the back of the train while you ride in one of the cars. Bikes go back there, too. The last train back from Kodomo-no-Mori leaves at 4:31 P.M.

Although the current English map doesn't indicate which restrooms have diaper-changing tables, the Japanese map does. Pick up one of these at the gate as you enter and look for a little icon of a baby in a diaper. Nursing mothers can ask to use cots in the first aid stations at Kodomo-no-Mori and at the Tachikawa Gate Bicycle Center. Hot water for formula is available on request at restaurants and first aid stations. The park only broadcasts announcements for lost children over the age of six, so keep a close eye on pre-school kids. Children must not wear diapers in the pools, including the kiddie pool.

WHERE & WHEN

Showa Kinen Park
昭和記念公園 (Showa Kinen Koen)
3173 Midoricho, Tachikawa-shi, Tokyo 190–8530
☎ (0425) 28–1751, (0425) 21–0300
(Telephone Service)
東京都立川市緑町3173　〒190-8530
OPEN: 9:30 A.M. to 5 P.M. March 1 to Oct 31; 9:30 A.M. to 4:30 P.M. Nov 1 to Feb 29
CLOSED: Dec 31, Jan 1, and the 4th Mon and Tues of Feb
FEES: *entrance* ¥390 for adults, ¥270 for children. *Rainbow Pool fees*: ¥2,200 for adults over age 15, ¥1,200 for children 6 to 15, ¥300 for children 4 to 6.

Rides and rentals:

Park train	¥250 for adults, ¥100 for children
Bicycles	¥400 for adults, ¥250 for children for 3 hours
Cycle boats	¥700 for 30 minutes
Rowboats	¥350 for 30 minutes
Canoes	¥500 for 30 minutes
Putter golf	¥1,550 for 18 holes, ¥820 for 9 holes
Disc golf	¥210 for for 3 hours plus ¥300 deposit
Petanque	¥100 for 30 minutes
Croquet	¥310 for 1 hour plus ¥200 deposit
Lawn bowling	¥210 for 1 hour plus ¥200 deposit
Horseshoes	¥100 for 1 hour plus ¥100 deposit
Strollers	¥150

Most sports can be played from 9:30 A.M. till 1 hour before the park closes, except putter golf, which stops at 3:30. Croquet and lawn bowling are only available on weekends and national hols from Dec 1 to Feb 29.

DIRECTIONS: a 3-minute walk from the south exit of Nishi Tachikawa station (JR Ome line). On weekends and national hols the park exit of the station opens and the walk is less than 1 minute. 15-minute walk from Tachikawa station (JR Chuo line). By car, take Itsukaichi Kaido and turn south onto Tachikawa Dori. Turn right at Akebono 2 crossing and the park will appear on your right after a few hundred meters.

PARKING: two lots hold about 2,000 cars, daily rate

COMMENTS: all ages, English map, first aid center can be used to nurse

Hiking for Little Legs

Todoroki Ravine • Tama Riverbank

Descending the spiral staircase that leads into **Todoroki Ravine**, you enter a different world. The babbling of a shallow stream drowns out the noises of suburban Tokyo, while the canyon's abundant greenery effectively obscures most signs of civilization. Though just 20 minutes by train from Shibuya, this small nature preserve offers a rare opportunity to take a walk in the wilderness. The autumn leaves are glorious, and it's also a great way to beat the summer heat. You'll probably want insect repellent, and even a change of clothes, especially for young children.

The first few hundred meters provide a taste of adventure; the narrow trail incorporating steppingstones and logs follows the stream toward the Tamagawa river, gradually growing less rugged. Ducks live near the upper entrance, the most pristine section of the park. Below Kanpachi Dori, a large road that crosses the ravine, the path becomes a meter-wide cement walkway with a low fence to prevent children from falling into the stream. On the left are restrooms, picnic tables, and the glassed-in entrance to an ancient tomb. While it's hard to see much inside without a flashlight, diagrams on a nearby sign show how the local chieftains were once buried with their possessions.

Follow the stream as it meanders through the ravine, swirling beneath trees. A small shrine and two dragon-spout waterfalls signal that you have reached the staircase that leads to Todoroki Fudo, a Buddhist temple. The coolness of the waterfalls makes this peaceful spot a good place for a break. The benches covered with bright red cloth are for the customers of Setsugekka, a tea shop selling traditional tea and sweets in the afternoons and early evenings. The stairs to the temple are steep; the building itself has a graceful design and peaceful courtyard. It is affiliated with

SIX

HIKING FOR LITTLE LEGS   Tour 26

Manganji temple, a little way up Meiji Dori, which dates back to 1470. Wash your hands under the dragon spout and toss a coin into the collection box for good luck, then head back down the stairs and follow the brook as it flows through a wealthy suburban neighborhood with driveways built over the river. At the small waterfall where it joins another stream, turn right, then left at Tengenbashi, the first red brick bridge. You will pass Heights Nakajima, a small apartment building, and after a short walk and some stairs you'll be at Tamazutsumi Shogakko bus stop, just across the street from the wide banks of the Tamagawa river. Walking from Todoroki station to this point will take 25 minutes to an hour, depending on how quickly you hike.

If you've had enough walking, catch the bus to Futakotamagawaen (see Other Things to Do in the Area). It's just seven stops, but be warned that it can take awhile on summer weekends when traffic is heavy. Those who still want to hike will enjoy strolling the banks of the **Tamagawa river**. Graceful wading birds splash in the quiet channels of the river; on the banks people play soccer and baseball, ride along the bike path, stretch out for a suntan, or practice musical instruments. On Sundays, you can often hear *taiko* drums from across the river. Weekdays, you might get a glimpse of the Tokyo Giants, whose baseball practice ground is just downstream.

Along the route you'll also see a few fishermen, and yes, they actually do catch something, mostly large carp and small minnows. Carry collapsible poles and buckets in your backpack (you can find these at most sporting goods stores) and join in the fun. Spend a peaceful hour or two watching the water flow by while you fish. One entertainment-maximizing option is to plan your trip here to coincide with one of the area festivals.

The ravine has a firefly festival around the temple grounds the first Sunday in July. More than 30,000 people visit an 18-meter-high black tent constructed in the ravine to showcase the luminous insects. *Yatai* stands sell concessions and amusements. More spectacular is the Tamagawa Fireworks Festival in July or August, when nearly 200,000 people gather along the riverbanks to watch more than 6,000 rounds of fireworks being shot off.

Other Things to Do in the Area

Instead of beginning at the ravine, go one stop further along the train line to Kaminoge station and visit the **Goto Museum** garden. Parts of this garden are strictly manicured in traditional Japanese style, with undecorated gates, lines of small Buddhist statues, bamboo water spouts, contrived streams, and pines clipped and

221

forced into careful shapes; other sections are filled with bushes and leaves left to nature. You can buy an entrance ticket to both the museum exhibit and the garden or simply pay ¥100, skip the exhibit and go straight outside. The museum exhibit gallery is small, but the collection of Japanese and Chinese paintings, calligraphy, ceramics, and tea ceremony utensils is outstanding, with many objects registered as National Treasures or Important Cultural Properties. To see the most well-known part of the collection—paintings based on the *Tale of Genji*, a literary masterpiece of the Heian period—come during Golden Week (April 29 through May 5). The exhibits have English titles and explanations. We suggest you spend an hour exploring the grounds before traveling one stop on the Oimachi line to Todoroki station and the ravine.

Once you have traversed the ravine, explore the woods in **Tamagawa-dai Park**, a short bus ride along the Tamagawa river past the Yomiuri Giants' practice field. Children can investigate tiny stairways and secluded paths. An aquatic plant garden on the far east side makes for pleasant scenery, and one section of the park has a splendid view of the river. More historically important here are nine ancient burial tumuli and a small museum housing a replica of a tribal chieftain's tomb dating from 600 A.D. Walk inside to see how the chieftain was laid to rest. Outside the mouth of the tomb, figures dressed in period garb reenact a festival for the tribe's next leader as he assumes his new position. The period of Japanese history from 400 to 700 A.D. has actually been named for these keyhole-shaped burial tumuli, and many have been discovered in Ota and Setagaya wards along the Tamagawa.

Let your aspiring bus driver or pilot enact his or her sudden-braking, hairpin-curve-negotiating, or taking-off-and-landing fantasies at the **Train and Bus Museum** at Takatsu station a few stops down the Den'entoshi line. Crawl into a cockpit with all the controls you could hope for, complete with a flight simulator. Nothing is simulated about the cockpit, though; it's the real thing, disconnected from most of the passenger seats. The same goes for actual (retired) buses and trains.

The museum's three small buildings also house a panorama of miniature trains with scheduled shows, a wall-sized photo of Shibuya station in the 1960s that illustrates Japan's rapid changes, miniature electric trains you can steer around a track, and, for safety-consciousness, a track crossing, again the real thing.

We have never seen this place crowded, even on Saturdays. We also love the ¥10 admission. Buy your admission ticket from a retired train ticket vending machine and hold onto it. You'll need it to enter the other buildings.

EATING OPTIONS

Restaurants The Timberwood Café at the entrance to Todoroki Ravine has a lovely view of the greenery and a tempting selection of cakes. There are a handful of inexpensive sandwich shops and Japanese restaurants around Kaminoge station near the Goto Museum. The options are slim near the Train and Bus Museum and Tamagawa Dai Park.

Picnic Possibilities Todoroki Ravine has a nice place to spread a picnic blanket just across from the entrance to the temple. There are a few benches in the park along the Tama river; one particularly pretty (and popular) place is near the railway bridge to Futakotamagawaen station. You could also bring a blanket or plastic sheet and have a picnic on the riverbank. The Goto Museum has no picnic spot, but you can buy drinks at vending machines in the museum's rest area and give your kids a snack. At the Train and Bus Museum, you can eat on benches near the vending machines. People also eat in the retired streetcar just outside. Tamagawa-dai Park has a large open field perfect for picnics.

FOR INFANTS AND TODDLERS

The Goto Museum has a room you may use for nursing if it's unoccupied; inquire at the reception desk. Baby rooms, nursing facilities, food, and supplies can be found on the fourth floor of the Takashimaya building farthest from the station. On the hiking trail you'll need to adopt makeshift solutions, although there are some restaurants across the road from the Tama river that may be able to provide hot water for bottles. There is a changing table in the women's restroom downstairs in the last building of the Train and Bus Museum.

If you are completely dependent on your stroller or for some other reason are leery about the rugged terrain in the upper section of the ravine, it is still possible to visit this small canyon by starting at the Tamazutsumi Shogakko bus stop and walking up, or entering via the steep staircase halfway down. You'll also have trouble with the many staircases in Tamagawa Dai Park. The ground all along the course in this chapter is rough, and although it's not impossible with a stroller, we don't recommend it.

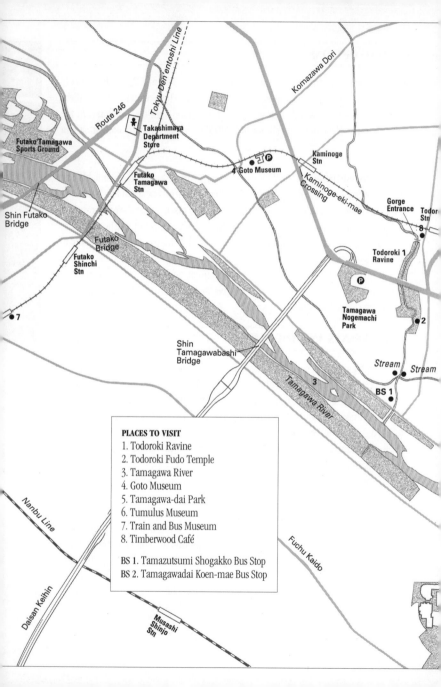

PLACES TO VISIT
1. Todoroki Ravine
2. Todoroki Fudo Temple
3. Tamagawa River
4. Goto Museum
5. Tamagawa-dai Park
6. Tumulus Museum
7. Train and Bus Museum
8. Timberwood Café

BS 1. Tamazutsumi Shogakko Bus Stop
BS 2. Tamagawadai Koen-mae Bus Stop

WHERE & WHEN

Todoroki Ravine

等々力渓谷 (Todoroki Keikoku)

2–39 Todoroki, Setagaya-ku, Tokyo

東京都世田谷区等々力2-39

OPEN: 24 hours

FEES: none

DIRECTIONS: a 3-minute walk from Todoroki station (Tokyu Oimachi line). Also accessible from Tamazutsumi Shogakko bus stop, served by bus #11 from Futakotamagawa station (Tokyu Oimachi and Shintamagawa lines) and Tamagawaen (Tokyu Toyoko and Mekama lines) every 20 minutes. By car, follow Meguro Dori south to Todoroki.

PARKING: no parking at the ravine but there is limited parking in nearby Tamagawa Noge-machi Koen and Todoroki Fudo

COMMENTS: all ages, no English

Goto Museum

五島美術館 (Goto Bijutsu-kan)

3–9–25 Kaminoge, Setagaya-ku, Tokyo

☎ (03) 3703–0661, 0662

東京都世田谷区上野毛3-9-25

OPEN: 9:30 A.M. to 4:30 P.M.

CLOSED: Mon, the day after a national hol, during exhibition changes, and Dec 26 to Jan 5

FEES: adults ¥700, students ¥500 for museum and garden. Garden only ¥100.

DIRECTIONS: a 5-minute walk from Kaminoge station (Tokyu Oimachi line). An easy-to-find map showing the way to the museum is posted in front of the station. By car, exit Kanpachi Dori at Kaminoge station crossing. The museum is on the 2nd small street on your right.

PARKING: free parking but the lot can only accommodate seven or eight cars

COMMENTS: all ages (for the garden), English pamphlet

Tamagawa-dai Park

多摩川台公園 (Tamagawadai Koen)

1–63–1 Den'enchofu, Ota-ku, Tokyo 145– 0071

☎ (03) 3721–1951

東京都大田区田園調布1-63-1　〒145-0071

OPEN: park always open; tomb museum (Kofun Tenjishitsu) 9 A.M. to 4:30 P.M.

CLOSED: tomb museum closes Dec 28 to Jan 4

DIRECTIONS: from the Tamagawa riverbank take bus #11 toward Tamagawaen. Get off at Tamagawadai Koen-mae bus stop. By train, a 5-minute walk from Tamagawaen station on the Tokyu Toyoko and Mekama lines. By car, the park is on Tamazutsumi Dori near the intersection with Nakahara Kaido.

PARKING: none in vicinity

COMMENTS: all ages, no English

Train and Bus Museum

電車とバスの博物館 (Densha to Basu no Hakubutsu-kan)

4–1–1 Futago, Takatsu-ku, Kawasaki-shi, Kanagawa-ken 213–0002

☎ (044) 822–9084

神奈川県川崎市高津区二子4-1-1

〒213-0002

OPEN: 10 A.M. to 5 P.M.

CLOSED: Mon (if Mon is a national hol, the following work day), also Dec 29 to Jan 3

FEES: 4 and up ¥10

DIRECTIONS: As you exit Takatsu station (Den'entoshi line), turn right and walk back along the side of the station until you come to the entrance. By car, see directions to Futako-tamagawaen. Pass the station and cross the Tamagawa river. Go straight at the next intersection, then turn left; Takatsu station is on your left with the museum behind it.

PARKING: none

COMMENTS: 5 and up, no English

City Seaside Campsite

Wakasu Kaihin Park • Yumenoshima Park and Tropical Greenhouse Dome

I magine this: your whole family cooking dinner outdoors, sharing stories about the big fish that got away. The catch of the day is on the grill as evening shadows flicker on the tent wall. In the background, the sound of waves and sleepy birds. Share with your children the fun of camping at **Wakasu Kaihin Park**. Here and at nearby Yumenoshima's tropical garden there's plenty of excitement for small campers, while mom and dad will love the convenience of the location, just a 20-minute drive from the center of Tokyo. Being close to town takes much of the stress out of an outdoor adventure—it's easy to go back because junior forgot his sleeping bag, or leave camp in search of *ramen* noodles when the fish aren't biting. And even the worst traffic jam won't stretch the ride home into more than an hour.

Surrounded by water on three sides, the park has a family campground and play area in one half; a golf course and a marina with a sailing school occupy the other half. The campground has room for over a hundred tents, so come with a crowd of friends or just your own clan. You can stay for a single day or spend up to three nights on the shore. Reserve space over the phone in Japanese at least one day in advance, (or as early as six months). During Japanese summer school holidays (July 21 to August 31), you must apply for reservations using an *ofuku* postcard (you can buy these at the post office) postmarked between April 15 and April 25. A lottery is held to allot camp space, but if any spots are left after the lottery you can reserve them by phone.

Bring your own tents and gear or rent what you need. In July, August, and September, Rentacomu, a rental company, sets up shop on the campground. Call (03) 3295–6666 in advance to reserve cookware, camp stoves, ice chests, folding tables, chairs, lanterns, sleeping bags, and lodge-style tents for overnight stays or tarp shelters for day outings. They also sell bait, but they operate only in summer. During the rest of the year, you can rent gear from many rental shops around town like **Duskin Rent All,** which also carries seasonal sporting equipment, household appliances, folding tables, and so on. Bring along an interpreter if you don't trust your Japanese. Many sporting good stores in Japan sell camping gear; the greatest concentration of shops is on the stretch of Yasukuni Dori that cuts through the Kanda-Ogawa-machi area of Chiyoda Ward.

The park's service center sells snacks and toys but no real food and no fishing bait or tackle. So be sure to bring a well-stocked ice chest, eating utensils, soap for washing up, plus, if you fish, enough line, bait, and lures to last your stay. If you've forgotten something essential, the nearest shop is a small supermarket 5 kilometers away among the apartment buildings of the Tatsumi area. Also, while there are sinks for washing hands and faces, there are no shower facilities at Wakasu. The showers at Yumenoshima Sports Center (see Other Things to Do in the Area) are probably the best way to wash up if you need to.

On the day of your camp out, check in at the Service Center. The office is past the little shop counter and down the hall on the left. Once you know your campsite number, find one of the wooden wagons on hand to help you carry your stuff from the car to the campground.

When your tent is up, venture out into other parts of the park. The campground is on the waterfront and near a long pier for fishing. Catch rock trout and horse mackerel in the spring, gilt head, half beaks, and gobies in the summer, bass in the fall, and turbot and trout in the winter. If the fish aren't biting, hit the bikes. There are two courses with separate cycle rental areas. The 4.5-kilometer course for kids who can handle two-wheelers takes you along the seaside perimeters of the park, past the golf course and marina to a round observation platform that makes a good place for a break. Relax and take in the waves, the sea gulls, the salt air, and the sailboats. People of all ages will appreciate the kiddie cycle track, which has all sorts of fascinating things to pedal, from old-style cars and two-seater pandas on wheels to single-seater "F1 racers" and bikes that have no pedals—they move as you bounce up and down on the seat. Kids can also have a lot of fun on the colorful metal playground equipment in the field behind the cycle rental areas.

Wakasu Kaihin Park makes a pretty full day for a growing family. But if you are staying for a few nights, head over to neighboring **Yumenoshima** before you leave. You can get there easily on the city bus that stops just outside the campground.

Yumenoshima's famous **Tropical Greenhouse Dome** provides many lessons for young visitors. Take a moment to learn about recycling garbage into energy. The tropical garden is not far from the Koto Ward Incineration Plant, where the heat created by burning garbage is used to produce super-heated water (125° C/257° F). The garden's converters take the energy from the water to warm the tropical plant dome in cold weather and cool it during hot weather.

Yumenoshima, or Dream Island, was once a final resting place for old wooden ships, scraps, junk, and trash from Tokyo. The city poured a meter-thick layer of topsoil on the landfill, cleaned up the canals that surround the island, and made the place a family park.

Step inside the three connected domes and enter a tropical rain forest. Dome A is crowded with woody ferns, water lilies from the Amazon, and orchids. It even has an elephant bamboo, the largest species of this fast-growing tree. In Dome B you walk through a cave behind a waterfall and wander past a thatched-roof hut, surrounded by palms and trumpet flowers, as well as fruit trees like banana, coconut, and mango. Dome C focuses on plants grown in the Ogasawara island chain, a subtropical zone to the south that is officially part of Tokyo. Look up. Some of the prettiest sights in Dome C touch the ceiling. Feast your eyes on rare screw pines and tall traveler's trees. Each section has a signboard with a brief description in English. An English pamphlet explains further, but individual plant names are given only in Latin and Japanese.

Don't miss the Venus flytraps and other carnivorous plants in the glass cases just outside the dome exit. Downstairs in the Information Gallery, displays teach about life in the tropics. Wall exhibits show pictures of people and animals living in the Ogasawara island chain and the world's three major tropical zones: Southeast Asia, Africa, and Central South America. Other displays explain how trees lose their leaves and show videos of tropical rain forests. An interesting video and aromatic exhibit lets you sample the fragrances of papaya and coffee flowers, jasmine blossoms and water lilies. Guess what kinds of plants are used to make household items like chocolate, furniture, chewing gum, soap, and perfume, then test yourself with a diorama that stretches across the back wall of the gallery. Push a button and the corresponding plant appears on the screen. None of the exhibits in the Information Gallery have English explanations or titles, but the pictures go a long way. The massive stump on the lawn outside the garden belonged to a giant lauan tree from Malaysia. Used for timber, these trees grow up to 50 meters tall. The greenhouses beyond that hold eucalyptus trees grown to provide food for the koalas at Tama Zoo (see Tour 22).

You can see the tropical dome and the area around it in less than an hour, but don't leave Yumenoshima just yet. The lush green park that surrounds the garden is a great place to jog, roller-skate, skateboard, cycle, or simply go for a stroll. Follow the path along the yacht harbor, stick to the smooth concrete pathways in front of the tropical plant dome, or pick your way through the trees on a winding path covered with wood shavings. There is an athletic track for serious exercisers and a wide, open circular field for letting the little ones romp. This is a good place to bring your dog for a game of fetch—unfortunately, no pets are allowed in Wakasu Kaihin Park.

Other Things to Do in the Area

Yumenoshima Sports Center occupies the southeast section of the park. For next to nothing you can swim, work out, have a sauna, and play volleyball, basketball, badminton, or table tennis. The facility also has a practice ring for sumo wrestling, dojos for judo and kendo, plus an outdoor target range for Japanese archery (but you need a license). There are three pools: a 25-meter pool for lap swims, a square pool with a water slide for beginners, and a kiddie pool. An English guidebook that you can get at the reception desk explains the facilities and payment procedures. Be sure to bring balls and all equipment required for the sport you wish to play.

A triangular building on the northwest side of Yumenoshima Park holds the remains of the **_Lucky Dragon #5_**, a misnamed wooden trawler that happened to be fishing for tuna in the vicinity of Bikini Atoll on March 1, 1954, when the U.S. Atomic Energy Commission tested a hydrogen bomb in the area. Most of the twenty-three crew members immediately showed signs of radiation poisoning and several of them died of related diseases. The Display House of the _Lucky Dragon_ has gory pictures depicting the illnesses of the crew and residents of small islands that were downwind from the explosion site. Many could cause small children to have nightmares. If you want to see the display house, it would be prudent to send a parent in first to judge whether the pictures are too graphic for your youngsters. There are no English titles or explanations for the pictures and wall charts, but a fifteen-page English pamphlet sold for ¥100 explains the incident and the fate of the crew of the _Lucky Dragon_ in adequate detail.

Koto Ward **water buses** depart on Tuesdays, Thursdays, weekends, and national holidays for two separate routes from the water bus pier at the far northwest corner of Yumenoshima. The Unga Course takes you via canals to Takabashi Pier near Morishita station (Toei Shinjuku subway line) and Kameido Pier between Kameido and Kinshicho stations (JR Sobu line). The Rinkai Course goes into the bay, swinging by Kurofunebashi before it stops at Takabashi Pier.

EATING OPTIONS

Restaurants Wakasu Kaihin Park has a pricey restaurant at the golf course club-house. There are no other restaurants within walking distance, but on weekends you might find *yatai* food stalls near the front of the main entrance selling any-thing from curry to fried noodles. Yumenoshima has a coffee shop in its Tropical Greenhouse Dome selling a very small selection of meals; tropical drinks and exotic desserts dominate the menu. The park also has a coffee shop with a limited menu on the second floor of the marina center and a Chinese restaurant in its Sports Center.

Picnic Possibilities Wakasu Kaihin Park is the place for a cookout. There are five circular campfire sites that can service several cooks at one time; you must reserve cooking space when you reserve your camp space. If the fire circles are not available, bring a camp stove. The Service Center sells snacks and drinks. You can also cook out at Yumenoshima's 10,000-square-meter barbecue area; bring everything you need, including a stove, and register at the park office on the day you arrive. Or bring a pic-nic and feast at a table or on a blanket. Vending machines near the plant dome and at the marina center sell drinks.

FOR INFANTS AND TODDLERS

Wakasu Kaihin Park has no special facilities for infant care, but roughing it is part of the camping experience. You can change a diaper on the baby bed just across from the restrooms in the Tropical Greenhouse Dome in Yumenoshima. Toddlers who are toilet trained can splash in the Yumenoshima Sports Center kiddie pool. No diapers are allowed in the pool. Strollers are not recommended for Wakasu Kaihin Koen. They are a little tricky on the wood-chip paths at Yumenoshima but you'll find lots of other stroller-friendly routes.

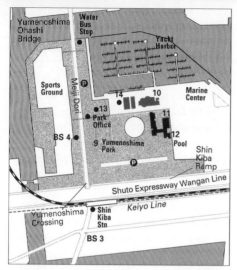

PLACES TO VISIT

1. Wakasu Kaihin Park
2. Service Center
3. Camp Site
4. Fishing Pier (breakwater)
5. Cycle Rental
6. Kiddie Cycle Track
7. Observation Platform
8. Playground
9. Yumenoshima Park
10. Yumenoshima Tropical Greenhouse Dome
11. Yumenoshima Sports Center
12. Pool
13. Display House of the *Lucky Dragon*
14. BBQ Area

BS 1. Wakasu Kyampujo-mae Bus Stop
BS 2. Wakasu Golf Links Bus Stop
BS 3. Shin Kiba Eki Bus Stop
BS 4. Yumenoshima Bus Stop

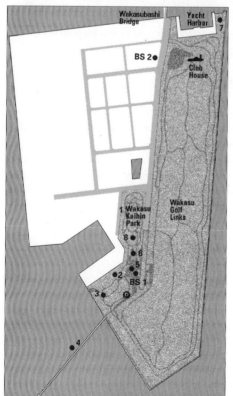

Wakasu Kaihin Park

若洲海浜公園 (Wakasu Kaihin Koen)

1 Wakasu, Koto-ku, Tokyo 136–0083

☎ (03) 5569–6701, reservation desk open 9 A.M. to 4:30 P.M.

東京都江東区若州1 〒136-0083

OPEN: 11 A.M. to 9 P.M. for day camp; 11 A.M. to 10 P.M. for overnight camp. Check-in at 11 A.M. Morning check-out is 10 A.M. and evening check-out is 9 P.M.

CLOSED: Tues, except during Japanese spring and summer school breaks. If Tues is a national or city hol, the park closes the following day. Also closed Dec 29 to Jan 3.

FEES:

	day camp	1 night, 2 days	2 nights, 3 days	3 nights, 4 days
check-out time	9 P.M.	10 A.M. or 9 P.M.	10 A.M. or 9 P.M.	10 A.M.
high school	¥200	¥400/600	¥600/800	¥800
junior high school	¥100	¥200/300	¥300/400	¥400
elementary school	¥100	¥200/300	¥300/400	¥400

Preschool children pay no entrance fee.

DIRECTIONS: from Shin Kiba station (JR Keiyo and Musashino lines or Yurakucho subway line) take bus #11 bound for Wakasu Kaihin Koen. Get off at Wakasu Kyanpujo-mae. It's about a 15-minute bus ride. By car, exit the expressway Bayshore line (Kosoku Wangansen) at the Shin Kiba ramp and head toward the Tokyo Heliport. The park is beyond the heliport. As you pull into the park you will see a parking lot for the golf course on your left; pass that and continue till you make a U-turn. The parking lot for the campsite will appear shortly on your left.

PARKING: 300-car lot charges ¥500 per entrance. The lot is open from 6 A.M. to 9:30 P.M.

COMMENTS: all ages, no English

Duskin Rent All

ダスキンレントアール

2–17–1 Meguro Honcho, Meguro-ku, Tokyo 152–0002

☎ (03) 3794–3431

東京都目黒区目黒本町2-17-1 〒152-0002

OPEN: 9 A.M. to 7 P.M.

CLOSED: Jan 1–3

DIRECTIONS: By car, on the south side of Meguro Dori between Yamate Dori and Kannana Dori. Look for a large blue building.

PARKING: available

Yumenoshima Park

夢の島公園 (Yumenoshima Koen)

3–2 Yumenoshima, Koto-ku, Tokyo 136–0081

☎ (03) 3521–8273

東京都江東区夢の島3-2 〒136-0081

OPEN: 24 hours

DIRECTIONS: a 10-minute walk from Shin Kiba station (JR Keiyo and Musashino lines or Yurakucho subway line). From Wakasu Kaihin Koen take bus #11 from Wakasu Kyanpujo-mae stop to Yumenoshima stop. By car, a 1-minute drive from the Shin Kiba ramp on the expressway Bayshore line.

PARKING: hourly rate, parking available for 350 cars from 8 A.M. to 9:30 P.M.

COMMENTS: all ages, no English

Yumenoshima Tropical Greenhouse Dome

夢の島熱帯植物館 (Yumenoshima Nettai Shokubutsu-kan)

3–2 Yumenoshima, Koto-ku, Tokyo 136–0081

☎ (03) 3522–0281

東京都江東区夢の島3-2 〒136-0081

OPEN: 9:30 A.M. to 4 P.M.

CLOSED: Mon (Tues if Mon is a national or city hol), Dec 29 to Jan 3

FEES: adults ¥250, middle school students ¥100, free for younger children and people over 65

DIRECTIONS: see Yumenoshima Park above. The Tropical Greenhouse Dome is in the northeast corner of the park.

COMMENTS: all ages, English pamphlet and some signboards

Yumenoshima Sports Center

夢の島総合体育館 (Yumenoshima Sogo Taiiku-kan)

3–2 Yumenoshima, Koto-ku, Tokyo 136–0081

☎ (03) 3521–7321

東京都江東区夢の島3-2 〒136-0081

OPEN: 9:30 A.M. to 8:45 P.M.

CLOSED: 1st and 3rd Mon of the month, except in Aug. If the 3rd Mon is a national hol, then the facility closes the following day. Also closed Dec 28 to Jan 4.

FEES: adults ¥300, children ¥140 for a 2-hour session in the pool, training room, archery ground, badminton or table tennis areas, the sumo dohyo, and the martial arts dojos. The sauna costs ¥650 for 2 hours and only high school students and adults are allowed to use it.

DIRECTIONS: see Yumenoshima Park above. The Sports Center is on the east side of the park.

COMMENTS: all ages, English pamphlet

Display House of the *Lucky Dragon*

第五福竜丸展示館 (Daigo Fukuryu Maru Tenji-kan)

3–2 Yumenoshima, Koto-ku, Tokyo

☎ (03) 3521–8494

東京都江東区夢の島3-2

OPEN: 9:30 A.M. to 4 P.M.

FEES: free

CLOSED: Mon

DIRECTIONS: see Yumenoshima Park. The Display House is on the northwest side of the park.

COMMENTS: older children, English pamphlet

Koto Ward Water Bus

江東区水上バス (Koto-ku Suijo Bus)

☎ (03) 3647–1111 (Koto Ward Office)

OPEN: call for schedule

DIRECTIONS: see directions to Yumenoshima Park above. Yumenoshima Pier is in the far northwest section of the park.

Scientific Adventure

Hands-on experiences teach more about science than textbooks. This section describes spots that may not be in your average guidebook, but spark enthusiasm in science and technology with exhibits that are enlightening and fun. Several of these tours take you to Yokohama, for one simple reason: there you'll find enough English explanations to answer your children's questions.

Our **Minato Mirai 21** *tour takes you to a Mitsubishi Heavy Industries museum, designed especially to attract the next generation to careers in science and technology. You'll also visit a maritime museum and walk the decks of a sailing ship. The area's best planetarium is part of* **Yokohama Science Center***, which has a space gym where would-be astronauts can train, as well as dozens of top-notch exhibits that teach about light and radio waves, meteorites, and more. Next door is a log cabin filled with climbing equipment for active children.*

At **Fujita's Vente** *you'll find the kind of high-tech entertainment you'd expect from one of the world's leading industrial countries. Robotics, holography, computer-aided music composition, laser technology, and virtual reality are all illustrated with enthralling games and activities in a futuristic environment.*

Future City: Minato Mirai 21

Landmark Plaza and Queen's Square Shopping Malls • Yokohama Maritime Museum • Mitsubishi Minato Mirai 21 Industrial Museum • Rinko Seaside Park

F resh sea breezes and futuristic fun spots make Yokohama's new Minato Mirai 21 development a great playground for people of all ages. The marble fountains, gleaming escalators, and hundreds of shops and restaurants in Landmark Plaza and Queens Square are the perfect cure for homesick mall rats. The area also boasts a restored sailing ship, a beautiful seaside park, and several good museums.

Only 45 minutes from Shibuya or Tokyo station, Sakuragicho is the gateway to Yokohama's attractions, including the gleaming Minato Mirai 21 development, which actually lives up to its name: "21st Century Future Port." Sleek, modern high-rise buildings house an entire community, with businesses, apartments, a convention center, shopping, hotels, medical care, and museums. Landmark Tower, seventy stories high, stands out like a modern colossus. As you leave the east exit of the station, you'll see a moving walkway that will get you there in 5 minutes. Get on, or walk below it to the ***Nippon Maru***, whose billowing sails beckon from a distance. Built in 1930, this ship was used to train cadets in the mercantile marine schools at Kobe's Kawasaki Shipyard, and later used to repatriate Japanese after World War II. English narration guides you through the decks and cabins. A single ticket from the vending machine outside the boat will allow you to explore the *Nippon Maru* and admire her rigging, then enter the **Yokohama Maritime Museum** and study seafaring in Japan. Bright, modern, interactive displays will make learning a pleasure: find out how sailboats harness wind power and how sailors once navigated by the stars, load and unload container ships with a toy crane, and see how the Port of Yokohama developed through pictures. The English explanations are just long enough to satisfy your curiosity on the main points. You'll probably want to spend a little over an hour on this part of your harbor adventure, then head for lunch at either the elegant shopping center that occupies the bottom four floors of Landmark Tower or Queen's Square's more child-oriented jumble of shops, eateries, event space, and offices.

Landmark Plaza Shopping Mall and the adjacent **Queen's Square** building complex have restaurants for every palate and pocketbook and stores that range from foreign favorites to popular Japanese chains. Landmark Plaza sells mainly clothing, shoes, and bags with boutiques like the Gap, Guess, Laura Ashley, Ferragamo, Bally, Bruno Magli, and Mikihouse and Tinkerbell for the kids. Bookworms shouldn't miss the Yurindo bookstore on the fifth floor, which offers an excellent selection of English books for both children and adults, as well as a good collection of German and French novels. An English floor guide to the shopping mall is available at the information counter on level three. Kids, however, generally prefer to shop in Queen's Square where a Warner Bros. Store, a Disney Store and a Snoopy store stand shoulder to shoulder. The Snoopy Store even has a small children's play area inside. Basement levels 2 and 3 conceal a five-part arcade, **Club Sega Yokohama**, with over 180 games arranged in different "communication spaces." However, we recommend a different way to spend your family time.

Across the street from the Landmark Plaza, the **Mitsubishi Minato Mirai 21 Industrial Museum** has attractions related to the areas sponsor Mitsubishi Heavy Industries has worked in, including environmental technologies, energy technologies, and space and underwater exploration. Mitsubishi built the museum to encourage youngsters to seek careers in scientific and technical fields, hoping to prepare the next generation to combat environmental problems. We rate it a ten for education value. Schoolchildren will want to come back again and again, for hours at a time. The museum is free for school excursions so that students may discover how central science and technology are to life.

Most exhibits have detailed English explanations; highlights include a Japanese H-II Rocket, a large model showing how garbage is turned into electricity, a display illustrating how a power plant works, and a detailed model of a deep-sea diving probe—Japan leads the world in ocean-probing technology. You can also see a model of Mitsubishi's pride and joy, a shield tunneling machine used in excavations for the Yokohama Bay bridge and the "Chunnel" connecting France and the United Kingdom. There is also a model of the graceful Bay bridge and a very simple but effective display explaining how trusses work, using the safety straps standing passengers cling to on moving trains.

Design your own seaworthy vessel on a computer-aided design (CAD) terminal with English capabilities and then try it out in a computer simulation. If you want a color printout of your boat, just put a ¥100 coin in the machine. There are also CAD terminals for designing airplanes but these are in Japanese only. Would-be pilots will enjoy the museum's surprisingly realistic simulated helicopter ride. Man the controls as the copter tilts and vibrates over Yokohama Bay and Mount Fuji. Reserve a turn at the CAD terminals and the helicopter simulation on the second floor the minute you walk in the door, and if you'd prefer English subtitles for the helicopter ride just ask. If the wait is long, just go out for lunch or visit another spot on the tour—you can reenter the museum with your ticket stub.

A short walk from all this futuristic high-tech excitement is the timeless relaxation of the seaside. Smooth gray flagstones line the edge of **Rinko Seaside Park** bordering on the harbor, green grass covers the gentle hill above. Watch the gulls, the boats, fishermen, and the waves from outside or inside: a small pavilion with wide windows and comfortable chairs is free for visitors during daylight hours.

These attractions should make for a long and interesting day, but there's

> When you're ready to leave, consider trading the long walk back to Sakuragicho for a 7-minute harbor cruise on a Sea Bass shuttle. Boats depart from Pukarisan-bashi pier just east of the park about every half hour. They dock at Sogo Department Store, which is directly connected to Yokohama station (see Tour 11 for more information).

plenty more to do at Minato Mirai, and we can almost guarantee you'll want to come back.

Other Things to Do in the Area

The large and luxurious **Yokohama Museum of Art** just north of Landmark Tower has a fairly extensive permanent collection that includes a small gallery with lesser-known works by some the world's most famous artists, including Picasso, Dali, Magritte, and Cezanne, but the bulk of the collection comprises works by Japanese artists. While the paintings are not as impressive as those in the National Museum of Western Art in Ueno, the museum's spacious corridors and elegant design provide an excellent setting for art appreciation. The viewing library has thirty English titles in its video collection and offers access to 50,000 digital images of masterpieces. Call or watch the media for information on the museum's frequent special exhibitions, which are often very good.

An excellent view of the harbor and, on good days, Mount Fuji, attracts visitors to the **Sky Garden** at the top of Landmark Tower, which despite its name is merely an expensive observation center. Ultra-swift elevators whisk you up to the 273-meter-high viewing platform in just 40 seconds.

Cosmo World is a good enticement for both children and shop-a-holics to move on. This mini-amusement park has about eight big rides and many smaller coin-operated ones for children under 120 centimeters. A ride on the 105-meter-high Ferris wheel, erected in 1989 as part of the Yokohama Expo, is a stomach-turning experience you won't soon forget. The Ferris wheel was torn down in 1997 to make way for the Queen's Square development, but will be rebuilt in 1998 somewhere on Shinkochiku, the wharf across the water from Cosmo World. At the time of this writing the exact location was undecided, but the sky-high Ferris wheel should be easy to spot.

The **Yokohama Pavilion** is home to **Yokohama Gulliver Land**, a detailed model of the future city that completely fills the large room in the center of the pavilion and gives a glimpse of daily life in Yokohama. Matchbox cars race along the expressway, passing a toy train as it stops at a miniature Sakuragicho station. Sweethearts stroll through Yamashita Park, gazing up at the Marine Tower or out to sea where the *Hikawa Maru* is anchored. Push a button to make a bright red festival dragon dance through the streets of Chinatown. Push another, and the wedding march plays as a bride and groom step triumphantly out of Christ Church. Tiny lights illuminate the city as an artificial night falls; morning brings a soft orange glow and the twittering of birds. Half an hour can easily pass before the enchantment wears off and you're ready to leave this free exhibition for a walk along the coast. If this is something you want to see, don't wait too long. According to the Minato Mirai 21 developers, Yokohama Gulliver Land will be torn down in 1999 to expand the adjacent exhibit hall.

There is a heliport in the northeast corner of Rinko park where, on weekends and national holidays, **Excel Air Services** offers very brief **helicopter rides** around Yokohama Bay (3 to 5 minutes) and between the Minato Mirai Rinji heliport and Urayasu heliport near Tokyo Disneyland (about 15 minutes).

Several places in Tokyo can help you prepare for earthquakes and fires, but for English speakers we recommend Yokohama's **Disaster Prevention Center**, where almost all exhibits have written explanations in English and the attendants speak well enough to get the important points across. A trip to the center will go far beyond any lecture on emergency preparedness. Shake your family out of complacency in an earthquake simulator that lets you experience one-third of the power of the 1-minute, 48-second Great Kanto Earthquake of 1923 and the 20-second Kobe Earthquake of 1995, both of which killed hundreds and demolished entire neighborhoods. Learn what to put in your evacuation kit, how to use a fire extinguisher, how to find your way out of an unfamiliar building in total blackness, and how to protect yourself from smoke.

The center teaches a few basics about first aid and CPR, but suggests you enroll in a course for more thorough understanding. There is a 50-minute English video on emergency preparedness that you can watch at the center or borrow to watch at home. A trip through the center takes 90 minutes, or about two and a half hours if you stay to watch the video.

EATING OPTIONS

Eating Out Food is a major attraction at Landmark Plaza, which has everything from Wendy's to a muffin shop, a French bakery, and elegant Japanese restaurants. Self-service restaurants in the fifth-floor food court offer a variety of dishes ranging from Italian to Chinese. The Queen's Square complex has over 25 restaurants, most in the three "at!" mini-malls. If you are looking for fast food and perhaps a chance to eat outdoors, visit the Y-Cruise food courts in "at! 2nd." At the end of Pukarisan-bashi Pier is Pier 21, a floating restaurant belonging to the Intercontinental Hotel. Lunch is casual with a limited, reasonably priced menu (¥800 to ¥1,800) and kids are welcome. All seats in the second-floor restaurant offer an excellent view of boats docking at the pier and sea gulls diving behind the huge ships plowing in and out of the harbor. At night the restaurant serves French food and prices climb to ¥6,000 to ¥8,000 for meals with several courses.

Picnic Possibilities Sit and watch the waves as you picnic at Rinko Park. You can bring food from home or buy something at the many takeout shops in Landmark Plaza. You'll have a good time even if the weather is bad, since a glassed-in lunchroom with tables, drink machines, and an excellent view of the harbor is open for park visitors from 6 A.M. to 6 P.M.

FOR INFANTS AND TODDLERS

Relatively empty streets, sidewalks for strollers, and plenty of things that interest tiny tots—from ocean-watching to button-pushing—make this a great place to come with small children. Changing and feeding present no worries. The fourth floor of Landmark Plaza has a few upscale children's clothing stores in the southeast corner;

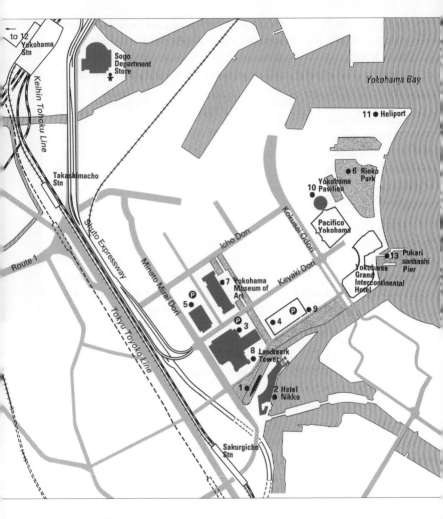

PLACES TO VISIT

1. The *Nippon Maru*
2. Yokohama Maritime Museum
3. Landmark Plaza Shopping Mall
4. Queen's Square
5. Mitsubishi Minato Mirai 21 Industrial Museum
6. Rinko Park
7. Yokohama Museum of Art
8. Landmark Tower, Royal Park Hotel Nikko
9. Yokohama Cosmo World
10. Yokohama Pavilion, Gulliver Land
11. Heliport
12. Yokohama Disaster Prevention Center
13. Pukarisanbashi Pier, Pier 21 Restaurant

near the center of the same floor is a baby room with hot water and diaper-changing facilities. You can also purchase some baby supplies at the shopping center's two pharmacies. Queen's Square has diaper-changing tables in restaurants for wheelchair users. The Yokohama Maritime Museum has cribs for diaper-changing in the main women's restrooms, as well as one in the corridor near the restrooms on the first floor. The Yokohama Museum of Art has a nursing room on the first floor and diaper changing in the first-floor women's room. Ask an attendant to open the nursing room for you. Children under five must be accompanied by an adult on the Cosmo World Ferris Wheel.

WHERE & WHEN

Landmark Plaza Shopping Mall
ランドマークプラザ
2–2–1 Minato Mirai, Nishi-ku, Yokohama-shi, Kanagawa-ken 220–0012
☎ (045) 222–5015
神奈川県横浜市西区みなとみらい2-2-1
〒220-0012
OPEN: shops 11 A.M. to 8 P.M., restaurants 11 A.M. to 10 P.M.; hours for some stores may differ
FEES: none
DIRECTIONS: 5 minutes by moving walkway from the east exit of Sakuragicho station (JR Keihin Tohoku and Negishi lines, Tokyu Toyoko line, Yokohama subway). By car, take the Minato Mirai exit from the Shuto expressway or follow the signs toward Sakuragicho from the end of the Daisan Keihin expressway.
PARKING: underground parking with capacity for 1,400 cars is available at an hourly rate; vouchers are given if you spend over ¥5,000 in the plaza
COMMENTS: English pamphlet, nursing room

Queen's Square
クィーンズスクエア
2–3–1 Minato Mirai, Nishi-ku, Yokohama-shi, Kanagawa-ken
☎ (045) 682–0109
神奈川県横浜市西区みなとみらい2-3-1

OPEN: most shops open 11 A.M. to 8 P.M.; several restaurants open until 11 P.M. or 1 A.M.
DIRECTIONS: see directions to Landmark Plaza; Queen's Square is next to Landmark Plaza
PARKING: paid parking available in a 1,700 car lot at an hourly rate; 2 hours free with receipts totaling ¥5,000 from Queen's Square stores.
COMMENTS: English pamphlet

Yokohama Maritime Museum & *Nippon Maru* Sailing Ship
横浜マリタイムミュージアムと日本丸
2–1–1 Minato Mirai, Nishi-ku, Yokohama-shi, Kanagawa-ken 220–0012
☎ (045) 221–0280
神奈川県横浜市西区みなとみらい2-1-1
〒220-0012
OPEN: 10 A.M. to 5 P.M. (until 6:30 July and Aug, until 4:30 Nov to Feb). *Nippon Maru* closes 30 minutes earlier than the museum.
CLOSED: Mon and days after national hols unless they fall on weekends; Dec 29 to Jan 1
FEES: adults ¥600, elementary and middle school students ¥300
DIRECTIONS: see Landmark Plaza; the sailing ship is a 2-minute walk from the south side of Landmark Tower
PARKING: none
COMMENTS: 5 and up, some English

Mitsubishi Minato Mirai 21 Industrial Museum

三菱みなとみらい技術館 (Mitsubishi Minato Mirai Gijitsukan)

Mitsubishi Heavy Industries Building, 3–3–1 Minato Mirai, Nishi-ku, Yokohama-shi, Kanagawa-ken 220–0012

☎ (045) 224–9031

神奈川県横浜市西区港みらい3-3-1
三菱重工業ビル 〒220-0012

OPEN: 10 A.M. to 5:30 P.M. (entry until 4:30)

CLOSED: Mon, days following national hols, New Year's, occasionally on other days for administrative purposes

FEES: adults ¥500, middle and high school students ¥300, elementary school students ¥200

DIRECTIONS: see Landmark Plaza; the museum is a 1-minute walk north from Landmark Tower

PARKING: there is ample parking in the basement of the building for an hourly rate

COMMENTS: older children, adequate English

Rinko Seaside Park

隣港公園 (Rinko Koen)

Minato Mirai 1-chome, Nishi-ku, Yokohama-shi, Kanagawa-ken 220–0012

神奈川県横浜市西区みなとみらい1丁目
〒220-0012

FEES: none

DIRECTIONS: see Yokohama Pavilion; the park is just east of the pavilion

PARKING: parking for 80 cars open from 10 A.M. to 9 P.M.

Yokohama Cosmo World

よこはまコスモワールド

2–1 Minato Mirai, Nishi-ku, Yokohama-shi, Kanagawa-ken 220–0012

☎ (045) 221–0232

神奈川県横浜市西区みなとみらい2-1
〒220-0012

OPEN: 11 A.M. to 9 P.M. on weekdays, 11 A.M. to 10 P.M. on weekends and hols

CLOSED: Mon

FEES: entrance is free, rides range from ¥100 to ¥600

DIRECTIONS: see Landmark Plaza; the amusement park is a 1-minute walk from the south side of Landmark Tower

PARKING: none on premises but lots nearby

COMMENTS: all ages, some English

Yokohama Pavilion

横浜パビリオン

Minato Mirai 1-chome, Nishi-ku, Yokohama-shi, Kanagawa-ken 220–0012

☎ (045) 221–0511

神奈川県横浜市西区港みらい1丁目
〒220-0012

OPEN: 10 A.M. to 5 P.M.

CLOSED: Mon, days following national hols, Dec 29 to Jan 3

FEES: none

DIRECTIONS: the pavilion is a 15-minute walk from the Landmark Plaza shopping center. You can also take bus #140 (get off at Pacifico Yokohama) from Sakuragicho station, or bus #141 (get off at Tenjii-mae) from Yokohama or Sakuragicho stations. The pavilion is a 2-minute walk.

PARKING: none but there are lots nearby

COMMENTS: all ages, no English

Landmark Tower Sky Garden

ランドマークタワースカイガーデン

2–2–1 Minato Mirai, Nishi-ku, Yokohama-shi, Kanagawa-ken 220-0012

☎ (045) 222–5030

神奈川県横浜市西区みなとみらい2-2-1
〒220-0012

OPEN: daily 10 A.M. to 9 P.M. (6 on Sat), Oct to June; 10 A.M. to 10 P.M. July to Sept; entry until 30 minutes before closing

FEES: adults ¥1,000, senior citizens ¥800, junior high/elementary students ¥500, preschoolers ¥200

DIRECTIONS: see Landmark Plaza; entrance

outside on the east side of the building, on the 3rd floor

PARKING: see Landmark Plaza

COMMENTS: all ages, no English

Yokohama Museum of Art

横浜美術館 (Yokohama Bijitsukan)

3–4–1 Minato Mirai, Nishi-ku, Yokohama-shi, Kanagawa-ken 220–0012

☎ (045) 221–0300

神奈川県横浜市西区みなとみらい3-4-1 〒220-0012

OPEN: 10 A.M. to 6 P.M. (entry until 5:30)

CLOSED: Thurs, days following national hols, Dec 29 to Jan 3, occasionally on other days for administrative purposes

FEES: adults ¥500, high school students ¥300, junior high/elementary students ¥100

DIRECTIONS: see Landmark Plaza; the museum is a 1-minute walk north from Landmark Tower

PARKING: paid parking available 10 A.M. to 9 P.M.

COMMENTS: all ages, some English, nursing room

Excel Air Service

エクセル航空ヘリクルージング

1–7 Minato Mirai; Nishi-ku, Yokohama-shi, Kanagawa-ken

☎ (047) 223–1155 (Yokohama Office), (047) 380–5555 (Main Office)

神奈川県横浜市西区みなとみらい1-7 〒220-0012

OPEN: reservation desk 9 A.M. to 5 P.M. Mon to Fri; 3 P.M. to 5 P.M. weekends and national hols. Helicopter availability varies by route and according to weather conditions.

CLOSED: Flights stop around Dec 25 to start again the 2nd Fri of Jan

FEES: ¥8,500 to ¥5,000 for adults and ¥6,000 to ¥3,500 for children between ages 3 and 12.

DIRECTIONS: Minato Mirai Rinji Heliport is in the northeast corner of Rinko Park near the parking lot.

COMMENTS: reservations recommended

Yokohama Disaster Prevention Center

横浜市民防災センター

(Yokohama Shimin Bosai Center)

4–7 Sawatari, Kanagawa-ku, Yokohama-shi, Kanagawa-ken 221–0844

☎ (045) 312–0119

神奈川県横浜市神奈川区沢渡4-7 〒221-0844

OPEN: 9:30 A.M. to 4:30 P.M.

CLOSED: Mon and the 3rd Tues of the month. When a scheduled day off falls on a national hol they stay open but close the following day. Also closed Dec 29 to Jan 3.

FEES: none

DIRECTIONS: a 10-minute walk from the west exit of Yokohama station (JR Tokaido, Yokosuka, Keihin Tohoku, Keihin Kyuko, Tokyu Toyoko train lines and Yokohama subway). Take the west exit of Yokohama station and go down the stairs into the Diamond shopping center. Walk straight through the long, shop-lined corridor. Near the end on the left side is the exit for the Hotel Rich. Take it and walk straight ahead for about 5 minutes, crossing the large intersection using the pedestrian walkway. You'll see the center next to Sawatari Chuo Koen. If you come by car, you may find it easiest to park in Sogo or one of the other department stores near the station and walk from there. There is also parking along the streets in some places. To get to Sogo, take expressway Yokohama, exit at Kinko interchange.

PARKING: none

COMMENTS: 5 and up, adequate English

Techno-Amusement in Sendagaya

Fujita Vente • Meiji Memorial Picture Gallery • Trim Sports Center

Crash! Listen to the sound of breaking glass as you put your hand through a paneless window. Giggle as holographic butterflies flutter around your fingers. Play a few notes, and the computerized piano will turn it into a lovely song. At **Vente**, construction giant Fujita makes technology enticing.

In the basement "amusement space," the best attraction, the virtual stage, is a video game, but you don't use a mouse or a joystick. Soccer balls come hurling forward on the screen and you "virtually" kick them with your leg. Sharks stalk you as you hunt for "virtual" sunken treasure. At another display, a video image of your face divides into nine squares. The parts scramble and you must move them back into place before a time bomb explodes. Twenty or so hands-on exhibits require thought and spark interest in learning, each one unique in its makeup, function, and purpose. You'll want to try them all; give yourself about an hour. Several require Japanese reading ability, but the attendants, some of whom speak English to a degree, will happily assist you.

The first floor of the building, also Fujita's headquarters, has a gift shop, a shop selling merchandise with the Bellmare soccer team's logo, a Ticket Pia (see Appendices), and a toy museum that has exhibits of domestic toys as well as shows from London's Toy and Model Museum. There is also a nice model

Look around and you'll see several examples of how Fujita uses technology to make their building more environmentally friendly. Just outside the basement-level entrance to the amusement space is the Earth Air Purifier (EAP II), a system that uses microbes in the soil to clean the air from the train track complete with scenery and switches. The second floor has a modern art museum that sometimes has exhibits of interest to children, like the World Picture Book Exhibition held every spring. There is also a theater that shows films related to the museum's exhibits.

Visiting **Meiji Memorial Picture Gallery**, a short walk away, is the fastest and most interesting way to learn about Japan's Meiji period and its importance in the country's history. After centuries of isolation, in the mid-1800s Japan finally opened its doors to the outside world and change flourished in every field. The gallery is like a huge historical picture book with eighty large paintings. Half are painted with tradi-

underground parking garage. To see how it works, place your hand on the panel in front of the EAP II. Tilapia swim in an aquarium nearby. These fish feed on spirulina algae that is filtered out of the building's sewage system. Above the tank you'll see the roots of a camphor tree that grows without soil. The roots are regularly sprayed with liquid fertilizer. Near that is a rainwater cascade; Vente stores rainwater in underground tanks for use in restrooms and an indoor pond for watering plants. There is even a mini bird sanctuary on the side of the building. Pick up English pamphlets on the amusement space and the building's "urban biospherics" to guide you around.

tional Japanese techniques and half are Western style, but all are the work of noted artists. The paintings highlight important events in the Meiji emperor's reign: his coronation, the relocation of Japan's capital from Kyoto to Tokyo, and significant battles fought during the period. Several of Japan's darker moments have been thoroughly euphemized, and parents may want to add comments on some of the negative things that happened in connection with the Sino- and Russo-Japanese wars, the occupation of Taiwan, and the annexation of Korea. Trends like advances in government, increased awareness of Western culture, and advances in women's education are also portrayed. Every painting is explained in detailed English. You'll need half an hour to zip through.

Classrooms for training in the tea ceremony *(sado),* Japanese flower arranging *(ikebana),* and calligraphy *(shodo)* are located in the basement. If your visit coincides with an *ikebana* or *shodo* class you may be able to watch. Just turn right out of the gallery's inner doors and go downstairs; the reception desk is on the left. Inquire about observing a class *(kengaku)* in your most polite Japanese—the genteel women at the reception desk use the most honorific forms of the language.

Although its name sounds more like an adult's indoor fitness facility, **Trim Sports Center** (also known as Hyakuen Koen or 100 Yen Park) is an outdoor park for kids. A level above the average neighborhood park, it offers exceptional wooden jungle gyms for three age groups: toddlers, primary school students up to second grade, and students third grade and up. The toddler section has a sandbox, too. Little ones can play safely with others in their own league. The jungle gyms get grander and more challenging for each age level. There is also a "mountain" with many kinds of wall-scaling rigs and climbing steps on one side and a refreshing waterfall on the other. Parents can relax in one of several log structures while the kids romp. A fountain and a large, well-tended flower bed make the setting all the more appealing. The attractive building at the back of the park is a ceramics school that offers courses for Japanese-speakers.

Other Things to Do in the Area

Meiji Jingu Skating Rink has ice-skating sessions and classes all year round. In the summer three outdoor pools, including a kiddie pool, open on the second floor.

On Sundays or national holidays, bike the 1.2 kilometer **Meiji Jingu Gaien Cycle Center** for a better view of the park. You can borrow cycles for free; they have everything from small bikes for children to mountain bikes, but no baby seats or tricycles.

EATING OPTIONS

Restaurants   Fujita Vente has vending machines selling drinks and ice cream inside its first-floor gift shop. There is seating for thirty in chairs of all different modern designs. Your kids will be even more impressed with the furniture than the junk food. Kimuraya, a restaurant on the same floor, has a higher-priced menu in more elegant surroundings. There are several restaurants and fast-food outlets near Yoyogi and Shinanomachi stations.

Picnic Possibilities   Tables in the rest houses at Trim Sports Center are good for picnics. Drinks and snacks are sold by the reception booth.

FOR INFANTS AND TODDLERS

Your stroller will come in handy when walking between the spots on this tour. There is a diaper-changing table in the family restrooms on the first floor of the Vente building. There are no infant care facilities at Meiji Jingu Memorial Picture Gallery or Trim Sports Center.

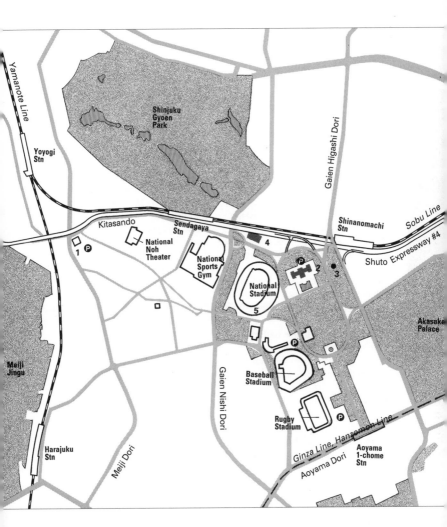

PLACES TO VISIT

1. Fujita Vente
2. Meiji Memorial Picture Gallery
3. Trim Sports Center
4. Meiji Jingu Skating Rink
5. National Stadium, Meiji Jingu Cycling Center

WHERE & WHEN

Fujita Vente
フジタ バンテ

4–6–15 Sendagaya, Shibuya-ku, Tokyo 151–0051

☎ (03) 3796–2486

東京都渋谷区千駄ヶ谷4-6-15　〒151-0051

OPEN: 10 A.M. to 6 P.M.

CLOSED: Thurs (Fri if Thurs is a hol), Obon (mid-Aug) hols, New Year's hols

FEES: none

DIRECTIONS: a 5-minute walk from east exit JR Yoyogi station (JR Yamanote and Sobu lines). An 8-minute walk from JR Sendagaya station (Sobu line). By car, you'll find it on the west side of Meiji Dori at the intersection with Kitasando.

PARKING: free space for 20 cars, but available only on weekends and hols

COMMENTS: 5 and up, English pamphlet

Meiji Memorial Picture Gallery
明治神宮聖徳記念絵画館

(Meiji Jingu Seitoku Kinen Kaiga-kan)

9 Kasumigaoka-cho, Shinjuku-ku, Tokyo 160–0013

☎ (03) 3401–5179

東京都新宿区霞岳町9　〒160-0013

OPEN: 9 A.M. to 4 P.M.

CLOSED: no hols but the hours are shortened during the New Year's hols

FEES: adults ¥500, high school students ¥300, middle and elementary school students ¥200

DIRECTIONS: a 5-minute walk from Shinano-machi station (JR Sobu line); a 10-minute walk from exit 2 of Aoyama 1-chome station (Eidan Ginza and Hanzomon subway lines). By car, take expressway #4 and get off at the Gaien exit. The parking lot for the picture gallery will be on your right.

PARKING: space for 2,000 cars, daily rate

COMMENTS: all ages, adequate English

Trim Sports Center
トリムスポーツセンター

9 Kasumigaoka-cho, Shinjuku-ku, Tokyo 160–0013

☎ (03) 3478–0550

東京都新宿区霞岳町9　〒160-0013

OPEN: 9:30 A.M. to 4:30 P.M. (March–Oct until 5)

FEES: adults ¥150, children ¥50

DIRECTIONS: see directions for Meiji Memorial Picture Gallery. The park is just across the street to the east of the gallery.

PARKING: daily rate, space for 2,000 cars

COMMENTS: all ages, no English

Meiji Jingu Skating Rink
明治神宮アイススケート場

(Meiji Jingu Ice Skate Jo)

5 Kasumigaoka-cho, Shinjuku-ku, Tokyo 160–0013

☎ (03) 3403–3456

東京都新宿区霞岳町5　〒160-0013

OPEN: 12 A.M. to 6:30 P.M. May 1 to Aug 31; 10 A.M. to 6:30 P.M. Sept 1 to April 30. Admission until 5:30.

CLOSED: rink is closed to general users during special events

FEES: adults and high school students ¥1,300, children ¥900; rental skates ¥500 (largest size available 30 cm). After 3 P.M., adults are ¥1,000 and children ¥700. Discount multiple ticket coupons are also available.

DIRECTIONS: a 4-minute walk from Sendagaya station (JR Sobu line). By car, just south of expressway #4 near Gaien-Nishi Dori.

PARKING: free parking available for about a dozen cars

COMMENTS: 5 and up, some English

Meiji Jingu Gaien Cycling Center
明治神宮サイクリングコース

10 Kasumigaoka Machi, Shinjuku-ku, Tokyo
160– 0013

☎ (03) 3405–8297

東京都新宿区霞岳町10　〒160-0013

OPEN: 9 A.M. to 3:30 P.M on Sun and hols only.

FEES: none

DIRECTIONS: bike rental southeast of the National Stadium in Meiji Jingu Gaien Park. See directions for Meiji Memorial Picture Gallery. The Cycle center is just across the street and southwest of the gallery.

PARKING: use parking lot near Meiji Memorial Picture Gallery.

COMMENTS: no baby seats or tricycles.

30

Yokohama Blastoff

Yokohama Science Center • Omoshiroi Log House

A good planetarium and six floors of scientific fun await amateur astronomers at the **Yokohama Science Center**, a great place for anyone who has ever dreamed of exploring distant galaxies. Try training for an interstellar career in the Space Gym, see how high you would be able to jump in the low gravity of the moon, learn about light and radio waves and meteorites. For foreigners there's an added bonus: complete and thorough explanations of the permanent exhibits in English, including subtitles for sections of the planetarium shows and English audio for the Imax theater.

Simulated stars sparkle across the ceiling as planetarium staff members point out major constellations and discuss some of the mysteries of the universe. The dome-shaped screen is also used for stomach-turning Imax shows, which let you experience the sensations of flight, speed, and motion without stirring from your seat. The Imax films change once a year, the star shows three times. Both are definitely top-notch. Buy tickets for the shows when you arrive and, if you are buying a ticket for Imax, tell the receptionist if you will be wanting to listen in English. Only fifty-seven of the three hundred seats in the theater are equipped with earphone plugs for the English narration. There are English subtitles for the star shows. The shows last about forty to 45 minutes each, but you'll want to spent much longer playing and learning at the science center.

Head for the fifth floor to experiment with the colors in light waves, learn about sunspots, and try out telescopes. Friendly staff members will help you stick a copy of your shadow to a wall or teach you about the characteristics of ultraviolet rays. The fourth floor was designed to spark ideas about the space colonies of the future. How would farming work? What would the houses look like? Detailed models show some possibilities. Come up with new answers yourself after conducting experiments that teach you about gravity, energy, and microscopes. Computers and satellite video clips help you visualize how the earth looks from space.

So you want to be an astronaut? Sharpen your skills and strengthen your muscles in the third-floor Space Gym. A variety of activities—like a walk through a jungle of lights and jumping equipment that simulates the weak gravity of the moon—make learning interactive and fun. Study gravity, motion, and the power of centrifugal force, or watch demonstrations of other scientific phenomena in the Science Theater.

The library on the second floor has science books (eighteen titles in English) and videos. There's also a set of experiments to teach visitors about the properties of air and how objects behave in a vacuum. Meteorite and rock specimens are on display in the basement, offering clues about the origins of the solar system. Special events and classes are held at different times during the year. Contact the planetarium in Japanese for schedules and application procedures.

When you're ready to move on, head outside, where you'll find a grassy area with a small play park. At the rear of the park is a hill; climb over it and you'll find **Omoshiroi Log House**, a playhouse made of cedar imported from Montana. This house is one of eighteen the city of Yokohama has built to give local kids a place to play together, safe from traffic and bad weather.

Three levels of crawl spaces and semi-enclosures provide the nooks and crannies that kids need for pretending to set up house or fight off a band of wayward pirates. Rope ladders and chutes, curious vertical log steps, and a circular slide exercise their muscles and prepare them for an early night of solid sleep. Quiet places for reading and art projects round out the log house concept: a natural place to build strong bodies and inspire creative minds.

Write your name and address in the ledger at the reception desk and slip off your shoes—play is barefoot here. You are asked not to eat, drink, or smoke in the house and to put toys back where you found them. The volunteers who staff the place do a great job of creating a wholesome atmosphere. Depending on how many friends you've brought along or made on the way, a kid can spend anywhere from 15 minutes to several hours here. And, like the planetarium, it's a place you'll want to come to again.

Other Things to Do in the Area

Film buffs and those who want to try time travel can head to Shochiku's **Kamakura Cinema World**, a theme park three stops away. For the reasonable entrance fee you get to peek at real films and TV shows in production and wander through open sets—a pretty good deal. We suggest you skip the attractions: they cost extra and few of them are worth it.

The mainly indoor theme park is divided into sections. The American Zone takes you back to the fifties; the Future Zone is a mooring dock for spacecraft. In the Japanese Cinema Zone Part 1, a mannequin dressed as Tora-san, hero of the *Otoko Wa Tsurai Yo!* film series, greets you in front of a reproduction of his family home in Tokyo's Shibamata in the 1950s. (See Tour 4 for more on Tora-san and Shibamata.) There's a large traditional market where vendors of old-fashioned Japanese sweets call out to passersby. Part II of the Japanese zone takes you back to the days of Edo, where you can see samurai and ninja sword fights and fully costumed courtesans. The preschool-level Kid's Zone features a Tom and Jerry stage set but has only one attraction. We don't recommend the place for toddlers; it is a little overwhelming and doesn't have much that will interest them.

English-speaking park attendants can come in pretty handy when you've lost your way or members of your party. Both are easy to do because of the park's complex layout and the crowds. Also be sure to ask for the English brochure at the ticket gate.

EATING OPTIONS

Restaurants   A small, modern coffee shop on the first floor of the Yokohama Science Center serves hamburgers, fries, ice cream, and drinks. There are few other restaurants in this residential neighborhood; the others are located in the station area. Kamakura Cinema World has restaurants on almost every floor.

Picnic Possibilities   In the basement of the science center (B1) is a clean, attractive rest area where you can eat food from home. Picnic tables in the grassy area outside are another good place to take a break. There is climbing equipment and a slide for kids. Remember that once you leave the science center you have to buy a new entrance ticket to get back inside. You can eat a lunch from home in the Kid's Zone on the top floor of Kamakura Cinema World.

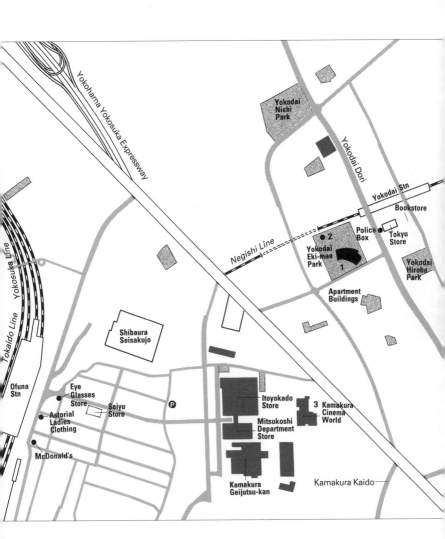

PLACES TO VISIT

1. Yokohama Science Center
2. Omoshiroi Log House
3. Kamakura Cinema World

FOR INFANTS AND TODDLERS

The science center has diaper-changing facilities in the first-floor women's restroom, but no nursing area. Bring your stroller if you like; elevators and a one-level floor plan mean there are no obstacles for wheelchairs or carriages. Moms often use the benches in the quiet library of the Omoshiroi House to change diapers or nurse. Cinema World has a diaper-changing table and nursing area in its Lost Child Center in the American Zone. There is also a stall with a changing table in the ladies' room across the hall.

WHERE & WHEN

Yokohama Science Center
横浜こども科学館 (Yokohama Kodomo Kagaku-kan)
5–2–1 Yokodai, Isogo-ku, Yokohama-shi, Kanagawa-ken 235–0045
☎ (045) 832–1166
神奈川県横浜市磯子区洋光台5-2-1
〒235-0045
OPEN: 9:30 A.M. to 5 P.M. (entry until 4) on weekdays and Sat. Opens from 9 on Sun and hols.
CLOSED: Mon (if Mon is a hol, Tues and Wed; if Sat is a hol, Mon and Wed), Dec 28 to Jan 1, and during exhibit changes
FEES:

	adults	students	over age 4
Entrance	¥400	¥200	—
Entrance & Planetarium	¥1,000	¥500	¥300
Entrance & Imax	¥1,000	¥500	¥300
Entrance, Planetarium & Imax	¥1,600	¥800	¥600
Six-month entrance pass	¥4,000	¥2,000	—

DIRECTIONS: a 3-minute walk from Yokodai station (JR Negishi line). By car, take Yokosuka-

Yokohama toll road and exit at Konandai. Take Yokodai Doro, which will lead you to Yokodai station. The science center is just a minute away.
PARKING: parking available for 50 cars only on weekends and national hols at a daily rate. The science center strongly advises coming by train as the lot fills quickly.
COMMENTS: 5 and up, adequate English

Omoshiroi Log House
おもしろいロゴハウス (Omoshiroi Rogo Hausu)
5–2 Yokodai, Isogo-ku, Yokohama-shi, Kanagawa-ken 235–0045
☎ (045) 833–1569
神奈川県横浜市磯子区洋光台5-2
〒235-0045
OPEN: 9 A.M. to 5 P.M.
CLOSED: 3rd Mon of the month and Dec 29–Jan 3
FEES: none—children through middle school are allowed to play
DIRECTIONS: see Yokohama Science Center
PARKING: none
COMMENTS: toddlers to younger elementary school students, no English

Kamakura Cinema World
鎌倉シネマワールド

6–1–1 Ofuna, Kamakura-shi, Kanagawa-ken 247–0056

☎ (0467) 48–1111

神奈川県鎌倉市大船6-1-1　〒247-0056

OPEN: 10 A.M. to 5 P.M. (entry until 3:30) weekdays; 10 A.M. to 7 P.M. (entry until 5:30) on weekends and hols

CLOSED: the theme park closes several days a year but the hols change annually. Call to confirm whether they are open.

FEES: adults ¥1,800, children ages 12 to 17 ¥1,500, children 4 to 11 ¥1,000, entrance only. Attraction cards are sold in several denominations at various machines inside the theme park.

DIRECTIONS: a 9-minute walk from the east exit of JR Ofuna station (JR Negishi line). As you exit, cross the street and turn left; walk along the road past Astorial Clothes Shop. Turn right at the eye wear store and continue until you reach the theme park. By car from Tokyo take expressway #1 to Haneda and change to the expressway Yokohane line bound for Yokohama. At the Moyori interchange switch to Yokohama-Yokosuka Doro. Exit at the Hino interchange and head toward Kamakura and Ofuna. From there it's a 30-minute drive on Kamakura Kaido.

PARKING: no parking at Cinema World, but there are area parking lots

COMMENTS: older children, English pamphlet, nursing room

Appendices

Tours for Mondays and the New Year Holidays

Mondays, especially rainy, summer Mondays, can be boring for kids as most museums, aquariums, children's centers, and other recreational attractions are closed. And Tokyo can be a lonely place for non-Japanese during the week or so the country takes off for New Year holidays. The good news is that several excellent places keep their doors open on Mondays and some even for part or all of the New Year's holidays. Here's a handy list of the ones you'll find in this book. New Year's schedules can change from year to year, so be sure to phone first.

Tours to Do on Mondays

Tours for Some of the New Year Holidays

Selected Activities for Rainy Days

Several of our tours include exceptional indoor venues for either learning and discovery or high-level play and arts-and-crafts activities. Some of the rainy-day places listed below could fill most of a day by themselves or might pair up well with other nearby places on the list in the same area. Three of our tours—9, 28, and 29—consist mainly (or exclusively) of indoor attractions.

Play and Create

• Meguro Citizen's Center Children's Hall Free (limited) parking, rarely crowded and just as much fun as the Children's Hall in Shibuya.	**Tour 12**
• Tokyo Metropolitan Children's Hall Lots of indoor play and you won't have to pay more than the minimum taxi fare from Shibuya station.	**Tour 13**
• National Children's Castle A bus from Shibuya station drops you off in front and a connected restaurant means you don't have to get wet to get lunch. Parking available.	**Tour 14**

Learn and Discover

• Fukagawa Edo Museum and Edo-Tokyo Museum Parking is limited at Fukagawa and non-existant at Edo-Tokyo so take the bus to cover the short distance between museums.	**Tour 2**

• National Museum of Japanese History   **Tour 3**
You can easily spend a whole day and still not see the
whole museum. Ample parking.

• Communication Museum and/or Printing   **Tour 8**
  Bureau Museum
A great day for stamp collectors! The Communication
Museum has no parking (you can sometimes find an
open space on nearby streets) but is close to a station.
The Printing Bureau Museum is far from the station
but has a fairly large, rarely full parking lot.

• Kabutocho Money Market   **Tour 9**
Rain needn't cancel your plans for this tour. Come by
train as there is no parking at either the Currency
Museum or Tokyo Stock Exchange but neither is far
from a station. Be sure to make reservations for the
English tour of the Stock Exchange.

• Tokyu Transportation Museum   **Tour 16**
In the Takatsu station building (Denentoshi Line) and
cheap.

• Yotsuya Fire Museum and Transportation Museum   **Tour 16**
The Fire Museum is connected underground to the
Yotsuya San-chome subway station. Active families
may want to visit the Transportation Museum on the
same day.

• Takashimaya Times Square Building   **Tour 16**
The rainy season is probably a good time to cave in
and let your kids assault their senses at the Tokyo
Imax Theater and Sega Joypolis.

• Shinagawa Aquarium and Heiwajima Kurhaus   **Tours 23**
Travel by car—both places have parking.   **and 24**

• Subway Museum   **Tour 23**
You can walk across the street from Kasai station to the
museum without getting wet.

• Future City: Minato Mirai   **Tour 28**
Three great museums for school-aged kids and two
enclosed shopping malls cluster together in this newly
designed section of Yokohama. You'll want to see the
whole tour—except Rinko Park.

• Yokohama Blastoff   **Tour 30**
This tour takes place indoors, so it is ideal for rainy
weather. Enjoy clear skies inside the planetarium and
jump over rain clouds in the space gym. Spend any
leftover energy in Omoshiroi Log House. Locations are
a short walk from Yokodai station; no parking.

A Note on Japanese National and School Holidays

If your children do not attend Japanese schools, you can avoid crowds and long lines
(to a degree) by staying home on public school holidays. During school trimesters,
Japanese students are off every Sunday and the second and fourth Saturday of the
month. In the future students will have every Saturday off, but at the time of this writing the Monbusho (Ministry of Education) had not yet decided when to make this
change. Many Japanese office workers work on Saturday too, another good reason to
make this the day you devote to seeing Tokyo.

School children also have three extended annual holidays, which vary slightly
according to the calendar year. Spring vacation, which marks the end of one school
year and the beginning of the next, is roughly two weeks long, extending from late
March to the end of the first week in April. Summer vacation lasts around forty day
from late July to the end of August. Winter vacation is generally the week before and
the week after January 1. Students and office workers take off on national holidays:
January 15, February 11, Spring Equinox (around March 20), April 29, May 3 to 5,
July 20, September 15 and Fall Equinox (around September 23), October 10,
November 23 and December 23.

Tickets and Event Listings

Ticket Pia and Ticket Saison sell tickets to performances, games, amusement parks, swimming pools, some museums, and movies, usually at a lower price than what you pay at the gate. Both ticket agencies have counters in various locations in Tokyo and Yokohama. To find the one nearest you, call Ticket Pia in English at ☎ (03) 5237–9999 or Ticket Saison in Japanese at ☎ (03) 5990–9999. The lines are often busy, but keep trying. Japan Railway's Midori-no-Madoguchi offices located in all major JR stations often sell packages that include train fares and entrance tickets, though many offer little or no discount.

Several English-language periodicals list upcoming performances and sporting events. The Tokyo Journal has a page describing events for kids and e-zine, Tokyo Q at <http://www/tokyoq.com> has the most up-to-date city wide listings in English. The Japan Times sports section always list the day's sporting events. Surprisingly, you can often get a ticket on the day of the game unless you want to see the Yomiuri Giants, Tokyo's most popular professional baseball team.

Department Stores: The Family Rest Stop

These department stores have baby rooms for nursing and diaper-changing and make a great last stop of the day. After browsing the children's department, head to the restaurant floor or the food courts in the basement and get dinner. Most stores are closed one day a week, a practice they often suspend during holidays and during the summer and winter gift-giving seasons.

Asakusa Area

Matsuya
松屋
Hanakawado 1-chome, Taito-ku, Tokyo
☎ (03) 3842–1111
東京都台東区花川戸1丁目
OPEN: 10 A.M. to 7 P.M.
CLOSED: no scheduled hols
CHILDREN'S DEPT. WITH INFANT CARE ROOM: 3rd floor

Kichijoji Area

Isetan
伊勢丹
1–11–15 Kichijoji Honmachi, Musashino-shi, Tokyo
☎ (0422) 21–1111
東京都武蔵野市吉祥寺本町11–1–15
OPEN: 10 A.M. to 7 P.M.
CLOSED: Wed
CHILDREN'S DEPT. WITH INFANT CARE ROOM: 5th floor

Nihonbashi Area

Mitsukoshi
三越
1–4–1 Nihonbashi-Muromachi, Chuo-ku, Tokyo
☎ (03) 3241–3311
東京都中央区日本橋室町4–1–1
OPEN: 10 a.m. to 6 p.m.
CLOSED: Mon
CHILDREN'S DEPT. WITH INFANT CARE ROOM: 4th floor

Takashimaya
高島屋
2–4–1 Nihonbashi, Chuo-ku, Tokyo
☎ (03) 3211–4111
東京都中央区日本橋4–2–1
OPEN: 10 A.M. to 6:30 P.M.
CLOSED: Wed
CHILDREN'S DEPT. WITH INFANT CARE ROOM: 5th floor

Shibuya Area

Tokyu
東急
2–24–1 Shibuya, Shibuya-ku, Tokyo
☎ (03) 3477–3311
東京都渋谷区渋谷24–2–1
OPEN: 10 A.M. to 7 P.M.
CLOSED: Thurs
CHILDREN'S DEPT. WITH INFANT CARE ROOM: 6th floor

Shinjuku Area

Isetan
伊勢丹
3–14–1 Shinjuku, Shinjuku-ku, Tokyo
☎ (03) 3352–1111
東京都新宿区新宿14–3–1
OPEN: 10 A.M. to 7 P.M.
CLOSED: Wed
CHILDREN'S DEPT. WITH INFANT CARE ROOM: 6th floor

Keio

京王

1–1–4 Nishi Shinjuku, Shinjuku, Tokyo

☎ (03) 3342–2111

東京都新宿区西新宿1–1–4

OPEN: 10 A.M. to 7 P.M.

CLOSED: Thurs

CHILDREN'S DEPT. WITH INFANT CARE ROOM: 7th floor

Odakyu

小田急

1–1–3 Nishi Shinjuku, Shinjuku-ku, Tokyo

☎ (03) 3342–1111

東京都新宿区西新宿1–1–3

OPEN: 10 A.M. to 7 P.M.

CLOSED: Tues

CHILDREN'S DEPT. WITH INFANT CARE ROOM: 7th floor

Takashimaya

高島屋

5–24–2 Sendagaya, Shibuya-ku, Tokyo

☎ (03) 5361–1111

東京都渋谷区千駄ヶ谷24–5–2

OPEN: 10 A.M. to 7 P.M.

CLOSED: Wed

CHILDREN'S DEPT. WITH INFANT CARE ROOM: 9th floor

Minato Mirai 21, Yokohama

Landmark Plaza Shopping Center

2–2–1 Minato Mirai, Nishi-ku, Yokohama, Kanagawa-ken

☎ (045) 222–5015

神奈川県横浜市西区みなとみらい2–2–1

OPEN: 11 A.M. to 8 P.M.

CLOSED: no scheduled hols

INFANT CARE ROOM: 4th floor

Yokohama Station Area

Sogo

2–18 Takashima, Nishi-ku, Yokohama, Kanagawa-ken

☎ (045) 465–2111

神奈川県横浜市西区高島18–2

OPEN: 10:30 A.M. to 7:30 P.M., Sun till 7 P.M.

CLOSED: no scheduled hols

CHILDREN'S DEPT. WITH INFANT CARE ROOM: 5th floor

Some Useful Phrases in Japanese

Conversation Control

Please speak more slowly.
Yukkuri to hanashite kudasai.
ゆっくりと話して下さい。

Please repeat that.
Mō-ichido itte kudasai.
もう一度言って下さい。

What does _____ mean?
_____ *wa dō iu imi desu ka?*
_____ はどういう意味ですか？

Phoning First

Are you open today?
Kyō wa aite imasu ka?
今日は開いていますか？

What are your hours today?
Kyō wa nanji kara nanji made aite imasu ka?
今日は何時から何時まで開いていますか？

Asking Directions

Where is the _____ train station?
_____ *eki wa doko desu ka?*
_____ 駅はどこですか？

Which way to _____ street?
_____ *dori wa dochira deshō ka?*
_____ 通りはどちらでしょうか？

Where is the rest room?
O-tearai wa doko desu ka?
お手洗いはどこですか？

How many minutes will it take on foot?
Aruite nan-pun gurai kakarimasu ka?
あるいて何分ぐらいかかりますか？

I want to go to _____ .
_____ *e ikitai no desu ga...*
_____ へ行きたいのですが

straight, right, left
massugu, migi, hidari
まっすぐ、みぎ、ひだり

Trains, Subways, and Buses

Which platform for _____ ?
_____ *yuki wa nan-ban sen desu ka?*
_____ 行は何番線ですか？

When is the next express train?
Tsugi no kyūkō wa nanji desu ka?
次の急行は何時ですか？

Does this train/bus stop at _____ ?
Kono densha/basu wa _____ ni tomarimasu ka?
この電車/バスは _____ に止まりますか？

Excuse me. I'm getting off here.
Sumimasen. Orimasu.
すみません。降ります。

transfer
norikae
のりかえ

central exit, north exit, east exit, south exit, west exit
chuo guchi, kita guchi, higashi guchi, minami guchi, nishi guchi
中央口、北口、東口、南口、西口

ticket machine
kippu uriba
切符売り場

I put in money but no ticket came out.
Okane o ireta no desu ga, kippu ga demasen.
お金を入れたのですが、切符が出ません。

Taxis

Take me to _____ please.
_____ *e onegai shimasu.*
_____ へお願いします。

Please open the trunk, I'd like to put a stroller inside.
Toranku o akete kudasai. Bebî-kâ o iretai no desu.
トランクを開けて下さい。ベビーカーを入れたいのです。

Please turn right/left at the next corner.
Tsugi no kado o migi/hidari e magatte kudasai.
次の角を右/左へ曲がって下さい。

Please go straight.
Massugu itte kudasai.
まっすぐ行って下さい。

Stop here.
Kono hen de ii desu.
この辺でいいです。

Making Reservations

I'd like to make brunch reservations for 2 adults and 3 children.
Otona futari to kodomo san-nin no buranchi no yoyaku o dekimasu ka?
大人二人と子供三人のブランチの予約をできますか？

I'd like to make a reservation for a tour in English.
Eigo no gaido no yoyaku o dekimasu ka?
英語のガイドの予約をできますか？

Days of the Week

Monday	*Getsuyōbi*	月曜日
Tuesday	*Kayōbi*	火曜日
Wednesday	*Suiyōbi*	水曜日
Thursday	*Mokuyōbi*	木曜日
Friday	*Kinyōbi*	金曜日
Saturday	*Doyōbi*	土曜日
Sunday	*Nichiyōbi*	日曜日

Dates

first	*tsuitachi*	一日
second	*futsuka*	二日
third	*mikka*	三日
fourth	*yokka*	四日
fifth	*itsuka*	五日
sixth	*muika*	六日
seventh	*nanoka*	七日
eighth	*yōka*	八日
ninth	*kokonoka*	九日
tenth	*tōka*	十日
tenth	*jūichi-nichi*	十一日
twelfth	*kūni-nichi*	十二日
thirteenth	*jūsann-nichi*	十三日
fourteenth	*jūyokka*	十四日
fifteenth	*jūgo-nichi*	十五日
sixteenth	*jūroku-nichi*	十六日
seventeenth	*jūshichi-nichi*	十七日
eighteenth	*jūhachi-nichi*	十八日
nineteenth	*jūku-nichi*	十九日
twentieth	*hatsuka*	二十日
twenty-first	*nijūichi-nichi*	二十一日
twenty-second	*nijūni-nichi*	二十二日
twenty-third	*nijūsan-nichi*	二十三日
twenty-fourth	*nijūyokka*	二十四日
twenty-fifth	*nijūgo-nichi*	二十五日
twenty-sixth	*nijūroku-nichi*	二十六日
twenty-seventh	*nijūshichi-nichi*	二十七日
twenty-eigth	*nijūhachi-nichi*	二十八日
twenty-ninth	*nijūku-nichi*	二十九日
thirtieth	*sanjūnichi*	三十日
thirty-first	*sanjūichi-nichi*	三十一日

Time

A.M.	*gozen*	午前
P.M.	*gogo*	午後
1:00	*ichiji*	一時
2:00	*niji*	二時
3:00	*sanji*	三時
4:00	*yoji*	四時
5:00	*goji*	五時
6:00	*rokuji*	六時
7:00	*shichiji*	七時
8:00	*hachiji*	八時
9:00	*kuji*	九時
10:00	*jūji*	十時
11:00	*jūichiji*	十一時
12:00	*jū-niji*	十二時
10 minutes	*juppun*	十分
20 minutes	*nijuppun*	二十分
30 minutes	*sanjuppun*	三十分
40 minutes	*yonjūppun*	四十分
45 minutes	*yonjūgofun*	四十五分
50 minutes	*gojuppun*	五十分

Buying Tickets

<u>2</u> adult tickets, <u>3</u> children's tickets please.
Otona <u>ni-mai</u> to kodomo <u>san-mai</u> kudasai.
大人2枚と子供3枚下さい。

<u>1</u> adult ticket, <u>2</u> children's tickets please.
Otona <u>ichi-mai</u> to kodomo <u>ni-mai</u> kudasai.
大人1枚と子供2枚下さい。

How much for a <u>four-year-old</u> child?
<u>Yon-sai</u> ji no kippu wa ikura desu ka.
4才児の切符はいくらですか？

Lost and Found

I lost my bag/a child's coat.
Watashi no baggu/kodomo no kōto o nakushi mashita.
私のバック/子供のコートをなくしました。

Where is the lost and found office?
Ishitsubutsu shūtokujo wa doko ni arimasu ka.
遺失物収得所はどこにありますか？

Restaurants

I'd like to order the same thing as the customer over there.
Ano hito to onaji mono o kudasai.
あの人と同じものを下さい。

I'd like to order something I saw in the window but I don't know the name.

Please come with me to the window.
Shō windō ni aru mono o chūmon shitai no desu ga namae ga wakarimasen. Issho ni kite kudasai.
ショーウィンドウにあるものを注文したいのですが名前が分かりません。一緒に来て下さい。

Child's meal please.
O-ko-sama ranchi o kudasai.
お子様ランチをください。

Please give us a little more time to order.
Mō chotto matte kudasai.
もうちょっと待って下さい。

Is it spicy?
Karai desu ka.
辛いですか？

May we have a high chair?
Kodomo yō no isu o kudasai.
子供用の椅子を下さい。

May we have an extra plate?
O-sara o ichi-mai yobun ni kudasai.
お皿を1枚余分に下さい。

Do you serve milk?
Miruku wa arimasu ka.
ミルクはありますか？

May we have a fork/spoon/knife?
Fōku/supūn/naifu o kudasai.
フォーク/スプーン/ナイフを下さい。

Excuse me. My child spilled something.
Sumimasen. Kodomo ga koboshimashita.
すみません。子供がこぼしました。

Infant and Toddler Care

Do you have a diaper-changing table/place where I can nurse my child?

Omutsu kōkan dai/junyū shitsu ga arimasu ka?

オムツ交換台/授乳室がありますか？

May I bring my stroller inside?

Bebî-kâ o mochikonde ii desu ka?

ベビーカーを持ち込んでいいですか？

Where can I put my stroller?

Bebî-kâ wa doko ni okeba ii desu ka?

ベビーカーはどこに置けばいいですか？

Is there a place nearby that sells diapers/baby formula?

Kono chikaku ni omutsu/akachan yō kona miruku o utte imasu ka?

この近くにオムツ/赤ちゃん用粉ミルクを売っていますか？

Where can I get some hot water to make formula?

Kona miruku o tsukuru oyu wa doko de moraemasu ka?

粉ミルクを作るお湯はどこでもらえますか？

Is there anything inside/in the show that will frighten a small child?

Kono naka no mono wa/kono shō wa kodomo ni kowasugimasu ka?

この中のものは/このショウは子供に怖すぎますか？

Lost, Hurt Children

My child is lost.

Kodomo ga maigo ni narimashita.

子供が迷子になりました。

My child is_____ years old.

Kodomo wa _____sai desu.

子供は_____才です。

My child is_____ centimeters tall.

Kodomo wa _____ senchi desu.

子供は_____センチです。

My child is a boy/girl.

Kodomo wa otoko-no-ko/onna-no-ko desu.

子供は男の子/女の子です。

My child has short/long hair.

Kodomo no kami no ke wa mijikai/nagai desu.

子供の髪の毛は短い/長いです。

My child has blonde/brown/red/black hair.

Kodomo no kami no ke wa kinpatsu/chairo/aka/kuro desu.

子供の髪の毛は金髪/茶色/赤/黒です。

The child is wearing blue/red/green/yellow/pink/purple clothes.

Kodomo no fuku no iro wa ao/aka/midori/kiiro/pinku/murasaki desu.

子供の服の色は青/赤/緑/黄色/ピンク/紫です。

My child is hurt.

Kodomo ga kega o shimashita.

子供が怪我をしました。

Where is the First Aid station?
Imushitsu wa doko desu ka?
医務室はどこですか？

Please call an ambulance.
Kyūkyūsha o yonde kudasai.
救急車を呼んで下さい。

Additional Vocabulary for Parents and Kids

adult	*otona*	大人
airplane	*hikōki*	飛行機
bicycle	*jitensha*	自転車
binoculars	*sōgankyō*	双眼鏡
camp fire	*kyanpu faiyâ*	キャンプ ファイヤー
camp site child	*kyanpu jō kodomo*	キャンプ場子供
entrance charge	*nyūjyōryō*	入場料
Ferris wheel	*kanransha*	環覧車
fishing rod	*tsuri sao*	釣り竿
garden	*niwa, teien*	庭.庭園
group discount	*dantai waribiki*	団体割引
helicopter	*herikoputâ*	ヘリコプター
ice skating rink	*aisu suketo rinku*	アイススケートリンク
light house	*tōdai*	灯台
magnifying glass	*mushi megane*	虫眼鏡
marionette clock	*karakuri dokei*	からくり時計
maze	*meiro*	迷路
merry-go round	*merî gō rando*	メリーゴーランド
net	*ami*	網
park	*kōen*	公園
parking lot	*chūshajō*	駐車場
petting zoo	*dōbutsu fureai kōnâ*	動物ふれあいコーナー
pond	*ike*	池
pool	*pūru*	プール
slide	*suberidai*	滑り台
swings	*buranko*	ブランコ
tent	*tento*	テント
toy store	*omocha-ya*	おもちゃ屋
water bus/ferry	*suijō basu*	水上バス

ID TAG

Please photocopy this form, complete it in Japanese, and give it to your child to use in case he/she gets lost.

私の名前は＿＿＿＿＿＿＿＿＿＿＿＿＿＿＿＿＿＿＿＿＿＿。迷子です。

Watashi no namae wa ＿＿＿. Maigo desu.

My name is ＿＿＿ and I am lost.

日本語を話せません。＿＿＿＿＿＿＿＿＿を話します。

Nihongo o hanasemasen. ＿＿＿ o hanashimasu.

I don't speak Japanese. My language is ＿＿＿.

父の名前は＿＿＿＿＿＿＿＿＿＿＿＿＿＿＿＿＿＿＿です。

Chichi no namae wa ＿＿＿.

My father's name is ＿＿＿.

母の名前は＿＿＿＿＿＿＿＿＿＿＿＿＿＿＿＿＿＿＿です。

Haha no namae wa ＿＿＿.

My mother's name is ＿＿＿.

住所と電話番号＿＿＿＿＿＿＿＿＿＿＿＿＿＿＿＿＿＿＿＿＿＿。

Jūsho to denwa bangōe: ＿＿＿.

My address and telephone number are: ＿＿＿.

Indices

Alphabetical List of Destinations

Destinations in Japanese （目的地インデクス）

Acknowledgments

This book was written with the insightful advice and assistance of six fun and adventurous kids: Yoichi Kobe, Amy Ozeki, Ken, Gene, and Yumi Sato, and Claire Maeda. We thank our families for all the happy times we shared testing Tokyo's museums and playspots, especially our husbands, Kazuhiko Kobe, Naobumi Ozeki, Takahiko Sato, and Masahiro Maeda, for their unwavering support. Special appreciation goes to Masahiro for his advice and frequent assistance throughout the many stages of this project.

We are grateful to Jennifer, Bryn, and Cort Young who visited many places in our first draft and offered excellent suggestions, and our editors, Barry Lancet, Michiko Uchiyama, and Janice Nimura, whose expertise shaped the final form of the book, and to Kazuko Matsuzaki for her diligent fact checking. We would like to express our sincerest gratitude to friends listed here who accompanied us on research days, recommended their favorite spots, or helped in other important ways.

Janelle Dessaint and Tess Kimura
Kazuko Kosuge
Takako and Ryohei Takahashi
Kazue Takahashi
Chikako Furuzawa
Kenji Doi
Robin Bulow
Rick Kennedy
Holley, Jeff, Russell, and Becky Kruetter
Victoria and Mitsumasa Aoki
Fumio and Yuri Okubo
Yoshiko and Nina Cataldo

Reiko, Mari, and Ryotaro Ogawa
David Ridges
Joanna Chinen
Robbie Walker and Kenny Okamoto
Norma, Kai, and Misha Bartruff
Ellen Yaegashi
Emiko Yang
Janie Yamamoto
Debbie Kobayashi
Janet Nishimura
Carol Miyazaki

とうきょうこ づ で
東京子連れお出かけガイド

KIDS' TRIPS IN TOKYO

1998年3月19日　第1刷発行
2001年4月 1 日　第2刷発行

著　者　アイビ・マエダ／リン・サトウ
　　　　キティ・コーベ／シンシア・オゼキ

発行者　野間佐和子

発行所　講談社インターナショナル株式会社
　　　　〒112-8652　東京都文京区音羽 1-17-14
　　　　電話：03-3944-6493

印刷所　大日本印刷株式会社

製本所　株式会社　堅省堂

落丁本・乱丁本は、小社業務部宛にお送りください。送料小社負担にて
お取替えします。本書の無断複写（コピー）、転載は著作権法の例外を
除き、禁じられています。

定価はカバーに表示してあります。
COPYRIGHT © by Ivy Maeda, Lyn Sato, Kitty Kobe and Cynthia Ozeki　1998
Printed in Japan
ISBN4-7700-2040-6

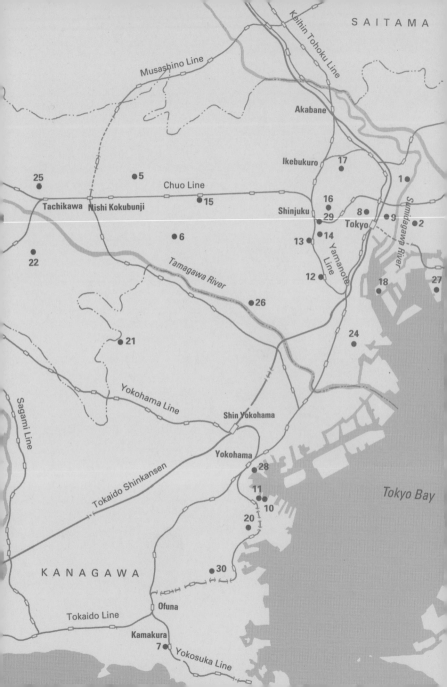